ROUTLEDGE LIBRARY EDITIONS: ROMANTICISM

Volume 19

RADICAL SENSIBILITY

RADICAL SENSIBILITY
Literature and ideas in the 1790s

CHRIS JONES

LONDON AND NEW YORK

First published in 1993 by Routledge

This edition first published in 2016
by Routledge
2 Park Square, Milton Park, Abingdon, Oxon OX14 4RN

and by Routledge
711 Third Avenue, New York, NY 10017

Routledge is an imprint of the Taylor & Francis Group, an informa business

© 1993 Chris Jones

All rights reserved. No part of this book may be reprinted or reproduced or utilised in any form or by any electronic, mechanical, or other means, now known or hereafter invented, including photocopying and recording, or in any information storage or retrieval system, without permission in writing from the publishers.

Trademark notice: Product or corporate names may be trademarks or registered trademarks, and are used only for identification and explanation without intent to infringe.

British Library Cataloguing in Publication Data
A catalogue record for this book is available from the British Library

ISBN: 978-1-138-64537-0 (Set)
ISBN: 978-1-315-62815-8 (Set) (ebk)
ISBN: 978-1-138-64252-2 (Volume 19) (hbk)
ISBN: 978-1-138-64253-9 (Volume 19) (pbk)
ISBN: 978-1-315-62988-9 (Volume 19) (ebk)

Publisher's Note
The publisher has gone to great lengths to ensure the quality of this reprint but points out that some imperfections in the original copies may be apparent.

Disclaimer
The publisher has made every effort to trace copyright holders and would welcome correspondence from those they have been unable to trace.

RADICAL SENSIBILITY

Literature and ideas in the 1790s

Chris Jones

London and New York

First published 1993
by Routledge
11 New Fetter Lane, London EC4P 4EE

Simultaneously published in the USA and Canada
by Routledge Inc.
29 West 35th Street, New York, NY 10001

© 1993 Chris Jones

Typeset in 10 on 12 point Baskerville by
Witwell Ltd, Southport
Printed in Great Britain by
TJ Press (Padstow) Ltd, Padstow, Cornwall

All rights reserved. No part of this book may be reprinted or reproduced or utilized in any form or by any electronic, mechanical, or other means, now known or hereafter invented, including photocopying and recording, or in any information storage or retrieval system, without permission in writing from the publishers.

British Library Cataloguing in Publication Data
A catalogue record for this book is available from the British Library.

Library of Congress Cataloguing in Publication Data
Jones, C. B.
Radical sensibility: lectures and ideas in the 1790s / Chris Jones.
  p. cm.
Includes bibliographical references and index.
1. English literature—18th century—History and criticism.
2. Great Britain—History—1789-1820. 3. Sentimentalism in literature. 4. Radicalism in literature. I. Title.
PR448.S4J66 1993
820.9′006—dc20   92-5389
                                                                      CIP

ISBN 0-415-07685-4

CONTENTS

Preface		vi
Abbreviated titles		xii
	INTRODUCTION	1
1	VARIETIES OF SENSIBILITY	20
2	TOWARDS REVOLUTION	59
3	SENSIBILITY IN REVOLUTION: GODWIN AND WOLLSTONECRAFT	85
4	SENSIBILITY IN REACTION	108
5	HELEN MARIA WILLIAMS: RADICAL CHRONICLER	136
6	CHARLOTTE SMITH AS RADICAL NOVELIST	160
7	WORDSWORTH AND SENSIBILITY	185
	Notes	219
	Bibliography	223
	Index	229

PREFACE

This book stems originally from research into William Godwin and the novel of the 1790s which I started as a postgraduate in Birmingham in the late 1960s. The granting of two sabbatical terms has allowed me to extend the subject in a very changed theoretical climate. My study of Godwin's letters convinced me that he shared with many of his correspondents a conception of the mechanisms of sympathy and the feelings which was associated with the movement known as Sensibility. While there has been considerable treatment of this formation in the early eighteenth century, I found few satisfying accounts of its later phases. It seemed to me that in following its transformations during the 1790s I might gain a perspective on its earlier development which could clarify some of the contradictions which emerge from modern studies of sensibility, some of which treat it as a predominantly conservative formation, others as potentially radical.

I am indebted to scholars too numerous to mention in distinguishing particular formations of ideas and tracing the interaction between ideas and historical events in the 1790s. Without Nicholas Roe's work on the radical years of Coleridge and Wordsworth and Stephen Gill's biography of Wordsworth I might not have dared to speculate on the suppressions of *The Prelude*. I am equally conscious of sins of omission. Michael Meehan's work came to hand after I had drafted the book. His establishment of a 'school of Shaftesbury' extending into the 1790s added to my confidence in my own thesis, but we have divergencies in focus and in our interpretations of the later material which deterred me from entering into lengthy dis-

PREFACE

cussion. I have cited only the works of those scholars with whom agreement or disagreement seemed most important to my argument, but my understanding of the period has also been greatly informed by the works and conversation of Marilyn Butler, Donald Reiman, David Erdman, and Gary Kelly, and the historical studies of E. P. Thompson, H. T. Dickinson, and Albert Goodwin. My research has been aided by the scholars who have been sifting and interpreting the treasure-house of manuscripts of the Godwin/Shelley circle in the Bodleian Library, principally Don Locke, Peter Marshall, and William St Clair.

I was initially drawn to the study of the history of ideas, nourished by the writings of Lovejoy, Wellek, Willey, Bate, and Abrams. At Birmingham, under the professorship of Richard Hoggart, I became interested in the work of Raymond Williams, especially in his analysis of the ways in which literature expresses social conflict and change. His idea of the interactions of 'social characters' in the context of a 'structure of feeling', all of which could be conceptualized, still seems to me more convincing than subsequent theories of 'ideology' which present vast monolithic systems creating and reproducing ideological 'subjects'. Some recent developments, by stressing the Saussurean principle of definition by opposition, seem to be bringing back a sense of the historical conflict of ideologies, in which even Marxism might participate, instead of holding aloof in the sphere of 'science'. Some of Diane Macdonell's examples of language as the site of ideological struggle are very close to my own attempts to demonstrate the ideological conflicts within the movement of sensibility.

Raymond Williams's suggestive formulation 'structure of feeling', which he conceptualizes in the formulae of the dominant ideology, put under stress but never wholly countered by opposing views, has many similarities with the concept of sensibility. Many eighteenth-century writers seem to lay claim to it, but with subtle differences. We may, thanks to T. S. Eliot, still retain the idea of sensibility as a union of emotion and thought, but we have largely lost that sense that the feelings are 'naturally' drawn to virtue and social good, which made sensibility such a morally positive term in the eighteenth century. The modern construction of the affectual realm is today occupied by a psychoanalytic theory in which the individual pursues personal completion through mirages of identification and projection within relations patterned on the nuclear family. Eighteenth-century constructions such as Shaftesbury's situated the individual in affective relationship beyond the family with his kind and with the entire system of being of which the individual could feel a part. There is perhaps some continuity. A seal pup is likely to awaken sympathies associated with the image of a club poised over its head rather than a fishing family impoverished by the depredation of fishing grounds. This sympathy could be theorized in terms of 'man's exploitation of nature', and ultimately some notion of a 'balance of nature', evoking the universal harmony hymned by Shaftesbury and Wordsworth. Conservation can appear progressive when campaigning against waste and pollution caused by vested interests, conservative when opposing experimental medical science. The emotion generated by the concept of nature, capable of inspiring civil disobedience and even 'terrorist' campaigns, is arguably a legacy of the Romantic period, and, beyond that, the movement of sensibility. When the French Revolution seemed to incorporate the causes of eighteenth-century humanitarianism, many followers of sensibility adopted a more radical expression of their faith. It is in these writers, and in the conflicts within the movement which their political affiliation provoked, that I see the most interesting transformations of sensibility.

Eighteenth-century sensibility can be seen as a structure of feeling in two related ways. In the spirit of structuralism we might say that, though feeling is an individual experience, the expression of feeling adopts symbolic formulae already articulated. Certainly the expression of feeling in literature of the period can be seen as formulaic, indeed notoriously so. It echoed the efforts of philosophers such as Shaftesbury and Hume to describe the workings of the social passions in their efforts to empower natural feeling as the basis of progressive civil society, religous faith, and aesthetic judgment. This structure of feeling related not only to the expression of personal feeling but to the basis of the social bond, and brought religous, moral and aesthetic realms into a homologous relationship. The replacement of terms like 'sentiment' and 'benevolence' by 'sensibility' can be seen as a search for a more inclusive term which would imply active, authentic, personal response to all representations which appealed to the social feelings. This construction was opposed by those who championed the more traditional authority of conscience, law, egotism, or power, but there were also internal tensions. The expansion of the social feelings could be seen as a mark of progress only to be expected of a society which enjoyed the best constitution in the world and a confirmation of its perfection. It could be seen by the less complacent as a spur to further progress in the directions indicated by Shaftesbury as the natural goals of social feeling: greater equality and individual freedom.

For Williams, the structure of feeling, while imaging terms common to antagonistic ideologies, does change, in a deep movement of collective sensibility in which the icons which focus common values are undermined and replaced. I would suggest that this process can happen less gradually than he suggests under the pressure of historical events like those of the 1790s. In Wordsworth's Preface to *Lyrical Ballads* we have the first complaints against the 'outrageous stimulation' provided by developments in information technology and mass media which disturb a 'structure of feeling'. He might also have added to his list the influence of government in controlling the extended information system by overt and covert means. The 1790s saw a concerted effort by politicians well aware of the power of words to subvert previously acknowledged images and values which were then seen to threaten the status quo. The vacuum created by their subversion produced different antagonists. In attacking the radical egalitarian aspects of benevolism they opened the way for an individualistic acquisitiveness which equally sapped their power. Today we are well aware of the manipulation of media images and political catch-phrases, sometimes provided by rent-a-don agencies; in the 1790s the management of public opinion, rather than interest-groups, was even more important to a government prosecuting an unpopular war in an unrepresentative Commons. The caricature of sensibility supported by the wave of anti-Jacobin novels and tales divested it of any legitimate claims to active intervention. They emptied the term of any social idealism, emphasizing its individualism and the emotional self-indulgence which was seen as its inevitable concomitant. They especially attacked the efforts of feminists to claim rights based equally on reason and feeling. The aggressive female abandoned to passion became a central figure of anti-Jacobin propaganda as it exploited the fears of patriarchy.

My study of Godwin had impressed me with the permanent damage that the anti-Jacobin campaign could inflict on a literary reputation. I was drawn to estimating the damage similarly inflicted on the concept of sensibility over the whole range of its applications. In hoping to contribute to the modern project of reviewing the accepted terms of literary and intellectual history by investigating the historical circumstances of their formation, I also felt some kinship with Romantics like Shelley, in taking up the lance of the Elfin Knight in defence of the fair form of Sensibility. Wherein had she erred but in thinking too well of humanity?

The study of a movement whose works were vilified, if not burned, and dismissed from the canon of polite literature, and whose adherents disowned their former connections, presents many difficulties. Continuities of ideas become more important than attributions in tracing the prevailing influence of radical sensibility, and the rarity of important texts, even in expensive modern editions, leads to dependence on central institutions like the overburdened British Library and the Bodleian. The method I have pursued has been to trace the history of ideas in their more explicitly radical expression and then to explore their use in less explicit contexts. Godwin and Wollstonecraft show the most explicit radical developments of the ideas of sensibility; others use these ideas and follow similar developments, sometimes denying their radical implications.

I owe a great debt of gratitude to the Bodleian Library, and especially to Mr Barker-Benson and his staff, with whose aid I can catch the Irish Mail and at noon study a manuscript of the Godwin circle. I am also grateful to the staff of the British Library, Birmingham University Library, Keele University Library, and the Library of the University of Wales, Bangor. I would like to thank Lord Abinger for permission to quote from the Abinger MSS in the Bodleian Library, and the Trustees of the Wedgwood Museum for permission to quote from the Wedgwood papers deposited at Keele University Library. My research has been materially helped by grants from the University of Wales, Bangor.

A version of the material on Helen Maria Williams was published in *Prose Studies* 12, 1 (1989) as 'Helen Maria Williams and Radical Sensibility'. I am grateful to the editors for allowing me to reproduce much of that material. An account of the main lines of my research in progress was delivered to the Leicester Conference on 'The French Revolution and British Culture' in

PREFACE

1989 and is scheduled to be published by Routledge in a collection of papers from the conference. Some of the material on Godwin and *The Enquirer* was delivered to the 1989 Leeds Conference on '1789/Prose/Politics'.

I am much indebted to specific volumes of the Bollingen *Collected Coleridge,* the editors of the Cornell Wordsworth series, especially James Averill and Stephen Gill, and to the latter's Oxford English Authors volume of Wordsworth's poetry and prose.

Finally I would like to thank my wife and family for tolerating my nocturnal habits of scholarship and periodic absences.

ABBREVIATED TITLES

Prelude　　　References are to the 1805 text given in Wordsworth, W. (1979), *The Prelude 1799, 1805, 1850*, ed. J. Wordsworth, M. H. Abrams, and S. Gill, New York, Norton.

OTHER CITATIONS

Char　　　Shaftesbury (1711), *Characteristicks of Men, Manners, Opinions, Times*, 3 vols.

CL　　　Coleridge, S. T. (1956-71), *Collected Letters of Samuel Taylor Coleridge*, ed. E. L. Griggs, 6 vols, Oxford, Clarendon.

DS　　　Wordsworth, W. (1984), *Descriptive Sketches*, ed. E. Birdsall, Ithaca, Cornell University Press.

Enquiries　　　Hume, D. (1888), *Hume's Enquiries*, ed. L. A. Selby-Bigge, Oxford, Clarendon.

EW　　　Wordsworth, W. (1984), *An Evening Walk*, ed. J. Averill, Ithaca, Cornell University Press.

Howe　　　Hazlitt, W. (1930-4), *The Complete Works*, ed. P. P. Howe, 21 vols, London, Dent.

Lect　　　Coleridge, S. T. (1971), *Lectures 1795 on Politics and Religion*, ed. L. Patton and P. Mann, London, Routledge & Kegan Paul.

LY　　　Wordsworth, W. (1978), *The Letters of William and Dorothy Wordsworth. The Later Years*, ed. De Selincourt, rev. A. G. Hill, Oxford, Clarendon.

OA　　　Wordsworth, W. (1984), *The Oxford Authors: William Wordsworth*, ed. S. Gill, Oxford, OUP.

ABBREVIATED TITLES

*PJ*93	Godwin, W. (1793), *Political Justice*, 2 vols.
*PJ*98	Godwin, W. (1946), *Political Justice*, 3rd ed., 1798, intro. and notes F. E. L. Priestley, 3 vols, Toronto, University of Toronto Press.
Prose	Wordsworth, W. (1974), *The Prose Works of William Wordsworth*, ed. W. J. B. Owen and J. W. Smyser, 3 vols, Oxford, Clarendon.
SP	Wordsworth, W. (1975), *The Salisbury Plain Poems*, ed. S. Gill, Ithaca, Cornell University Press.
Treatise	Hume, D. (1888), *A Treatise of Human Nature*, ed. L. A. Selby-Bigge, Oxford, Clarendon.

INTRODUCTION

The ideas associated with the concept of sensibility in the eighteenth century were a powerful force in the development of art, philosophy, and social thinking. Their origin in the latitudinarian divines of the seventeenth century, the Cambridge Platonists, and the work of Shaftesbury has been well researched 18by many scholars, and the image of the benevolent man which they inspired in the literature of the period has also received much attention.[1] The shift from a trust in reason to provide principles of action and judgment to an emphasis on the role of the feelings had repercussions in all fields of speculation. It provoked the literary movement which has been described as 'pre-Romantic', or which constituted, as Northrop Frye suggested, an 'Age of Sensibility'.[2] The devaluation of reason and classical structure in favour of effects which directly addressed the feelings led to theories of the Sublime and the Pathetic which dominated poetic appreciation. The development towards a more emotional and imaginative reaction to the sublime in nature has been the subject of many studies, mostly centred on poetry and aesthetics, of which the most influential has been M. H. Abrams's *The Mirror and the Lamp* (1953). Such was the impact of Abrams's work that nature became the dominant context for studying the philosophical developments of the period, to the detriment of the social element in the progressive theories of sensibility. While some aspects of sensibility seem nostalgic, the predominant impulse was progressive. The cult of original genius and the search for national primitives awakened interest in the Middle Ages and the misty Celtic past. Even in these antiquarian leanings the spirit of the movement was progressive, as it looked back to primitive societies

1

within a perspective of development. It sought for a similar emotional and imaginative response to nature as Ossian, a similar enthusiasm for splendid deeds and ideals of love and honour as the Age of Chivalry, yet moralized and refined by the advances of modern civilization. The idea that the purpose of art was to invigorate and purify the emotions, especially those connected with the social affections, influenced the development of an aesthetic most prominently expounded by Scottish writers. In social thinking, the trend was to see society less as a mechanism and more as a system of relationships based on social sympathy. Sensibility also gave an impetus to humanitarian and philanthropic crusades which sought reform in the treatment of orphans, prisoners, and slaves on an international scale.

The didactic and progressive tendency of sensibility lay in its expansion and refinement of emotional response, unlocking human potentialities undreamed of by former cultures. Henry Mackenzie defended novels in *The Lounger* by stressing this historical cultural dimension:

> As promoting a certain refinement of mind, they operate like all other works of genius and feeling, and have indeed a more immediate tendency to produce it than most others, from their treating of those very subjects which the reader will find around him in the world, and their containing those very situations in which he himself may not improbably at some time or other be placed. Those who object to them as inculcating precepts, and holding forth examples, of a refinement which virtue does not require, and which honesty is better without, do not perhaps sufficiently attend to the period of society which produces them. The code of morality must necessarily be enlarged in proportion to that state of manners to which cultivated eras give birth. As the idea of property made a crime of theft; as the invention of oaths made falsehood perjury; so the necessary refinement in manners of highly-polished nations creates a variety of duties and of offences, which men in ruder, and, it may be (for I enter not into that question), happier periods of society, could never have imagined.[3]

However sentimental Mackenzie was as a novelist, he was properly distrustful when writing as a critic, and his article goes on to detail all the faults of the school of sensibility which were highlighted in later attacks. In privileging generosity and benevolence, it neglected the cardinal virtues which should be paramount:

> The duty to parents is contrasted with the ties of friendship and of love; the virtues of justice, of prudence, of economy, are put in competition with the exertions of generosity, of benevolence, and of compassion: and even of these virtues of sentiment there are still more refined divisions, in which the overstrained delicacy of the persons represented always leads them to act from the motive least obvious, and therefore generally the least reasonable.

The enthusiasm of sentiment tends to remain in the imagination for many devotees who 'pay in words what they owe in actions' and often leads to a 'sickly sort of refinement' which 'creates imaginary evils and distresses, and imaginary blessings and enjoyments, which imbitter the common disappointments, and depreciate the common attainments of life'. This last criticism bears particularly on Rousseau, though Mackenzie does not mention him in listing the French authors of sentiment. Rousseau had been singled out by the reviewer in the *Monthly Magazine* in the previous year as a dangerous example of the excess of passion, refuting Hugh Blair's contention that genius and taste in literature were linked with moral refinement. When Scott reviewed the novel of sentiment in his piece on Mackenzie in *Lives of the Novelists* he refused to class Rousseau's works as sentimental: they 'partake of the insanity of their author, and are exaggerated, though most eloquent, descriptions of overwhelming passion, rather than works of sentiment' (Williams 1968: 79). During the 1790s the attacks on the excesses of sensibility became more pointedly directed at its subversive and individualistic tendencies and by the end of the century the concept and its associated vocabulary were virtually unusable except for purposes of satire.

What were the reasons for this sudden demise of a concept which had seemed to bear all the optimistic hopes of a better, more sensitive society? The undiscriminating use of the term itself and the typical products of the Minerva Press might support the idea that like any literary vogue it had run its course and come finally to parody itself, a common life-cycle in literary modes. Yet the criticism of the 1790s was not predominantly aesthetic but political, social, and moral. Moreover the critics of sensibility in the 1790s were often ambivalent in their criticism. Anti-Jacobin writers attacked sensibility as socially subversive, yet Burke, the greatest anti-Jacobin of them all, laid claim to a heart full of sensibility. Coleridge, attacking the 'bastard sensibility' of emotional self-indulgence, wanted to stress active benevolence, which for many was the main injunction of sensibility. Mary Wollstonecraft attacked Burke's sensibility as instinct deserted by reason and criticized the 'artificial sensibility' fostered in women; yet she commended 'natural sensibility' and in her many honorific definitions of the term came close to Burke's description of a natural sensitivity and taste which did not depend on reason. Even evangelicals, with their stress on innate depravity, wished to enlist sensibility as an ally. Hannah More praised a 'chastised' sensibility and Wilberforce valued its power in improving an enthusiastic faith. Sensibility was clearly not a uniform or unitary concept when it could be both championed and attacked from so many points of view and I think modern scholarship has erred in trying to impose such a unitary interpretation on to it.

Up to the 1970s scholars seem to have followed the lead of the anti-Jacobin writers and characterized sensibility as a subversive force, individualistic and emotionalistic. Though a 'natural history' of the idea might seem to confer some sort of respectability, little in the way of a *social* criticism was credited to attitudes too indulgent and too liable to betray, under a modish extravagance of fervid language, a cold and mercenary selfishness. R. F. Brissenden, in his valuable study *Virtue in Distress*, credits the writers of sensibility with more substantial concerns, yet the status of their concepts declines from 'ideals' to 'ideas', and then to 'fantasies':

> [I]deals and ideas such as these – notions of man's innate benevolence, of his 'humanity', of his capacity to sympathise, of his ability and his right to exercise his own judgment, to formulate alone and unaided his moral sentiments – functioned not only as powerful fantasies but also as complex and sometimes precisely defined concepts which were developed and investigated in the work of philosophers, scientists and imaginative writers.
>
> (Brissenden 1974: 33)

INTRODUCTION

In his view these ideas provided the basis of a powerful social critique in the early eighteenth century but by the Revolutionary period this had degenerated into escapist individualistic fantasy. For Brissenden the development from 'sentiment' to 'sensibility' during the period marks the degeneration of the concept as it came to signify an attitude characterized more by feeling than by reason. Brissenden's version of sensibility also includes a self-acknowledged inability to engage with the real world. I have used the two terms interchangeably, as much from a conviction of their continuity as from the inconvenient absence of an adjectival form of 'sensibility'.

Later scholars have tended to characterize sensibility as a conservative movement, especially in its dealings with the feminine. Looking through the list of typical fictional characters of sensibility with anything of a modern feminist consciousness one must be struck by the predominantly masculine licence to be natural. Not for women were the escapades of a Tom Jones, spontaneously benevolent and amorous, nor the lubricious emotional epicureanism of a Yorick. The 'natural' female was constructed on different lines. For most writers feminine sensibility had to be regulated before it could be seen as an asset, while for some sensibility itself was a kind of natural control implanted particularly in the female breast as a divine compensation for their inaccessibility to reason. The first definition of this particularly eighteenth-century sense of the term quoted in the *Oxford English Dictionary* is Addison's remark about modesty being 'such an exquisite Sensibility, as warns a woman to shun the first Appearance of every thing which is hurtful'. For Mary Poovey, the attitudes associated with sensibility are part of a conservative patriarchal formation which appealed to 'natural' feelings aligned with traditional roles and subordinations. In *The Sign of Angellica* (1989) Janet Todd has traced the way in which the self-representation of the woman as writer was affected by the age's preoccupation with female propriety. John Sheriff sees a conformist trend in the development of the ideas of sensibility affecting both sexes, especially in Hume and Adam Smith. Assuming a linear progression from Shaftesbury and Hutcheson to Hume and Smith, he sees a shift from a reliance on good nature to 'a morality based on feeling and social custom' (Sheriff 1982: 17). For him the ethical philosophy of the mid-century was dominated by a Humean relativism which 'held that the code of morality to which each society and era gives birth superseded nature as the base of morality' (1982: 96).

John Mullan's study of sensibility (Mullan 1988) seems to have influenced several other books, in its stress on the physical manifestations of sensibility as a defining feature of the concept. It restricts the meaning of sensibility to what might be termed body-language, and a notion of sympathy which arises from intense forms of relationship, such as the communion of author and reader. It suggests that the ideas which previous theorists had associated with the term – of intuitive apprehension, of the primacy of the social passions and the trust in individual response – were the product of this unnaturally close communion. When sentimental heroes appeal to such virtues in the ordinary relations of real society they find that division and coldhearted selfishness rule. In indicating the direction which sensibility took in response to this impasse, Mullan has recourse to physiologists and neurologists to illustrate an absorption in the intricate mechanisms of sensation. Mullan takes Hume's description of sympathy in the *Treatise* as his starting-point, and sees everything after this as a descent from some ideal sentimental bond which might be extended as a model for society as a whole. Even Hume's later ideas in the *Enquiry* are, for Mullan, a sad departure from his earlier intensity as the theory of sympathy gives way to ideas of benevolence and utility. Janet Todd similarly speaks of the development of sensibility away from the familial fellowship of Humean sentimentalism as it became 'anti-community, a progressing away from, not into, Humean social sympathy' (Todd 1986: 136).

It seems to me that the effort to confine the notion of sensibility in these ways is damagingly simplifying. While all these varieties or manifestations of sensibility undoubtedly existed, they were conflicting trends within a formation which became, for short time in the 1790s, a site of contention between radical and conservative discourses. The radical ideas which Brissenden saw as deeply involved with the concept of sensibility did not dissolve into neurasthenic navel-gazing or transcendental reverie, or at least not before putting up a struggle. Some writers of the period continued to support ideas of moral egalitarianism, the autonomy of the individual, the priority of universal benevolence, and the capacity of men to act on an apprehension of social justice which was as natural as the 'social felings' which were the basis of society and constituted man a social animal.

Sensibility is a Janus-faced concept. Apparently an appeal to unconditioned natural feelings, it was also a social construction which translated prevailing power-based relationships into loyalties upheld by 'natural' feelings. Lawrence Stone's influential account of the process within the context of the family fails to engage with this mutation (Stone 1979). While his evidence shows an apparently more liberal attitude towards mutual affection as a basis for marriage and a greater recognition of the wishes of the children on the part of parents, the extent to which the wishes of the parent become an emotional imperative to the child cannot be estimated. Stone sees this internalization of the demands of patriarchy as a feature of an earlier period, but I would suggest that it persisted into the period which he sees as dominated by 'affective individualism'. The affectualization of the child-parent bond, like that of the wife-husband bond, all too often rendered submission an exalted act of emotional loyalty. Lear's lines 'Better thou / Hadst not been born than not t'have pleas'd me better' is the reproach of a father exerting an authority that appeals to an emotional bond, yet is capable of fearsome financial reprisals. The Marriage Act of 1753 did, as Stone admits, legally strengthen the hand of parents in their children's choices. Some of Stone's evidence, however, does reveal instances of liberality which cannot be deconstructed into the exercise of parental authority by other means. The movement of sensibility encouraged such liberality, and seems a better explanatory hypothesis than Stone's 'affective individualism'. The relinquishing of patriarchal authority is too important to be ascribed to an extension of the religious tolerance demanded by Dissenters. Their claims for freedom of worship and equality of representation were accompanied by an emphasis on the hierarchical relationships of the sexes and the family even stricter than the aristocratic norm. The individualism which was recognized as a 'natural' right could only be so recognized because it was seen as a 'social' and progressive characteristic of a free society which valued its freedom as much as its solidarity. The much-vaunted freedom of eighteenth-century Britain in comparison with other countries was linked with a conception of individualism which, while it licensed the claims of Dissenters, affirmed the innate sociability of man.

The other side of the Janus face of sensibility is indeed a cult of the unconditioned and the 'natural', yet one which saw social goals as the natural end of individual action. The basis for this optimistic fusion of the individual and the social can be seen in the Shaftesburyan line of sensibility. It is a theoretical construction which owed much to the code of behaviour in free aristocratic society. Shaftesbury, in championing freedom and criticizing social and religious traditions, argued only for the equality and naturalness of his cultured milieu, but his formulations were taken out of this context to become the basis of a radical, even revolutionary, ideology. What Robert Voitle describes as Shaftesbury's 'final version of the moral sense' uses terms which in the late century could provoke persecution and imprisonment. This speaks not only of a *Sense of Partnership* with Human Kind' but includes 'that sort of *Civility* which rises from a just *Sense* of the common *Rights* of Mankind, and the *natural Equality* there is amongst those of the same Species' (Voitle 1984: 332).

Codified by Hutcheson, benevolism was taught in educational institutions and popularized in literature. As a native progressive social philosophy it modified the reception of other critical ideas. Most of the writers of radical sensibility were influenced by Rousseau, especially by his criticism of the artificialities and inequalities of high society. Yet most rejected his flight from society and progress. Paine had attacked monarchical and aristocratic government and pointed to the progress which 'society' could make without their intervention. More importantly, the writers of the Scottish Enlightenment had developed theories of social progress which started from the assumptions of Hutcheson and linked progress with the liberalization of traditional power-relationships. Their theories stressed the progressive nature of man and the natural evolution of his institutions. Within their bulky treatises the topics which interested sensibility received voluminous treatment marked by typical differences of conservative and liberal leanings. All of them had to grapple with the fact that man, following his Hutchesonian natural sociability, had produced the 'commercial society' as the final stage of social evolution, which, in its selfishness and divisiveness, was profoundly anti-social. Only Smith robustly accepted the primacy of the selfish motive in economic and social progress. Others like Kames and Ferguson nostalgically harked back to the social virtues of more primitive stages and called for something analogous to warfare to maintain the vitality of public spirit. Millar took a more optimistic attitude to political progress. He supported Fox, joined the Friends of the People, contributed to the *Analytical Review*, and was persecuted for progressive opinions during the 1790s. Their theories of progress and their appeal to natural sociability find echoes in writers of the 1790s such as Godwin and Wollstonecraft. Godwin thought that the inequalities of 'commercial society' were perhaps necessary to awaken individual enterprise and the powers of mind, but that the progress of mind was now rendering obsolete the institutions which perpetuated inequality. Coleridge followed him in this, and in his vision of a society without personal property, though he justified it by reference to the communism of the primitive Christians. Radical sensibility largely disowned the appeal to commerce and materialistic interests which were a feature of Painite and Dissenting propaganda. While this high-mindedness invites charges of naivety, many writers at least implicitly acknowledged the importance of wealth, but only as a condition of independence or a source of beneficence.

Radical writers of sensibility stressed qualities in direct contrast to the popular degenerate model of the 'man of feeling' in emphasizing action and intervention. While giving precedence to the passions, they held, with Shaftesbury and Hutcheson, that self-centred passions, like the 'partial' affections towards family and local connections, could be regulated by a universal benevolence seeking the widest communal good. In championing individual sensibility they affirmed the authority of personal experience over precept and custom. In their ideas of equality they challenged the hierarchical distinctions of Burke's grand community of the living and the dead in which feudal loyalties assumed the authority of natural feelings. When the French Revolution offered a prospect of the triumph of their principles, British radicals were naturally drawn to its defence, yet, as the Revolution ran its course, all the premises of radical sensibility were thrown into doubt. Their struggles to sustain the radical faith in man's natural benevolence and sociability were largely unavailing as Robespierre imposed virtue by the guillotine and fusillade, and reaction triumphed in wartime Britain. Many writers who had seemed to favour a liberal sensibility, like

Hannah More, were quick to abandon its more radical features. Those who held fast to its liberal tenets, like Helen Maria Williams, Mary Wollstonecraft, and Charlotte Smith, became more extreme in their radicalism. In seeking a firm basis for their social criticism this latter group moved closer to the rationalism of William Godwin, to some extent compromising the distinguishing intuitive characteristic of sensibility, the claim that it preceded reason and judgment. During the 1790s Godwin himself, in acknowledging the insufficiency of reason as a motive to action, was moving closer to the ideas of sensibility. In their attempts to combat the hegemony of conservative sensibility the proponents of radical sensibility shared similar problems to those which dogged Godwin after he had asserted in *Political Justice* that Fénelon rather than a mother, father, or benefactor should be rescued from the burning palace. While criticizing the assumption of conservative sensibility that feelings towards husbands, parents, benefactors, rulers, and fatherland were beyond rational qualification and commanded instinctive loyalty, they certainly did not wish to deny the real value of such affections when they were soundly based. In the name of individual sensibility they qualified and attacked traditional sentimental images which enshrined conservative values just as Godwin attacked traditional social institutions in the name of individual reason.

In tracing the lineage of the radical sensibility of the 1790s I have adopted a 'history of ideas' approach, though it is not the study of a 'unitary idea' or the disclosure of some all-embracing world-view which reconciles diversities into universal harmony. The moral philosophy of the eighteenth century is as rich as any other age in its conflicts, its 'creative mis-readings', and its sheer misunderstandings of others' terminology and ideas. The ideas of sensibility can be described loosely in a way which will accommodate a variety of approaches, or they can, as Brissenden states, be linked with precise philosophical definitions. It would be a mistake to assume that the imaginative writers of the eighteenth century did not have access to the formulations of philosophers whose works were standard in the school-rooms, universities, and Dissenting Academies of the time, and were cited in the leading periodicals. Modern critical fashion is wary of works dealing with ideas, preferring to deal with literature which more obviously invokes artistic predecessors, betrays personal

INTRODUCTION

characteristics and ambivalences, and joins in the dance of signifiers in unrestrained intertextuality. The literature of the eighteenth century which invokes 'human nature' or 'the passions' offers a particularly tempting field for tracing modern patterns of desire and projecting a modern mistrust of reason. In wishing to restrain interpretation to the historical context I am also aware of the danger of trusting too much to a supposed continuity based on the repetition of verbal formulae. Conceptual formations change under the stress of history. Elements are discarded or substituted, different elements and connections privileged. It is often the imperialistic ambition of studies of this kind to establish master-paradigms which make sense of experience at both individual and national levels. But such iconic master-paradigms, like the discrimination of phonemes and the harmonies of music, exist only at a vertiginously high level of generality, and only Plato could claim that a change in the mode of music entailed a change of politics. Concepts and conceptual formations do not have a 'natural' history, nor is their development to be ascribed to a purely intellectual dialectic. They exist in conflict with counter-concepts against which they define themselves. The ideological battleground of the conflict is history, the events which not only invite appropriation by rival discourses, but often resist such appropriation. The French Revolution was initially appropriated by the discourse of radical sensibility. Its subsequent history resisted this appropriation and favoured the conservative paradigm. Such events could be seen as the knots and burrs of organic processes, the precipitates which create new valencies and new possibilities of combination. Hindsight might allow us to talk of events being 'constructed' by the 'dominant discourse', but it is in the struggles by which it achieves dominance that we can sense the pressure of history on its evolution. Dominance is seldom won without scars; areas of stress are problematized and often prove the site of fresh developments or new conflicts. For individuals the reversal of powerful conceptual formations causes a profound anxiety that can itself be conceptualized in a 'dark night of the soul' paradigm – for those who have come through it. Concepts, ideas, are the 'fictions' by which experience is naturalized to yield continuity, explanation, and plot, and it is in the transformations of these paradigms that history becomes meaningful. Conversely it is by relating these fictions to history that the transformations of paradigms can be explained. It is today almost heretical to suggest that a historical signified may lurk beneath the sign, that desire or feeling may have an object apart from the infinitely regressing deprivations of childhood, or that the sublime is more than an apotheosis of such privation. If the orthodoxies of Derrida and Lacan can be seen as methods of salvaging a disillusioned personal authority from the failure of 1968, a similar disillusionment can be seen in the writers of the 1790s. The object of feeling, the focus of the 'sublime' experience, is dissociated from communal aspirations to become the exponent of personal, often nostalgic, emotion. Feeling itself, from being a widely cited basis of authority, grows opaque to conceptualization, and the opposition of feeling and reason becomes dogma. In his treatise on the sublime, Burke ridiculed the fantastic notion that the order of society might rest on something as untrustworthy as our aesthetic sense and proclaimed that reason, pragmatism, and interest governed the conduct of men in society. This might serve to explain his part when, posing as the man of feeling, he achieved a pyrrhic victory, severing all connections between feeling and reason.

One of the points of distinction between writers in the tradition of sensibility is the degree to which they were willing to allow reason or reflection a role in moral behaviour. While they are linked by their reliance on a natural pre-rational apprehension of the 'beauty' of virtuous actions and dispositions and on the feelings as the source of benevolent actions, they differ as to the amount of rational investigation into the tendencies of actions involved in moral decisions. To those like Smith and Burke who apparently believed that the passions which lead men to action are divinely implanted instincts which ensure the good, and especially the stability, of the whole, little reflection on individual acts is required. Man's natural reverence for his superiors and partiality towards his family and immediate circle are justified by the Providential scheme whereby this unthinking loyalty is made the means of sustaining the whole system of society. It is even blasphemous to imagine that humanity can improve on this universal administration and extend beneficence to those whose situation excludes them from private partiality. Varieties of the Providential argument, from the sophisticated Hartleyan arguments of Coleridge to the more anti-humanist attitude of the Evangelicals, were the most common antagonists to radical sensibility's trust in the active powers of human benevolence. Hannah More (1801: 7: 39) attacked universal philanthropy as 'founded on the mad pretence of loving the poor better than God loves them'. Mary Wollstonecraft criticized Burke for accepting as the injunctions of sensibility tenets which were the result of such Providential as well as prudential reasoning: 'Affection for parents, reverence for superiors or antiquity, notions of honour, or that worldly self-interest that shrewdly shews them that honesty is the best policy: all proceed from the reason for which they serve as substitutes; – but it is reason at second-hand' (Wollstonecraft 1790: 71-2). Godwin, in his similar attacks on unreflecting habits of action, emphasized the role of reason so strongly that his links with the school of sensibility have been seen as tenuous, yet his system in *Political Justice* was recognized as a variant of that of Hutcheson and his later writings clearly show this affiliation.

The debates of the 1790s were characterized by a politicizing of issues raised within the school of sensibility to the extent that one's stand on matters such as the conduct of the private affections, charity, education, sympathy, genius, honour, and even the use of the reason, became political statements, aligned with conservative or radical ideologies. Under the suppression of direct political expression, these issues became a code in which conservative and progressive thinkers proclaimed their allegiances and worked out terms of accommodation. Godwin foresaw the amazement with which future generations would look back at the way philosophical ideas like universal philanthropy were subjected to the scorn and acrimony of political caricature. Yet he himself had welcomed the participation of philosophy no longer as a spectator but as an actor in the great national events of the Revolution. Philosophical concepts, however integral to a particular system, became utopian and revolutionary when released from the social contexts in which they had seemed self-evident.

The project of both radical and conservative after the confrontations of the 1790s was to stabilize the language, to accommodate the demands of the mind and those of reality. For many, this negotiation was staged on the scene of sensibility and in the context of domestic relationships functioning as paradigms of political struggle. Similar struggles were fought on philosophical terrain. Wordsworth maintained through the 1790s a faith both in man's active powers and in the beneficent power of nature – were they not harmonious aspects of the one life which animated man and nature? He found that Providence offered a more secure basis of hope as he digested the failures of man's aspirations, whether guided by reason or a rebellious imagination. The more restricted affections became his surest confirmation of man's essential benevolence, rather than the aspirations for universal amelioration of the early 1790s which had been justified by reason. Yet in works like *The Convention of Cintra* Wordsworth tried to invest the partial affections of family and patriotism with the same moral sublimity as the universal cause of the French Revolution and tried to reconcile them with the claims of reason. While conservatism triumphed politically, the coded war of sensibility transformed the linguistic and conceptual weapons by which it maintained its hegemony.

After the French Revolution it is easy to find examples of the ideological use of terms associated with sensibility. Hazlitt conducts an extended post-mortem on the failure of such idealism, seen particularly clearly in his *Memoirs of Thomas Holcroft*:

> Kind feelings and generous actions there always have been, and there always will be, while the intercourse of mankind shall endure: but the hope, that such feelings and such actions might become universal, rose and set with the French Revolution . . . The French Revolution was the only match that ever took place between philosophy and experience: and waking from the trance of theory to the sense of reality, we hear the words *truth, reason, virtue, liberty*, with the same indifference or contempt, that the cynic who has married a jilt or a termagant, listens to the rhapsodies of lovers.
>
> (Howe: 3: 156)

Hazlitt's cynicism is often theatrical and self-centred – the image of the 'jilt' here establishes the pattern of personal betrayal which Hazlitt often linked with the betrayal of Revolutionary hopes – but he directly testifies to the impoverishment of a range of vocabulary associated with radicalism and with sensibility. The same technique is used in *The Plain Speaker*:

> I was taught to think, and I was willing to believe, that

genius was not a bawd – that virtue was not a mask – that liberty was not a name – that love had its seat in the human heart. Now I would care little if these words were struck out of my dictionary, or if I had never heard them.

(Howe: 12: 135)

The brittle consensus of eighteenth-century benevolism had been broken and with it the optimistic idealism of its language. The classic texts of benevolism fell into neglect. Hazlitt in elegiac mood painted his father reading Shaftesbury's *Characteristicks*; Wordsworth in 1815 thought Shaftesbury unjustly depreciated. Samuel Parr in 1801 lamented that Hutcheson was now no longer widely studied, though Godwin continued to recommend his works.

Hazlitt looks back nostalgically to a time when the language of sensibility was aligned with liberal social doctrines, yet the ideological complexion of eighteenth-century sensibility is far from consistent. The difficulties of categorizing it are evident in modern studies. Mullan makes the rather astonishing claim that Hume's idea of sympathy was not bound by the patterns of social relations in the dominant classes of Hanoverian Britain but was an attempt to generalize the affective basis of these relations to a whole society and to 'human nature' in the abstract (Mullan 1988: 23). Only when he deals with Richardson does he notice the marks of sensibility being used to construct an ideological model of womanhood. Gary Kelly in his *English Fiction of the Romantic Period* is also in trouble over the ideological leanings of sensibility. For him it is predominantly a critical reformist movement, yet in dealing with Mary Wollstonecraft he calls sensibility 'that culture of courtliness in disguise' (Kelly 1989: 40). Mary Wollstonecraft is the cause of this inconsistency and she, as well as most of her critics, has difficulty distinguishing clearly between the conservative and radical senses of sentimental terminology.

Three trends in sensibility, the potentially radical, the conservative, and the self-indulgent, seem to coexist throughout the century, often uneasily cohabiting within the same text or providing parameters for the development of an author's attitude. Only in the 1780s and 1790s do these strands of a wide consensus unravel. Vicesimus Knox, for instance, wrote appreciatively of sensibility in the 1780s. One of his essays championing the education of women has recently been extracted as a challenge to prevailing ideas of female learning (Jones 1990: 106-9). During the 1790s he contributed a series of articles to the *Morning Chronicle* heavily critical of the government's conduct towards both Poland and France. Yet he became editor of the archetypal 'coffee-table' book *Elegant Extracts* and tried to suppress his radical works. For many the journey through the 1790s was not a political re-education in which the ideas of Paine or Godwin were superseded by a diametrically opposite set of ideas. Many retained or professed to maintain the same ideas of liberty and freedom as they had in their radical days. Burke's concern for cohesion and Godwin's gradualism both gave good grounds for postponing the millennium in the historical cirumstances of the time. A progressive sensibility deprived of more universal goals could still take the private sphere as its scene of beneficence and maintain a radical critique of society in more indirect ways. The continuities between a radical and a conservative sensibility, seemingly so irreconcilable, are readily explained if the quarrels between Burke and Godwin, Rousseau and Wollstonecraft, are seen as disputes between different viewpoints within the same formation.

The social dimension of the potentially radical strain of sensibility has, I think, been insufficiently recognized and confused with the more traditional social responsibilities acknowledged in conservative writing. Critics frequently point out that Mary Wollstonecraft and other authors involved with the concept of sensibility stress reason and duty to society, and often view this as part of the instability of the concept and of the writers themselves. In fact the impulse to benefit the widest system of which one is a member and the use of reason to ensure this end stem from the earlier philosophical representatives of the tradition, Shaftesbury and Hutcheson, whose ideas remained current until the end of the century.

The common anti-Jacobin narrative paradigm aligns sensibility with selfishness, sees the cultivation of an enthusiastic aesthetic taste as self-indulgent, and deep sympathetic emotions as dangerous. In the early writings of Edgeworth and Austen a sensibility attuned to the expansive sympathies propagated by poetry and music, and ready to engage in a love-relationship which transgresses social prohibitions, leads typically to tragedies like fainting on wet ground and contracting a fatal fever, or to marital infidelity and death in infamy. If the protagonist has any redeeming features, it leads to re-education to the norms of society, the learning of prudence, and submission to the traditional roles and obligations of society. Marianne Dashwood ends up mistress of a family, well integrated into the conservative patriarchal order, and reconciled to the prosaic Colonel Brandon, a realistic and fortunate, if unexciting, fate. We may compare this with a fiction of Mary Hays, a fervent apostle of Godwin and Mary Wollstonecraft. In her story of Henrietta from *Letters and Essays Moral and Miscellaneous* (1793; Hays 1974) the heroine's fervid sensibility experiences similar misfortunes to those of Marianne. She similarly succumbs to fever and a despair which she recognizes is liable to lead to death. Conquering this suicidal self-obsession, she determines to find fulfilment in the service of society. But the scene of Henrietta's usefulness is not in the world of subservience and custom. Like her author, she goes to London to join the march of intellect, the pursuit of 'moral and religious truth'. The varieties of sensibility are all linked, and considerable force is needed to compress them into one type or typical narrative trajectory. Neither radical nor conservative sensibility denied the pleasures of taste, sympathy, and enthusiasm. Radical sensibility could offer just as much in the way of discipline and social usefulness as the conservative alternative, and aim at that extensive benefit to society which was derided as illusory by conservative writers.

The anti-Jacobin satirists did their work only too well in ridiculing and suppressing the threat of radical sensibility. After the turn of the century the whole movement had been branded with weakness and irresponsibility. Women like Hays and Wollstonecraft who had aspired to sublimity of thought and action were 'unsex'd females'; men who responded to emotional impulses of benevolence were effeminate; both were dangerous. After the satirical pounding it sustained, it is little wonder that we now have difficulty in responding seriously to the language of sensibility.

Richard Parker, the 'President' of the mutineers of the Nore, appealed to sensibility as he died 'a Martyr in the cause of Humanity' for aiding armed rebellion. His 'Dying Declaration' states:

> I preserve my fortitude, and am enabled to do this by

considering that as a human being I stand subject to human passions, the noblest of which is a tender *sensibility at every species of human woe.* Thus influenced, how could I indifferently stand by, and behold some of the best of my fellow creatures cruelly treated by some of the very worst. I candidly confess I could not, and because I could not, fate consigns me to be a victim to the tenderest emotions of the human heart.

(Dobrée and Manwaring 1937: 226)

It comes as something of a shock to find language so often parodied, reminiscent of an erring heroine of sensibility, in the mouth of a mutineer, yet Parker was in deadly earnest. It is reported that his judges were moved to tears by his speech, just as Jeffrey is supposed to have wept in private over the 'mawkish' poetry of Wordsworth, but in neither case was the judgment rescinded.

The strongly evaluative use of gendered terms like 'masculine' and 'effeminate' became a feature of the reviewer's vocabulary, and had reference to more than stylistic considerations. The 'masculine' virtues of courage and strength employed in the defence of an inherited patriarchal structure were dominant. Wordsworth's picture of ideal man in *The Prelude* is anachronistically feminized if it is considered a nineteenth-century work, with its appeal to a heart 'tender as a nursing Mother's' and a life full of 'female softness' (xiii.207-8). More typical is the debate between Caroline Helstone and Shirley on the attraction of men like Rousseau and Cowper, and their decision in favour of men like Wellington. The demise of sensibility had immense consequences for gender definition. I have even been advised that a study of the concept can only be adequately performed by a woman. Feminist issues are prominent in the development of the attitudes of sensibility, and crucial in its defeat, but as a movement of ideas it engaged philosophers, artists, novelists, and poets in a wider egalitarian enterprise.

The book falls into two sections. In the first four chapters I have attempted to follow the historical evolution of sensibility as a complex of ideas, to indicate some of its main preoccupations and internal conflicts. The last three chapters deal with writers whose works span the 1790s and show their responses to historical events and the war of ideas. Wordsworth is the last of these

INTRODUCTION

and is the major literary figure of the period deeply affected by the tradition of sensibility. Much of the preceding material can be seen as a context which can be used to interpret his development.

1
VARIETIES OF SENSIBILITY

Although the word itself was not common before the mid-century, sensibility took over the ambiguities which clustered around the term 'sense' and became almost exclusively associated with the philosophers of the 'moral sense' school. Locke had focused attention on the senses as the only avenues of knowledge, and tended to emphasize perception and cognition. Sense-impressions beget ideas in the mind, commonly envisaged as pictures to be re-evoked by memory, analysed by reason, and recombined by wit and fancy. He also counted reflection as a source of ideas about the operations of the mind itself. Reflection, he admitted, was not a sense in the way in which he usually used the term, since it had nothing to do with external objects, but he believed it so very similar that he described it as an internal sense, from which we gain ideas of reasoning, willing, the idea of perception itself, and, in conjunction with the outer senses, ideas of pain and pleasure, existence, power, and succession. Later philosophers, applying an empirical psychology of introspection, tended to crowd into this category of inner sense or reflection all sorts of special senses which they felt to be implanted by nature or the creator, some of them suspiciously similar to the 'innate ideas' which Locke had hoped to banish from philosophical discussion. The aesthetic and moral senses posited by Shaftesbury were like the other senses in their immediacy of perception, yet they performed functions formerly credited to the reason. They were also suspiciously allied to the sense of pleasure and pain, since the immediate perception of beauty or virtue entailed pleasure. Locke had denominated pleasure and pain simple ideas, unresolvable and unexplainable;

they governed the passions as responses to things which caused joy or uneasiness. Desire itself was painful, an uneasiness caused by the absence of an imagined delight, while joy was the delight of possessing a good. Shaftesbury and Hutcheson reacted against the self-centredness of this definition and argued for the existence of altruistic passions and for a natural approbation of actions and dispositions which were directed towards the good of the whole. Such was the popularity of Locke's work, however, that Hutcheson had to argue particularly strenuously against the Lockean interpretation of the passion of benevolence. Later in the century Adam Smith produced another 'selfish' explanation of benevolence, that it was adopted to win the sympathy and favour of others. Fundamental to the whole debate over benevolence was the question of its limitations, whether man was capable of judging what was good for society as a whole, or whether he was to be contented with a domestic beneficence, confident that Providence would take care of the whole. Towards the end of the century a benevolence restricted to these 'inevitable charities' was stigmatized as selfish by many writers of sensibility.

Shaftesbury's distinctive emphasis is on the system of which the individual is a part. His aesthetic ideas stress the importance of seeing the part in relationship to the whole, and the moral sense judges of actions as they affect the whole system of which the individual is a part. Man has a moral sense which has an immediate apprehension of right and wrong, just as the aesthetic sense makes him aware of beauty and deformity:

> Let us suppose a Creature, who wanting Reason, and being unable to reflect, has, notwithstanding, many Good Qualities and Affections; as Love to his Kind, Courage, Gratitude or Pity. 'Tis certain that if you give to this creature a reflecting Faculty, it will at the same instant approve of Gratitude, Kindness and Pity; be taken with any show or representation of the social Passion, and think nothing more amiable than this, or more odious than the contrary. And this is *to be capable of Virtue*, and *to have a sense of Right and Wrong*.
>
> (*Char*: 2: 53)

In a celebrated passage this spontaneous judgment is referred to the 'heart', which, 'however false or corrupt it be within itself', can always find the 'Difference, as to Beauty and Comeliness, between one *Heart* and another, one *Turn of Affection*, one *Behaviour*, one *Sentiment* and another' (*Char*: 2: 53).

But if this spontaneous judgment of the heart approves of behaviour which benefits the system as a whole, then it has to have some relation to the reason. Shaftesbury points out 'how far WORTH and VIRTUE depend on a knowledge of *Right* and *Wrong*, and on a use of Reason sufficient to secure a right application of the Affections' (*Char*: 2: 34–5). The use of this reason is to direct benevolence to its proper objects. It might also have a role in regulating the 'economy' of the passions in preserving a balance between the '*Self-Affections*' and the '*natural Affections* which lead to the good of THE PUBLIC' (*Char*: 2: 86). Those thinkers who wished to direct natural benevolence to the most comprehensive objects had to incorporate a regulative and exploratory faculty into their account of the functioning of the moral sense and social passions, since the most usual natural affections might lead to the exclusive favouring of the most immediate objects: self, family, and friends. Shaftesbury finds it necessary to remark 'that even as to *Kindness* and *Love* of the most natural sort (such as that of any Creature for its Offspring) if it be immoderate and beyond a certain degree, it is undoubtedly vitious' (*Char*: 2: 27), and he condemns that 'PARTIAL AFFECTION, or social Love *in part*, without regard to a Society or a *Whole*' (*Char*: 2: 110).

Shaftesbury's discussion introduces the two elements which were to dominate the debate within the school of sensibility, and have been seen as constituting the different camps of 'rationalists' and 'sentimentalists'.[1] On the one side there is the stress on a natural capacity to respond to behaviour which is attuned to the good of the system. Typically this is presented as the response of a spectator to 'images' of such things as affections and sentiments. On the other side there is the stress on the reason or regulative faculty as the guide of an active social passion which seeks a goal expressed in utilitarian terms as the greatest good of the most extended system. Hume and Smith contribute to the sentimental side of the argument by minimizing the role of the reason and the impulse towards 'universal' benevolence, and by emphasizing the natural sympathies which bind society together in traditional groupings. The natural sympathies are discovered and defined by an empirical study of history and society as it now exists, and by the capacity of the individual for benevolence as it is envisaged in their individualistic, empirical philosophy. Both tend to glorify the narrow and customary allegiances which Shaftesbury had distrusted. They have some moral qualms about the mechanisms which they describe, since neither ignores the existence of injustice in society, but they are willing to leave moral justification to a creator who, by an unseen hand or implanted sense of 'utility', reconciles partial injustice with the good of the whole. Neither sees the individual as naturally capable of acting from the motives of universal benevolence. It is noticeable, however, that both support their assertions of man's capacity for benevolent sympathy by appealing to images from the drama and literature in ways which contradict the limitations of their own systems, bearing witness to the fact that Shaftesburyan ideas were dominant in aesthetic theory.

In the 1790s the two conflicting yet interconnected strands of sentimentalist thought were polarized in the confrontation between Burke and Godwin over the French Revolution. Although they have been seen as opposites, it is still possible to discern the family resemblances between them. Burke's appeal to feeling and prejudice does not exclude the exercise of a pragmatic reason in adjusting the mechanisms of the State, and his ideal statesman is a cautious reformer. Godwin too is no atomistic reasoner, since a fervid passion for the common good animates all the actions of his ideal reformers, whose commitment to gradualism can in theory amount to a full acquiescence in the caution of Burke's statesman. But, as the eventful decade progressed, the issues became so politicized that any *rapprochement* was impossible, and a triumphant conservative reaction seemed to confirm the most cynical contentions of Hume and Smith. It is, however, necessary to see the debate as one within the school of sensibility to appreciate how issues which had formed merely the matter of amicable argument, and ideas which had been seen as compatible, became the rival doctrines of political opponents. Reason versus passion, universal benevolence versus partial affection or enlightened selfishness, individual judgment versus the opinions and customs of society, the artistic imagination versus just moral and social ideas: while these issues had been debated within the philosophical and fictional writings of the century, their clash was now seen against the background of the French Revolution, its promise to mankind, and its threat to unreformed Britain. The pressure which was exerted on the radical camp was such as to reveal rifts between reformers which had not been evident earlier. Priestley could argue amicably with his colleagues about natural selfishness or benevolence in the 1780s and debate the merits of their repective proponents, Hartley and Hutcheson, since the goal of both was identical. Hartley had actually demonstrated the evolution of the moral sense from man's basic self-interest as the result of association. But when the dust settled from the conflicts between 'Jacobins' and conservatives, it was the ideas of Hartley and Priestley which formed the basis of philosophical radicalism and produced the image of the man of political economy – a selfish engrosser of ideas and pleasures who had to be educated and cajoled by rewards and penalties into the service of the public. The reason, which had been the guide and regulator of benevolence for Godwin, became the instrument of selfishness and materialism, still a weapon against aristocratic privilege, but informed by none of those benevolent ideas which Godwin had hoped would equalize men upwards to share the benefits of a further evolution of the aristocratic ideal.

The ideas of Francis Hutcheson serve as a source for both Godwin's development of the role of the reason and for the denigration of the reason in Hume's system. Hutcheson, in codifying Shaftesbury's ideas and bringing them into relation with other philosophical schools, shows a proselytizing zeal which attempts, by a certain wilful confusion of terminology, to annex other varieties of moral thought. He attempts to identify his use of 'reason' with that of the Rational Moralists like Balguy, who held that reason directly apprehended moral distinctions, and also claims an affinity between his moral sense and the Conscience of religious moralists like Butler. Generally, Hutcheson's distinctive and confusing contribution to sentimentalist thought is to emphasize the regulative aspect of benevolence and to underscore Shaftesbury's universalist premises, while hardly ever using the term 'reason' for the faculty which ensures these goals. Hutcheson often uses the term 'reflection' where Shaftesbury might have used 'reason', since he is anxious to locate his moral sense within the reflective rather than the sensitive operations of the human mind as described by Locke. The 'reflection' is for Hutcheson a general term for 'those powers and determinations of mind by which it perceives, or is conscious of all within itself, its actions, passions, judgments, wills, desires, joys, sorrows, purposes of action' (Hutcheson 1753: 1: 6).

Hutcheson insists that passions and affections, not reason, are the causes of actions, but that the moral sense approves of benevolent actions and especially of those actions producing the widest good. The 'exciting' reason of an action is a passion, the 'justifying' reason is drawn from the moral sense (Hutcheson 1971: 121). The moral sense delivers an immediate apprehension, yet it can apparently calculate the extent of an action's benevolence and the regulation necessary for its production. Reason or 'reflection' seems to have an essential role to play here, since it informs us of the tendencies of actions and it is only by reflection that we form useful abstract conceptions about the superiority of universal goals. Godwin's principle of justice is one of these abstract principles, but Hutcheson suggests that they

> only serve to suggest greater ends than would occur to us without reflection and by the prepollency of one desire toward the greater good, to either private or public, to stop the desire toward the smaller good when it appears inconsistent with the greater.
> (1971: 124-5)

The natural affection of public spirit itself seems to be capable of regulating the other lesser affections and, of course, gaining the approbation of the moral sense. As reason is powerless to incite to virtue, abstract principles and moral persuasion can have no power over those who have no public affections. Only those who possess them can be moved to virtue and appreciate the pleasure arising from them. Hutcheson's purpose is not to persuade to virtue, but to remove those 'opinions of opposite interests', confident that, thus enfranchised, 'a natural disposition can scarcely fail to exert itself to the full' (1971: 107). One who fails to grasp the connection between his own happiness and public good and follows only his selfish ends must 'have perpetual remorse and dissatisfaction with his own temper, through his moral sense' (1971: 127-8).

The incommunicability of the pleasures of benevolence to those who do not share them is a good answer to those who would characterize his benevolence as selfish, yet it posed considerable problems for later educationists, like the Edgeworths, who wanted to recommend benevolence as a source of pleasure, yet distrusted the excesses of sensibility. Notoriously, sensibility was often considered as the possession of a cultivated élite, whose delights 'To those who know thee not, no words can paint', as Hannah More explained in her poem *Sensibility* (1785). If the 'natural disposition' is so favourable to virtue, then progress seems to be inevitable if the benevolent affections and the moral sense are given free play, disabused of artificial moral principles inculcated by custom, society, and religion, and exercised and refined by moral experience. Shelley, who had a similar trust in man's 'natural disposition', looked forward in *Prometheus Unbound* to the day when human nature was 'its own divine controul' (Shelley 1977: 205), yet the woman of sensibility, that much-praised paragon of self-control, required a total transformation to become Shelley's new woman, 'frank, beautiful and kind' and 'From custom's taint exempt and pure' (1977: 193). Perhaps the more obvious way of interpreting Hutcheson in a progressive way was to emphasize the importance of reason as an ally of benevolence and the moral sense in discovering what courses really benefited mankind. This was less certain, however, as reason was assailed by opinion, dominated by the constructs of the age. Hutcheson could count among his intellectual progeny both Godwin and Hume. While Godwin develops his stress on reason or reflection as the regulative aspect of the moral sense, connected with ensuring universal benevolence, Hume develops the idea of the non-appetitive nature of the reason. Hume may also have been influenced by the importance which Hutcheson ascribed to 'opinion' in human action and the way in which he stresses, with Locke, that opinion is likely to be affected by untrustworthy associations of ideas, which 'raise the Passions into an extravagant Degree, beyond the proportion of real Good in the Object: and commonly beget some secret Opinions to justify the Passions' (Hutcheson 1969: 95).

Hume similarly diminishes the importance of reason in the formation of opinion and motivation of action and trusts to a notoriously ill-defined sentiment, feeling, or passion, made uniform in human nature by the creator, and evident in the empirical study of history. In the account of moral behaviour in the *Treatise*, Hume relies on the workings of sympathy. In sympathy we partake of the joys and sorrows of those we observe. The mechanics of the process are based on observation of the outward signs of emotion which we recognize because of the similarity of all human expression. We almost instantaneously interpret these signs as expressions we ourselves use, and convert the ideas of these emotions into the emotions themselves. Godwin was later to make a point of the similarity of men's constitutions leading to sympathetic and benevolent feelings, and if he recommended the *Treatise* to other friends as pertinaciously as he did to Tom Wedgwood, this might well be the source of Wordsworth's account of the conversion of observed experience into re-evoked emotion in the Preface to *Lyrical Ballads*. Hume believes that we are similarly affected by a dramatic performance or literary presentation which makes a vivid impression on our minds but, outside aesthetic experience, the operation of sympathy is controlled by the same factors which control the vividness of impression in cognitive response: we react more vividly to images that are close to us in relationship, in space, and in time, and, more importantly, we react with greater sympathy to those whose pleasures we can vicariously enjoy than those whose sorrow might engage our feelings.

Sympathy is most assured when the object is connected with ourselves:

> Whoever is united to us by any connexion is always sure of a share of our love, proportion'd to the connexion, without enquiry into his other qualities. Thus the relationship of blood produces the strongest tie the mind is capable of in the love of parents to their children, and a lesser degree of the same affection, as the relation lessens. Nor has consanguinity alone this effect, but any other relation without exception. We love our countrymen, our neighbours, those of the same trade, profession, and even name with ourselves.
> (*Treatise*: 352)

Habit has an important part to play in this distribution of affection, since it strengthens the conception of any object. When Hume goes on to investigate our capacity to sympathize with objects other than those intimately connected to the self, his first objects are the rich and the powerful: 'Nothing has a greater tendency to give us an esteem for any person, than his power and riches; or a contempt, than his poverty and meanness' (*Treatise*: 357). Hume does not immediately resolve this esteem into sympathy with imagined power. The main attractive adjunct to prosperity that he adduces is the pleasure of the imagination which relishes the objects with which the rich surround themselves 'such as houses, gardens, equipages; which, being agreeable in themselves, necessarily produce a sentiment of pleasure in everyone, that either considers or surveys them' (*Treatise*: 357-8). This concurrence of the pleasures of art and imagination in sanctioning the wealth and power of the mighty later gave many thinkers doubts about the moral basis of the artistic imagination. Hume asserts that 'men of wit always turn the discourse on subjects which are entertaining to the imagination; and poets never present any objects but such as are of the same nature'. Philips had written on cider in a manner which would never consort with beer, and no doubt if wine had been a native product that would have monopolized his song. So we may 'comprehend the delicacy of the imagination among the causes of the respect, which we pay the rich and powerful' (*Treatise*: 358). Hume maintains that this respect for the rich and powerful is reinforced by their connection with their forebears: 'For what is it we call a man of birth, but one who is descended from a long succession of rich and powerful ancestors, and who acquires our esteem by his relation to persons whom we esteem' (*Treatise*: 361). Hume can dismiss his (selfish) hypothesis that our esteem is based on the hope of actually partaking in these advantages, and rest on the conclusion that:

> there remains nothing which can give us an esteem for power and riches and a contempt for meanness and poverty, except the principle of *sympathy*, by which we enter into the sentiments of the rich and poor, and partake of their pleasures and uneasiness. Riches give satisfaction to their possessor, and this satisfaction is convey'd to the beholder by the imagination, which produces an idea resembling the original impression in force and vivacity.
>
> (*Treatise*: 362)

However 'natural' the mechanisms of sympathy are, Hume's examples are dominated by the aristocratic and patriarchal distinctions of his own day, which might suggest that they too are similarly natural. Dealing with transitions of the passions and the imagination from one object to another he emphasizes a hierarchical order. 'Our passions', he finds, 'descend with greater facility than they ascend.' It is 'more natural for us to love the son upon account of the father, than the father upon account of the son; the servant for the master; . . . the subject for the prince'. On the other hand the imagination finds it easier to ascend from the inferior object to the more considerable, from the satellites of Jupiter to the planet itself, and on that principle is founded the practice of giving wives the husband's name and all the ceremonies giving social precedence to the illustrious (*Treatise*: 341-2).

Our sympathy with distress, for Hume, is again most certain when the object is a friend or relation and, when extended to others, is governed by the extent of their distress and the force with which it is presented. A weak sympathy with distress is likely to cause contempt:

> A certain degree of poverty produces contempt; but a degree beyond causes compassion and good will. We may undervalue a peasant or servant; but when the misery of a beggar appears very great, or is painted in very lively colours, we sympathise with him in his afflictions, and feel in our heart evident touches of pity and benevolence.
>
> (*Treatise*: 387)

Once again the imagination is appealed to in dubious moral circumstances. A lively presentation of distress, such as Burke's theatrical presentation of the discomfiture of Marie-Antoinette, is likely to evoke more sympathy than other worthy objects. Hume's sympathy with distress is further limited by his assertion that, if the distress is too great, the result will be aversion. We may look with compassion on a man due to be executed, but are overcome with revulsion when contemplating the torture of the rack.

There is no suggestion in the *Treatise* that man is naturally capable of restraining his partial affections or his selfishness by an extended idea of the good of society. We cannot 'hope for any inartificial principle of the human mind, which might controul those partial affections, and make us overcome the temptations arising from circumstances' (*Treatise*: 488). Consequently justice is an 'artificial' virtue, supported by public praise and blame, and fostered by education and politicians. Hume does emphasize what Adam Smith called the 'remarkable distinction' between justice and the other virtues, which might well have influenced Godwin. Whereas the exercise of benevolence is left to the individual's choice, justice is so important to the fabric of the community, having regard to property rights and contracts, that there is a paramount obligation on everyone to obey it. Godwin might well have been inspired by the conception of a whole society bound to ideas of just actions, but by a natural impulse, not indoctrination or coercion. As Dugald Stewart later commented, Godwin had adopted the obligation of justice but applied it to the system of benevolence.[2]

Whereas Hume does not extend his ideas of natural sympathy to support the whole organization of society, Adam Smith erects a model of established society completely cemented by bonds of feeling and sympathy. It is the universal desire for sympathy which keeps men within the bounds of socially acceptable behaviour. In his *Theory of Moral Sentiments*, originally published in 1759, man 'does not want to be great, but to be beloved' (Smith 1976: 166), and to find perfect sympathy in others: 'to see the emotions of their hearts in every respect beat time to his own' (1976: 22). In order to provide such sympathy, the spectator must endeavour to 'bring home to himself every little circumstance of distress which can possibly occur to the sufferer. He must adopt the whole case of his companion, with all its minutest incidents, and strive to render as perfect as possible that imaginary change of place on which his sympathy is founded' (1976: 21). It is indeed a mark of our progress in civilization that sympathy is so common, since savages, because of the harsh conditions shared by all, show little compassion and expect none. Smith emphasizes the ability of the imagination to enter into the feelings of another without distinction of rank or relationship, and in this respect his sympathy may seem less restricted than that of Hume, especially since he asserts that in imagination we might indeed suffer with the prisoner on the rack. Yet Smith's sympathy is even more regulated than Hume's. The perfect sympathy which he has evoked as the yearning of the heart is, in fact, impossible. Naught loves another as itself, and if we wish to procure a realistic amount of sympathy then we must moderate our passions to that degree with which an impartial spectator might be expected to sympathize (1976: 22-3). If Smith is a representative of sensibility, here he is closer to Eleanor than Marianne Dashwood. Since, in Smith's version of Hume's theory, moral distinctions are reducible to a feeling of approbation or disapprobation, sympathy has a moral aspect and the imagined impartial spectator is a moral arbiter whose sympathy is equivalent to moral approbation. Smith sometimes suggests that this impartial spectator is superior to the fashions, follies, and injustices of contemporary society, but, judging from his examples of sympathy, it appears that this impartial spectator is completely attuned to the sentiments which uphold the present state of society.

Like Hume, Smith asserts that we more readily sympathize with the rich and powerful, and implies that the latter have a duty to parade their clothes, equipage, and other luxuries for the admiration of the vulgar. The 'disposition to admire and almost to worship the rich and the powerful and to despise or at least to neglect, persons of poor and mean condition' is, he admits, detrimental to morals (Smith: 1976: 61), but it is justified in supporting the stability of the social structure: 'Nature has wisely judged that the distinction of ranks, the peace and order of society, would rest more securely upon the plain and palpable difference of birth and fortune, than upon the invisible and often uncertain difference of wisdom and virtue' (1976: 226). The stability of society is also served by the restriction of charity to the narrow circle of habitual connections, since 'the peace and order of society is of more importance than even the relief of the miserable' (1976: 226). Sympathy, as 'affection', binds together the bonds of family, tribe, region, and nation, for 'what is called affection, is, in reality, nothing but habitual sympathy' (1976: 220). Such allegiances are certainly not linked with a love of mankind in general: 'the love of our own country seems not to be derived from the love of mankind . . . We do not love our country merely as a part of the great society of mankind; we love it for its own sake, and independently of any such consideration' (1976: 229). Similarly, our respect for kings is something that surpasses legal obligation and approaches worship: 'That kings are the servants of the people, to be obeyed, resisted, deposed, or punished, as the public conveniency may require, is the doctrine of reason and philosophy; but it is not the doctrine of nature' (1976: 53). The way in which natural feeling supports the hierarchical distinctions of society here anticipates Burke's claim that it is 'natural' to 'look up with awe to kings, with affection to parliaments, with duty to magistrates, with reverence to priests, and with respect to nobility' (Burke 1803: 5: 161).

With regard to criminal justice, Smith's sympathy is far from soft; our sympathy with the victims of crime produces 'an immediate and instinctive approbation of the sacred and necessary law of retaliation' (Smith 1976: 71). Smith's ideas of natural sympathy and natural emotions seem to be so patently derived from existing society that he has little of Hume's difficulty in deciding on what basis justice operates as a motive of action. He picks up Hume's distinction of justice as a paramount obligation, without which the whole edifice of society would fall, and immediately decides that 'nature has implanted in the human breast that consciousness of ill-desert, those terrors of merited punishment which attend upon its violation, as the great safeguards of the association of mankind'. It is sometimes questionable whether Smith should be enrolled among the followers of sensibility at all, since his estimate of natural human benevolence is so low:

> Men, though naturally sympathetic, feel so little for another, with whom they have no particular connexion, in comparison to what they feel for themselves; the misery of one, who is merely their fellow-creature, is of so little importance to them in comparison even of a small conveniency of their own . . . that if this principle did not stand up within them in his defence, and overawe them into a respect for his innocence, they would, like wild beasts, be at all times ready to fly upon him; and a man would enter an assembly of men as he enters a den of lions.
> (1976: 86)

Smith criticized Hutcheson for underestimating the selfish aspect of human behaviour, and, given his own account of man's benevolent propensities, it is perhaps little wonder that his work gives a model of the man of humane sensibility as an amiable perpetual victim too good for this world:

> There is a helplessness in the character of extreme humanity which more than anything interests our pity . . . We only regret that it is unfit for the world, because the world is unworthy of it, and because it must expose the person who is endowed with it as a prey to the perfidy and ingratitude of insinuating falsehood, and to a thousand pains and uneasinesses, which, of all men, he the least deserves to feel, which generally too he is, of all men, the least capable of supporting.
> (Smith 1976: 40)

Smith admits that those unjustly condemned by society would find the impartial spectator partly of mortal extraction, since they could only find consolation in another world of more candour, humanity, and justice than the present; where their innocence is in due time to be declared, and their virtue to be finally rewarded.

Smith contributed largely to the characteristic features of the novel of sensibility, notably in the greater complacency with which novelists dispatched to a secure heavenly judgment heroines or other females who had been unlucky enough to experience the fate of Clarissa, and especially in the character of the man of sensibility. This Harleyesque character became the archetypal man of feeling of the later period, especially among more conservative writers, and it has been justly censured by critics as a degeneration of the type. It has been persuasively argued that such examples as Yorick, Harley, and Dr Primrose, while attractive in their amiable human weaknesses, are implicitly criticized by their creators for an over-reliance on untrustworthy natural feeling. Sheriff argues that this authorial criticism is consistent with philosophical and moral positions espoused by their authors in other contexts. Thus Yorick is implicitly criticized for his lack of that consistent and firm Conscience which in Sterne's sermons is the guide and regulator of human conduct, while Dr Primrose and Harley are criticized for their lack of that awareness of social reality, custom, and opinion which Hume and Smith had emphasized. Sheriff writes of the 'compromise' made between the ideas of the sentimentalists and the rationalists:

> Ethical philosophers like Hume and Smith and literary artists like Sterne and Mackenzie took from sentimental ethics and the concept of good nature only natural sympathy; from the ethics of the rationalists and the exaltation of reason they took only an awareness of social custom and opinion. They believed that with these two ingredients, fairly consistent moral conduct in society was possible.
>
> (Sheriff 1982: 96)

The Hume/Smith position was by no means widely accepted. Reid objected to the demotion of reason as the arbiter of morality and to the vagueness of Hume's appeal to passion and feeling. Both he and Adam Ferguson restated the Shaftesbury/ Hutcheson faith in natural social feelings as against what they felt was a modified system of selfishness. Ferguson's *Essay on the History of Civil Society* (1767) seems at points to be waging a running battle with Smith as it attacks those features of contemporary society which Smith saw as essential to its stability and progress. Deriving moral sentiment from natural sociability and fellow-feeling, he sees 'savage' society as the original social compact:

> Prior to the establishment of property, and the distinction of ranks, men have a right to defend their persons, and to act with freedom; they have a right to maintain the apprehensions of reason, and the feelings of the heart; and they cannot for a moment converse with one another, without feeling that the part they maintain may be just or unjust.
>
> (Ferguson 1966: 34–5)

Our natural 'sensibility' to right and wrong, when 'joined to the powers of deliberation and reason', constitutes the 'basis of a moral nature' (1966: 33). Though Ferguson's main intention is to show the progress of society, and he spends some time debunking the supposed perfections of Greece and Rome, the natural sociability of primitive tribal society has a moral appeal which admonishes the supposed advances of modern society. Rather than finding a defect of sympathy and sensibility among primitive peoples, he regards them as more alive to the emotions of public spirit and disinterested benevolence. The fact that the American Indians 'appeared to have no apprehensions of gratitude, as a duty by which the one was bound to make a return', is a mark not of moral and sentimental depravity but of the most exalted equality and freedom:

> It was their favourite maxim, That no man is naturally indebted to another; that he is not, therefore, obliged to bear with any imposition, or unequal treatment. Thus, in a principle apparently sullen and inhospitable, they have discovered the foundation of justice, and observe its rules, with a steadiness and candour which no cultivation has been found to improve. The freedom which they give in what relates to the supposed duties of kindness and friend-

ship, serves only to engage the heart more entirely, where it is once possessed with affection . . . The love of equality, and the love of justice, were originally the same.

(1966: 88)

In that time he finds virtues which have fled civilized society with its unnatural divisions. 'The case, however, is not desperate', he comments, 'till we have formed our system of politics, as well as manners; till we have sold our freedom for titles, equipage, and distinctions; till we see no merit but prosperity and power, no disgrace but poverty and neglect' (1966: 40). Ferguson concedes that modern societies show the natural development of original propensities. Thus the sociable herding instinct leads to the establishment of nations and care for subsistence leads to accumulation and commerce. Nevertheless he objects to narrow definitions of pleasure, since the exercise of benevolence is 'the first and the principal constituent of human happiness' (1966: 53). He considers that modern states are fostering competition and commerce to excess, isolating the individual and depriving him of the satisfactions of public service. He anticipates Godwin's individualistic criticism of governments which, by institutionalizing virtue, assume the responsibility which should properly lie with the individual. The praise of free commerce which develops from this position is abruptly curtailed and qualified. In the expectation of a superior exposition of this doctrine (perhaps delayed until 1776), he comments:

> I willingly quit a subject in which I am not much conversant, and still less engaged by the views with which I write. Speculations on commerce and wealth have been delivered by the ablest writers, who have left nothing so important to be offered on the subject, as the general caution, not to consider these articles as making the sum of national felicity, or the principal object of any state.
>
> (1966: 144-5)

Ferguson's *Essay* outlines a position similar to that of most Scottish social historians, though he is more outspoken in his condemnation of commercial society and his preference for a primitive stage which, Duncan Forbes has argued, can be equated with the Scottish clan system. His emphasis on a principle of progression and a 'desire for perfection' (Ferguson

1966: 8) within man leads him to the same 'essentialist' position as that of Godwin and later perfectibilists in that, though his evidence for progress is historical, its goal cannot be a matter of imitation, or of reliance on established standards and written documents. To arrive at the best state of nature, he argues, man

> cannot find it perhaps in the practice of any individual, or of any nation whatsoever; not even in the sense of the majority, or the prevailing opinion of his kind. He must look for it in the best conception of his understanding, in the best movements of his heart; he must thence discover what is the perfection and happiness of which he is capable.
> (1966: 9)

Though he gives Montesquieu obsequious praise, he doubts the inevitable connection of a 'spirit' with a particular constitution. The principle of virtue associated by Montesquieu with a republic is admitted to be a wonderful ideal, but 'perhaps we must have possessed the principle, in order, with any hopes of advantage, to receive the form' (Ferguson 1966: 67). The 'moderation' ascribed to aristocratic states is scanned as the 'moderated arrogance' of one class and the 'limited deference' of the other (1966: 68). The principle of honour associated with monarchies points out the duties and dignities associated with each rank, so that society is 'intangled together' with reciprocal obligations, but subjects are not 'combined by the sense of a common interest', neither do they possess the 'sense of equality, that will bear no incroachment on the personal rights of the meanest citizen; the indignant spirit, that will not court a protection nor accept as a favour, what is due as a right; the public affection, which is founded on the neglect of personal considerations' (1966: 70). It is equally fallacious to rely on laws as the bastion of liberty, since they are open to evasion if 'they are not enforced by the very spirit from which they arose . . . the influence of laws . . . is not any magic power descending from shelves that are loaded with books, but is, in reality, the influence of men resolved to be free' (1966: 263-4).

The spirit of modern commercial society dissolves all ideals of virtue and honour into a scramble for riches and power '[w]here the desire of a supposed happiness serves to inflame the worst of passions, and is itself the foundation of misery'. Virtue has fled the field of public life, since only Sparta made virtue an object of policy. Society is only redeemed by the alloy of good and evil in every individual and the virtue of private life where 'its frequency, as a spontaneous offspring of the heart, will restore the honours of our nature' (Ferguson 1966: 162).

Later, when the success of the *Essay* had established Ferguson more securely in the order of power and riches, he was less scathing in his attacks on modern society and more cautious in his expectations of advances towards perfection. In his *Principles of Moral and Political Science* (Ferguson 1792) he continues to distance himself from Smith's exclusivity of feeling by asserting 'a principle of sympathy and indiscriminate concern in the condition of a fellow creature, whether prosperous or adverse, to which, as congenial to man, even where it operates towards any other animal, we give the name of humanity' (1792: 1: 125). But though moral feelings are still based upon 'sensibility', they are given their direction by opinion, and influenced by considerations such as power, honour, and riches. Ferguson is more easy in his role of investigating not 'what men ought to do, but what is the ordinary tract in which they proceed' (1792: 1: 263). His use of the word 'must' in the following passage has the typical ambiguity of an exhortation to reluctant resignation and a statement of empirical historical fact: Mankind, he asserts, 'must be contented to act in the situation in which they find themselves placed; and, except when urged by great occasions, seldom project, and rarely at once obtain, any great innovation' (1792: 1: 263). The balance of ambiguity has shifted from the *Essay*, when the 'inevitable' progress of society was regarded with a moral indignation which made resignation difficult. On revolution as a historical phenomenon he refused to give a verdict, considering it 'the great problem of political wisdom' in which 'maxims of science and reason or principles of justice are inculcated in vain'. It is an example of 'the powerful instincts of nature' in the multitude which the philosopher cannot pronounce justified or unjustified without establishing general principles which compromise the rights of the citizen or the rights of governments (1792: 2: 291). War, however, he thought necessary to the preservation of virtue, since it fostered public spirit. The cardinal virtues revive when property is jeopardized.

Ferguson shows a greater Rousseauistic or Hutchesonian influence in his *Essay* than most of the other Scottish social historians, who were less certain of the original benevolence of man or more sanguine about the rise of freedom and individualism. John Millar, whose influential *Origin of the Distinction of Ranks* appeared four years later, to be followed by his *An Historical View of English Government* (1787), saw the development of commerce and industry as inseparably bound up with the development of the arts, liberal humanitarianism, and individual freedom. While he has the same reaction as Ferguson to modern selfish materialism his optimistic reading of history sees a progression towards a more egalitarian and moral society.

Self-aggrandizement and self-preservation are the motive forces of history in Millar's account of the early political process. The leader of a group of conquering and quarrelsome barons becomes sovereign of the conquered territory by offering feudal protection to threatened barons and then to the minor proprietors against the barons. A similar conflict between monarch and aristocracy had led to the establishment of the rights of subjects in modern times, though if Charles I had maintained a standing army as his fellow continental monarchs had done we would have suffered the same fate of absolute rule. Less distrustful than Ferguson of established laws and documents, he valued the charters and bills of rights by which the people had, through their traditional power of granting taxes, limited the power of the monarch since the times of the witenagemot. He has something to offer Burke in defending the continuity of the Constitution not only through the 1689 settlement but even in the period of the Norman invasion. For an avowed Whig, he shows a surprising reluctance to condemn the 'Norman Yoke', which he sees as merely the introduction of conditions common to the rest of Europe and already largely established in pre-Norman Britain. Like Paine, he maintains that natural rights are not lost in civil life, but he admits that they are modified. Restraints there must be, but neither 'greater nor more numerous, than are necessary for the general prosperity and happiness' (Millar 1803: 295). The principle of utility evident in this formulation was for Millar the mark of difference between himself as a Whig and the Tory reliance on authority. Utility, however, is not a distinctive Whig principle. Notoriously employed by Paley, it claims descent from both Hutcheson and Hume, the latter a Tory, if a 'speculative' one as Millar dubbed him. Millar was not, however, guided by any test of longevity or extent of acceptance in his estimate of utility. Utility was governed by the progressive interests of society, and progress was towards the wider diffusion of wealth and power, and the growing preponderance of 'the people at large' who demanded 'the equalization of ranks, and the diffusion of popular privileges' (1803: 307). The idea of contract, often cited as Locke's radical legacy to the Whigs, receives as short shrift from Millar as it later did from Godwin. It can be reduced to the idea of a binding promise, such as Burke used to deny the present generation the right to renegotiate a century-old contract of submission. Millar's concept of utility, like Godwin's principle of justice, makes short work of contract theory: 'a promise inconsistent with any great interest of society is not productive of moral obligation' (1803: 301). The similarity between the ultra-radical Godwin and the cautious Scottish Whig on a theme which brought the former lasting opprobrium throws into relief other points in which they coincide.

Millar, like many in the mid-century period, was torn between the idea of interests, rights, and feelings as individualistic and selfish, or at least self-interested, and the Shaftesbury/Hutcheson idea that they were 'social' and directed towards the good of society as a whole. He seems to follow Smith in his use of a spectator to evaluate benevolence, but in such a way as to highlight the selfishness of the spectator's expectations. Those who show benevolence, he says, 'gratify the selfish feelings of the spectator, and call forth a sort of gratitude from every person who conceives himself within the sphere of their beneficial influence' (Millar 1803: 274). But virtue has a 'natural' attraction which is innocent of views of interest. It has 'a native beauty and excellence, which is felt and acknowledged by all the world; which, from the immediate contemplation of it, and without regard to its consequences, is the genuine source of pleasure and satisfaction' (1803: 272). Yet after considering this reaction as natural and unreasoning he dismisses the question whether these are 'simple and original' feelings or 'excited from different views and reasonings' as metaphysical. As it affects practical morality this is 'of little importance' (1803: 273).

Millar's may be viewed as one of the best-balanced accounts of historical and contemporary events. Like Ferguson, he held that a 'division of ranks' or at least a principle of subordination was necessary in society, but he did not go so far as Ferguson as to assert that it was the natural growth of the practice of choosing a leader in war and that it thereafter followed the preordained progress of society towards establishing hierarchy and dependence, eventually to be dissolved by a commercial free-for-all when distinctions of personal virtue were irretrievably lost. If government depends on opinion, then it is a historical fact that a principle of subordination is natural, as Burke might say, a saving grace, to society. But the terms of this subordination are always changing with the changing interests of society. Millar valued the 'feelings of the human mind which give rise to authority' as a 'wise provision of nature for supporting the order and government of society' but they must be 'regretted and condemned' when they are made 'as happens, very often the instruments of tyranny and oppression' (Millar 1803: 310). Millar himself supported interventionist movements like the anti-slavery campaign and reformist politicians like Fox. He backed the Rockingham Whigs in their battle against Crown influence, but gradually came to the view that the aristocracy had become the partners of monarchical oppression instead of its opponents and championed the rights of the people, supporting the extension of the franchise. He did not hesitate to praise the French Revolution as a triumph of philosophy and science and only regretted that in the general wreck of opinions it had overthrown those regulations which defended the civil rights of the inhabitants (1803: 308). A member of the Society of the Friends of the People and a contributor to the *Analytical Review*, he suffered much criticism for his reformist activities, and his son, who was more extreme in his views, was forced to emigrate to America where he died a victim of the climate. According to John Craig's biographical note, Millar was still sanguine of a good result to the Revolution even after Napoleon came to power. Craig also credits him with 'a heart overflowing with benevolence and sensibility' and the expression of his sensibility, like his moral philosophy, seems to have been influenced by Smith in the pains he took 'to repress every exterior mark of affliction, every thing which might appear a demand on the sympathy of his friend' (Millar 1806: cxxiii).

Millar's work was widely read and traces of his ideas of historical evolution are evident in the work of Mary Wollstonecraft, Godwin, and Coleridge. They all, however, wanted to carry his view of history to a different conclusion, in which the enlightenment brought by the diffusion of wealth overcame the materialistic motives of commerce and produced a triumph of benevolence and humanity. Though Millar dealt with the topics of sensibility, he rarely committed himself to statements about the benevolent nature or capabilities of man or woman, dealing more in historical constructions which gave scant support for any other than the selfish hypothesis. His *Division of Ranks* charts the effects of historical progress on several relationships of great interest to sensibility, those of father and child, master and slave, man and woman, king and subject. He generally demonstrates a humanizing of the original power-relationship into terms of greater equality, yet he also sees the dangers of the breakdown of established order and subordination in the equality of competing interests established by commercial society. Filmer's derivation of the absolute authority of the monarch from that of the father draws a diatribe against the attempt 'to defend one system of oppression by another' (Millar 1806: 138) and the assertion that such power is regulated by the interests of the governed. If either is extended further it 'immediately degenerates into usurpation, and is to be regarded as a violation of the rights of mankind' (1806: 138). Yet he fears that proper domestic subordination is threatened by the new independence of wage-earning children.

When he deals with the progress of woman from a disregarded chattel to the object of chivalric devotion and later to the friend and companion of man, Millar is one of the few eighteenth-century writers who see the conservative model of the woman of sensibility not as an expression of her essential nature but as a social construction. In an age of regular government improving in 'useful Arts and manufactures' woman becomes less the object of those romantic and extravagant passions which are the offspring of a disordered society, and becomes capable of 'securing the esteem and affection of her husband, by dividing his cares, by sharing his joys, and by soothing his misfortunes' (Millar 1806: 89-90). She is indeed possessed 'of peculiar delicacy and sensibility' but Millar leaves it an open question whether this is 'derived from original constitution, or from her way of life' (1806: 89). It is education which gives women modesty, diffidence, and industry in domestic economy, and leads them to adhere 'to that particular standard of propriety and excellence which is set before them' (1806: 90). It is their confinement to the family which causes them 'in a particular manner, to improve those feelings of the heart which are excited by these tender connections' (1806: 91). The succeeding age of 'opulence and elegant arts' sees them emerging into society to partake in and minister to the pleasures of society, which leads to 'licentiousness and dissolute manners' (1806: 101). The Christian tradition of Europe has so far averted the excesses of Roman and Eastern social decay, but gallantry has become a 'serious occupation' (1806: 108).

Millar sees sympathy and benevolence as largely restricted to the 'conjugal, the parental, and filial relations' as a sphere 'adapted to the limited capacities of the human heart' (Millar 1803: 217). The undermining of these feelings by the progress of society refutes for him the 'benevolent philosophers' who look forward to 'endless degrees of perfection' in human nature produced by education and culture (1803: 232-3). But though he has little faith in the possibility of more extensive benevolence, he perpetually bemoans its absence. The justice which is the leading principle of commercial society is 'not that nice and delicate justice, the offspring of refined humanity, but that coarse, though useful virtue, the guardian of contracts and promises, whose guide is the square and the compass, and whose protector is the gallows' (1803: 94). The observance of this sort of justice can be prompted by by man's own 'pecuniary interest' but 'before a man can become eminently generous or benevolent, he must resolve to sacrifice that interest to the good of others' (1803: 245). Such a sacrifice cannot be looked for in the 'scramble, in which the hand of every man is against every other' (1803: 249). The manners of society and the desire to please bring about an appearance of humanity, but Millar condemns its insincerity as a 'petty traffic, which aims merely at the purchase of reciprocal good offices' (1803: 247) and a 'tinsel reciprocation of small benefits' often interrupted by 'those opposite and jarring passions which arise amid the active pursuits of a commercial nation' (1803: 248). Nevertheless, he believes that some 'limited and regulated charity' is consistent with the manners of 'a refined and polished people', though 'the higher exertions of benevolence are out of the question' (1803: 254-5). Considerable irony plays about phrases like 'refined and polished people' as he goes on to compare modern mercantile companies with avaricious Roman governors and emphasizes the common attitude of barbaric and modern times towards a friend, which may be summed up in the 'famous prudential maxim, of constantly behaving to him as if he were one day to become your enemy' (1803: 260).

Millar's scheme of progress is dominated by Smith rather than Hutcheson. If fellow-feeling and shared ideas of just social behaviour form the original social bond, they enter into historical progress in only a vestigial form. Man might have a direct apprehension and love of virtue, but benevolence, except in the favoured circumstances of home-life in a period before opulence, is rarely operative. Benevolence and sympathy have become social fashions cloaking the urgent demands of a selfish rapacity. Generosity, charity, humanity, all depend on feelings which are termed 'ebullitions of tender-hearted and thoughtless generosity' (Millar 1803: 255), yet the lack of such feelings is bitterly regretted, and their presence celebrated in such outstanding individuals as Fox, to whom the *Historical View* is dedicated. The process of enlarging personal freedoms seems to bring along with it the Hobbesian selfishness of commercial competition, and Millar's enthusiasm for the liberty of slaves, his work on behalf of those oppressed by the law, his arbitration and conciliation in legal disputes, even the sensibility and benevolence of his private life, become anachronisms in an opulent commercial society.

Henry Home, Lord Kames, whose *Sketches of the History of Man* appeared in 1774, is far closer to Shaftesbury and Hutcheson in the moral basis of his philosophy, championing the moral and aesthetic senses and arguing for the natural sociability of man: 'do not benevolence, compassion, magnanimity, heroism, and the whole train of social affections, demonstrate our fitness for society, and our happiness in it?' he asks (Kames 1813: 2: 35). Yet he too has doubts about the capacity for universal benevolence and acknowledges not only the force of the self-regarding passions posited by Shaftesbury and Hutcheson, but also the existence of an active 'principle of malevolence' which is 'carefully disguised after the first dawn of reason; and is indulged only against enemies, because there it appears innocent' (1813: 2: 23–4). Like Ferguson, he values patriotism as the root of all the virtues, and, while this involves him in a similar apology for warfare as part of the divine plan, it also leads him to extend the range of benevolence to include the idea of country and to other possible extensions of sympathy.

In the history of man the social passions prevail for the most part, and time has 'perfected men in the art of subduing their passions, or of dissembling them' (Kames 1813: 2: 43). If our antisocial propensities can be thus subdued it might seem that society can be an educative force leading to individual improvement and itself capable of progress towards perfection: 'How devoutly to be wished, (it will be said,) that all men were upright and honest, and that all of the same nation were united like brethren in concord and mutual affection!' (1813: 2: 43). But Kames warns men against such pleasing dreams. The anti-social passions have been implanted to give men wholesome 'agitation' without which 'scarce any motive to action would remain; and man, reduced to a lethargic state, would rival no being above an oyster or a sensitive plant' (1813: 2: 45). The life of social virtue and benevolence to Kames seems like a dull sort of Heaven in which the lack of resistance induces torpor. He values the masculine virtues demonstrated in rivalry and conflict: 'Farewell, upon that supposition, to courage, magnanimity, heroism, and to every passion that ennobles human nature!' (1813: 2: 48). In what he refers to as the triumph of man's natural timidity, even the mental faculties will lie dormant, deprived of objects to be desired or dreaded. War is necessary for man as 'the school of every manly virtue' (1813: 2: 126), although he recognizes that perpetual war turns man into a beast of prey. Consequently Providence has arranged that war and peace alternate in a healthy cycle. Even though peace is advantageous to monarchs, making their subjects docile and materialistic, Providence 'renders kings blind to their true interest, in order that war may sometimes take place' (1813: 2: 127). He suggests that the British have a substitute for warfare in the turbulence of elections and the violence of faction, but the military virtues are seen as the only antidote to the threatening vices of luxury and voluptuousness introduced by commerce.

Honour is an important principle to Kames. It not only marks out the behaviour suitable to one's rank but upholds essential ideas of dignity. He has a long footnote arguing for the legalization of duelling, though the text remonstrates against its frequency (Kames 1813: 1: 335). The moral sense apparently shares the same class-bound sense of honour which dictates appropriate behaviour. In a passage which brings to mind the encounter of Falkland and Tyrrel in *Caleb Williams* Kames writes of the possibility of being insulted by a brutal fellow even to a blow, and being moved to stab him to the heart, scarce forbearing 'so long as to bid him draw', and feeling no remorse but only 'sorry for having been engaged with a ruffian' (1813: 3: 193).

Patriotism is the utmost extent to which our individual loyalty can be extended, and even this expansion of affection is managed with some difficulty. For Kames our social feelings are very limited, certainly do not rise to universal benevolence, and can only comprehend a small territory as an object of patriotic love: 'Our relations, our friends, and our other connections, open an extensive field for the exercise of affection: nay our country in general, if not too extensive, would alone be sufficient to engross our affection' (Kames 1813: 2: 22). Like Ferguson, his model is classical, this time republican Rome rather than Sparta, a small commonwealth with strict rotation in office from which no citizen is disqualified. He admires the cantons of Switzerland, with their sumptuary laws prohibiting luxury, but sees that Berne is declining into selfishness as the bailages appropriated to members of the great council become too lucrative. Like most of the Scottish social historians he shows moral predilections that seem to conflict with the providential history he is charting, as the natural goal of historical progress would seem to be the limited monarchy of Britain. Monarchies, with their great inequalities of rank and fortune, 'engender luxury, selfishness and sensuality' (1813: 2: 103). A large proportion of the book is taken up with his scheme for a national militia which would save the country from this fate by reinforcing the manly virtues.

Though Kames supports the idea of a strictly limited benevolence, the complications of his moral philosophy, in its plethora of implanted principles and passions, allow a more extended benevolence to be contemplated than Hume or Smith considered. The moral sense is the voice of God within us 'requiring from us no exercise of our faculties but attention merely' (Kames 1813: 3: 121) and establishing morality on the 'solid foundation of intuitive perception' (1813: 3: 120). We are impelled to obey the dictates of the moral sense by 'the principles of duty and benevolence' (1813: 3: 140). Duty here seems to regulate benevolence, specifying the objects towards which we should actively exercise the offices of affection and loyalty:

> It is our duty to honour and obey our parents; and to establish our children in the world, with all advantages,

> internal and external: we ought to be faithful to our friends, grateful to our benefactors, submissive to our masters, kind to our servants; and to aid and comfort every one of these persons when in distress.
>
> (1813: 3: 126)

Benevolence and sympathy become duties, imperative in the relationship of parent and child, becoming less urgent with lesser degrees of relationship and dwindling to indifference in the case of strangers: 'Our relations in distress claim that duty [benevolence] from us, and even our neighbours: but distant distress, without a particular connection, scarce rouses our sympathy, and never is an object of duty' (1813: 3: 132).

But Kames needs benevolence and social affection to perform more than this. The mind must rise to patriotism, so he introduces the faculty of generalization, by which 'our country, our government, our religion, become objects of public spirit, and of a lively affection' (Kames 1813: 3: 141). This patriotism is not a mere attachment to the physical locality in which one was bred: that is a passion 'far inferior, and chiefly visible in low people' (1813: 2: 129). He also requires personal benevolence to perform the charity work so expensively and inefficiently administered by parishes and foundling hospitals. His objections to these are partly economic, since he is against the working population supporting the idle; partly moral, in that there is a lack of discrimination between the deserving and undeserving poor; and partly sentimental: foundling hospitals are no substitutes for parental care, and, even if families were really unable to support a child, adoption would surely save the child if the alternative was exposure. His motives do not include the concern for equality demonstrated by Ferguson's American Indians or Godwin's self-respecting fellow-beings, but are firmly within the tradition of a condescending and self-exalting charity. He proposes that the names of givers and of deserving objects should be posted on the door of the parish church. For this work, benevolence needs to cast free from duty and excite us

> to be kind, not only to those we are connected with, but to our neighbours, and even to those we are barely acquainted with. Providence is peculiarly attentive to objects in distress, who require immediate aid and relief. To the principle

of benevolence, it hath superadded the passion of pity, which in every feeling heart is irresistable.

(1813: 3: 137)

Such pity can only extend to individuals; it does not seem to have the support of the generalizing faculty, since this would overburden the individual's capacity for benevolence and cause harm to those who might sacrifice personal advantage in helping others. The dictate of the moral sense is, according to Kames, that the just temperament 'is a subordination of benevolence to self-love' (1813: 3: 137). Kames often speaks of benevolence not as a principle but as a passion in a Lockean sense, producing an uneasiness which has to be gratified for the benefit of those suffering from it, and equivalent to any other passion which might become a 'ruling passion' to the detriment of those so overruled. As this passion is dependent upon its object, it might be weakened or destroyed by lack of satisfaction: 'frequent disappointments in attempting to gratify our benevolence, would render it a troublesome guest, and make us cling rather to selfishness, which we can always gratify' (1813: 3: 141).

Benevolence and the social affections are priceless but precarious possessions for Kames, the source of man's firmest allegiances, yet apparently subject to complete reversal if experience disappoints them. He offers an outstanding example of the process by which relationships of power are reinterpreted in affective terms and potentially share in the instability of all affective relationships. While he writes within a perspective of progress there is little evidence that he envisages further beneficial advances in the state of society other than the education of women to be better mothers and companions and to better fulfil their God-given role as subordinate supporters of male enterprise.

Kames was also very influential in aesthetic theory. In his earlier *Elements of Criticism*, which first appeared in 1762, the moral bearing of literature and the function of sympathy in artistic creation and appreciation are developed in ways which demonstrate a similar conflict between principles which are capable of an expansive interpretation and applications which insist on their limitation by the forms of contemporary society.

Hume had exempted the sympathy raised by artistic means from his restrictions of sympathy because it was more vivid to the senses and carried more power than the mere sight of a distressed peasant. In fact this sympathy was a major proof of man's capacity for sympathy and benevolence, especially when supported by the contagious sympathies of a theatrical audience. Ferguson cited this capacity as proof of an original moral sense and Kames also sees it as 'a striking instance of providential care to fit man for society. In reading a play, or in seeing it acted, a young man of taste is at no loss to judge of scenes he never was engaged in, or of passions he never felt' (Kames 1813: 2: 35). The development of this natural sensibility was of great importance for morality, but Kames was aware of dissentient voices warning of the insufficiency of mere literary taste to nurture a sound morality. Such voices included traditional moralists like Johnson and also some who followed the trend of sensibility in emphasizing the role of the feelings in human behaviour. Burke, in his celebrated *Philosophical Enquiry into the Origin of our Ideas of the Sublime and Beautiful* (1757), had rejected the view that taste was an innate intuitive principle; it was equally composed of reason and educated judgment. That virtue was similarly the object of an inner sense and that it was recommended by its beauty he also dismissed as a 'whimsical theory' which threatened to 'remove the science of our duties from their proper basis, (our reason, our relations, and our necessities,) to rest it upon foundations altogether visionary and unsubstantial' (Burke 1990: 101-2). Yet the sublime and the beautiful did appeal directly and 'captivate the soul before the understanding is ready either to join with them or oppose them' (1990: 97), and there were virtues (but not necessarily 'virtue') connected with these principles. While beauty was connected with the sexual passions and the social affections and virtues, its effect was to relax the mental and physical faculties. For their exercise and development they required to be 'shaken and worked to a proper degree' by the sublime effects of terror which agitated the more powerful emotions connected with self-preservation (1990: 123). Images of terror are naturally attractive, and horrors and catastrophes in real life are even more attractive, as long as the spectator is not personally threatened. Burke refused to analyse this response into modifications of pity and benevolence in the customary manner of philosophers of sensibility, leaving the moral bearings of the sublime very questionable. It seemed to stem from a totally amoral fear and worship of power. Burke emphasized the element of fear in religious feelings and in the emotions with which superiors are regarded: 'awe, reverence, and respect' (1990: 123). These three terms are used in the *Reflections* to characterize our natural feelings towards kings, magistrates, priests, and nobility. While the *Reflections* might be held to assert a natural 'love' of the British Constitution these terms are derived in the *Enquiry* from the passion of fear inspired by a power-based social structure.

Kames, like Burke, stresses that it requires more than the cultivation of taste to provide a moral education. He also emphasizes the difference between taste and genius, two terms which the writers of sensibility tended to bring closer together in their accounts of the way in which genius, inspired by nature and passion, communicates this inspiration to the heightened appreciation of a sensitive reader. Genius, Kames warns, is 'allied to a warm and inflammable constitution, delicacy of taste to calmness and sedateness' (Kames 1805: 1: 10). Men of genius are commonly prey to every passion, but men of taste usually have a deep response to the moral duties which counterbalances irregular desire. He also seems to acquiesce in the idea that the sublime can have a non-moral basis. Our ambition to be honoured causes us to identify with great conquerors and this apparently laudable principle accounts for what Kames 'once erroneously suspected' to be 'a wrong bias' in human nature:

> the grossest acts of oppression and injustice scarce blemish the character of a great conqueror: we, nevertheless, warmly espouse his interest, accompany him in his exploits, and are anxious for his success: the splendour and enthusiasm of the hero transfused into the readers, elevate their minds far above the rules of justice, and render them in a great measure insensible of the wrongs that are committed.
> (1805: 1: 203)

This natural bias towards the worship of heroes like Coriolanus later led Hazlitt to his disillusioned account of the imagination as an aristocratic faculty, suppressing the many to elevate the principal. Kames approaches this 'aggrandizing' when he warns against dissipating the effect of the central figure and counsels 'placing the nobler parts most in view, and in suppressing the smaller parts' (1805: 1: 195).

Generally Kames considers aesthetic values as coterminous

with moral values. Both taste and the moral sense 'discover what is right and what is wrong: fashion, temper, and education, have an influence to vitiate both, or to preserve them pure and untainted' (Kames 1805: 1: 5). As in his social theory, sympathy is given a prominent place as 'the capital branch of every social passion' (1805: 1: 9), and while his account of its workings is developed from Hume he also extends its range in two important ways, in his account of 'ideal presence' and in the central role which it plays in his account of artistic creation, two of the many points in which he anticipates the theories of Wordsworth and Coleridge.

Attacking the unities of place and time three years before Johnson's more famous assault, Kames does more justice to the imaginative participation of the theatrical spectator than Johnson's account of an audience met together to hear a well-modulated recitation, entertaining no dramatic illusion whatsoever. Kames's spectator might well have been that described by Johnson as 'wandering in ecstasy' as he experienced the 'waking dream' of ideal presence. This illusion, which 'commands our belief' until we reflect on our real situation, is essential for moving the passions. In reading, 'the reader's passions are never sensibly moved, till he be thrown into a kind of reverie, in which state, forgetting that he is reading, he conceives every incident as passing in his presence, precisely as if he were an eye-witness' (Kames 1805: 1: 77). Morally ideal presence has an essential function in extending sympathy beyond the customary limits:

> It is wonderful to observe upon what slight foundations nature erects some of her most solid and magnificent works. In appearance at least, what can be more slight than ideal presence? And yet from it is derived that extensive influence which language hath over the heart, an influence which, more than any other means, strengthens the bond of society, and attracts individuals from their private system to perform acts of generosity and benevolence.
>
> (1805: 1: 82)

But this illusion is only maintained by incidents 'linked together according to the order of nature' (1805: 1: 84) and any improbability shatters it. Probability is a matter of generally accepted feelings and standards as well as of the order of nature, and the power of ideal presence to transcend these limits is an exceptional kind of added grace, such as pity gives to benevolence. Usually a strict notion of decorum dictated by 'natural' contemporary standards governs Kames's ideas of aesthetic and emotional reactions. In his view all men have a notion of a perfect 'common nature', however far below it they themselves fall, and judge of behaviour by this common standard:

> we have a conviction that this common nature is *right*, or *perfect*, and that individuals *ought* to be made conformable to it. To every faculty, to every passion, and to every bodily member, is assigned a proper office and a due proportion: ... if a passion deviate from the common nature ... it is wrong and disagreeable: but as far as conformable to common nature, every emotion and every passion is perceived by us to be right, and as it ought to be; and upon that account it must appear agreeable.
> (1805: 1: 88-9)

When he comes to consider those best qualified to judge of this common nature Kames turns, like Wordsworth, from aesthetic to social and moral considerations. Like savages, labourers are 'totally void of taste' since they lag behind the cultivation of a 'polite' nation. On the other hand the opulent and dissipated are equally disqualified since they have little appreciation of 'simplicity, elegance, propriety, and things natural, sweet, or amiable' (Kames 1805: 2: 399). The true judge has a 'good natural taste' preserved by regular living, 'using the goods of fortune with moderation' and by following 'the dictates of an improved nature' (1805: 2: 401). Lest this should seem too small a jury to try the case, Kames resorts to nature 'who hath marked all her works with indelible characters of high or low, plain or elegant, strong or weak' (1805: 2: 401) which all men perceive to some extent.

The complacency with which Kames appeals to this common standard of decorum in behaviour and in passion is reinforced by his comforting reassurance that each man has pleasures proportioned to his rank. Behaviour suited to a person's dignity and the station allotted to him by Providence is naturally pleasing to a spectator (Kames 1805: 1: 278). When he talks of the organic nature of a work of art one is aware of that union of organicism with conservatism which the Romantics are supposed to demonstrate, as the 'common nature' is one trained in the connections of ideas of a hierarchical society. Here he sounds most Coleridgean:

> Every work of art that is conformable to the natural course of our ideas, is so far agreeable; and every work of art that reverses that order, is so far disagreeable. Hence it is required in every such work, that, like an organic system, its parts be orderly arranged and mutually connected bearing each of them a relation to the whole, some more intimate, some less, according to their destination.
>
> (1805: 1: 23)

He traces this to an implanted principle of order which governs the arrangements of every man's perceptions, ideas, and actions. We 'view the principal subject before we descend to its accessories or ornaments, and the superior before inferior or dependent; we are equally averse to enter into a minute consideration of constituent parts, till the thing be first surveyed as a whole' (1805: 1: 19). This natural hierarchy of superior and inferior, principal and dependent, has as much relation to social as to intellectual criteria. Among the unnatural ways of associating ideas he instances both a metonymic excess in Mistress Quickly (the same example used by Coleridge to illustrate defect of 'method') and metaphorical excess as in the wit which works by 'joining things by distant and fanciful relations' (1805: 1: 19). The natural order of ideas is illustrated almost verbatim from Hume, implying a totally social frame of reference: 'the mind extends its view to a son more readily than to a servant; and more readily to a neighbour than to one living at a distance' (1805: 1: 16-17). The linkings of sympathy in society determine the transitions of our ideas and the priority granted to different objects. For Kames man is a mixed being of social and asocial, benevolent and selfish principles, and the benevolent passions towards kindred he admits as at bottom selfish. Friendship is 'less vigorous than self-love' and does not usually extend to a friend's children (1805: 1: 59). An act of charity can be performed 'partly in view to enjoy the pleasure of a virtuous act', which a note informs us is 'the most respectable of all selfish motives' (1805: 1: 39). Indeed benevolence 'may not improperly be said to be the most refined selfishness' (1805: 1: 152).

Kames continually formulates general propositions fraught

with expansive possibilities only to show that they are applied in a strictly limited context. The same can be said of many of the writers of the mid-century who gestured towards wider possibilities of sympathy, intellectual and aesthetic exploration, and individual freedom and genius, only to restrict their implications to a framework of ideas and a society which was recognized as the standard of virtue and the summit of practicable political liberty. One famous example is Young's *Conjectures on Original Composition* (1749), given prominence today because of the keywords in its title and its influence in Germany. It is quite apparent that, apart from a cloudy commitment to 'feeling' and 'virtue', Young has no standards by which to judge or recognize individual genius, can well conceive of it losing its way when it departs from the beaten track, and is anxious to conclude with a thoroughly conventional celebration of a Christian death bed. Kames's works remained standard well into the nineteenth century, and he was recognized as a leading proponent of the 'culture of the heart'. Though his construction of sensibility is dominated by contemporary social and aesthetic standards, some of the mechanisms which he invokes as 'natural' do conflict with conservative restrictions and point towards a later expansive sensibility that exploited the richness of subjective response. Though he separates genius and taste in his early paragraphs they are linked in their dependence on sympathy. Just as sympathy is promoted in the audience, so the artist must have that outstanding degree of sympathy that enables him to completely identify with another character. In a passage which looks forward to the debates of Wordsworth and Coleridge on dramatic language he asserts that 'each passion hath a certain tone, to which every sentiment proceeding from it ought to be tuned with the greatest accuracy'. In order to reach such perfection:

> it is necessary that a writer assume the precise character and passion of the personage represented; which requires an uncommon genius. But it is the only difficulty; for the writer, who, annihilating himself, can thus become another person, need be in no pain about the sentiments that belong to the assumed character: these will flow without the least study, or even preconception.
>
> (Kames 1805: 1: 364)

Lest we should think that this licenses the creation of Iagos and Iachimos as well as Desdemonas and Imogens, Kames warns against representing characters who can expect no sympathy from the audience. Just as objects of terror may be represented, but not objects of horror, so only disgust is raised by the insufferably monstrous character of Iago or of Sin in *Paradise Lost*. The best hero for a tragedy is one whose fault is 'venial' and whose misfortunes can therefore 'warmly interest the spectator' (Kames 1805: 2: 298). Such is the force of Kames's humanity that he even questions sculptural representations of Negroes carrying dials or fish supporting basins of water, since they give 'the appearance of giving pain to a sensitive being' (1805: 2: 387). Realism is much constricted by these moral demands, which are also the demands of sympathetic feeling. Our feelings should also be brought to reinforce and not to question the arrangements of Providence. Plays like *Romeo and Juliet* which turn too much on unhappy chances tend to bring Providence into disrepute, though a 'regular chain of causes and effects directed by the general laws of nature never fails to suggest the hand of Providence, to which we submit without resentment, being conscious that submission is our duty' (1805: 2: 302).

During the century the ideas of sensibility permeated aesthetic thought. The aim of art was to appeal to the emotions, especially through the sublime and pathetic, which became the dominating subjects of aesthetic debate. Wharton's question 'What is there transcendently sublime or pathetic in Pope?' (Elledge 1961: 2: 719) was tantamount to dismissing him. Wharton also thought that art should appeal to the social emotions and, in comparing the *Iliad* and the *Odyssey*, he singled out the virtue of extended benevolence when recommending the latter. Instead of admiring 'the destroyers of peace and the murderers of mankind', the *Odyssey* moved readers towards the 'duties of universal benevolence, of charity, and of hospitality' which are 'inculcated with more emphasis and elegance than in any ancient philosopher, and I wish I could not add than any modern' (1961: 2: 708).

By the 1780s the more liberal trends of sensibility were in the ascendant in aesthetic theory. While there is no one text which represents these ideas as a coherent system, the best approach to this is Hugh Blair's *Lectures on Rhetoric and Belles Lettres* of 1783. Based on lectures delivered in Edinburgh since the

1760s, they include ideas from Lowth, Campbell, Beattie, Hume, Hutcheson, and especially Kames, which support his liberal position. It is a compilation in which these ideas can be seen most comprehensively at a time just before conservative pressures were felt. His stress on moral virtue as the common foundation of the powers of production and appreciation of art goes far towards Shelley's account of the homology of poetry and morality, while his discussion of natural taste develops the universalistic tendencies which reach their fullest expression in Wordsworth's Preface to *Lyrical Ballads* and *The Prelude*.

Blair defines good taste as a power compounded of natural sensibility to beauty, and of improved understanding. It is towards the improvement of understanding that his lectures tend, and in their analysis of figures of speech, prose style, and organization, the analytic reason is mightily exercised, while the judgment is employed in criticism and comparison of well-chosen extracts. Yet the basis of taste is sensibility, that response to beauty which has no connection with reason. Beautiful objects or scenes 'strike us intuitively' and often 'strike in the same manner the philosopher and the peasant, the man and the boy' (Blair 1813: 1: 18). There are marked inequalities of taste among men, due pricipally to education, culture, and the sensitivity of their organs and internal senses. Though cultivation and judgment may produce a 'correct' taste, Blair champions the natural spontaneity of a 'delicate' taste. The man of correct taste continually refers to a standard of good taste which ensures that he is 'pleased himself precisely in that degree in which he ought and no more' (1813: 1: 28). Delicacy of taste leans more to nature and feeling, yet such perfection of natural sensibility is not granted to all. It 'implies those organs or powers which enable us to discover beauties that lie hid from a vulgar eye' (1813: 1: 27). A person of delicate taste feels strongly and 'feels accurately', seeing distinctions and differences where others see none.

Another prerequisite of good taste, and indeed of good art, is a 'good heart':

> Wherever the affections, characters or actions of men are concerned (and these certainly afford the noblest subjects to genius), there can be neither any just or affecting description of them, nor any thorough feeling of the beauty of that description, without our possessing the virtuous affections.

> He whose heart is indelicate or hard, he who has no admiration of what is truly noble or praiseworthy, nor the proper sympathetic sense of what is soft and tender, must have a very imperfect relish of the highest beauties of eloquence and poetry.
>
> (Blair 1813: 1: 26-7)

If poetry is 'the language of passion, or of enlivened imagination' (1813: 3: 80), the passions it deals in are predominantly virtuous ones. Epic poetry, which is designed to 'extend our idea of human perfection', warms our hearts with sentiments of 'valour, truth, justice, fidelity, friendship, pity, magnanimity'; it awakens 'the generous and public affections', and purifies the mind from sensual pursuits. Since high virtue 'is the object which all mankind are formed to admire', epic poems 'are, and must be, favourable to the cause of virtue' and furnish a testimony which refutes sceptical philosophers' attempts to weaken 'the essential distinctions between vice and virtue' (1813: 3: 196). Though he admits that the education of taste alone does not provide a moral education, the exercise of taste is 'in its native tendency, moral and purifying', while the poet or public speaker cannot attain the sublime without possessing the virtuous affections in a strong degree: 'He must feel what a good man feels, if he expects greatly to move, or to interest mankind' (1813: 1: 15). Genius is the creative and inventive faculty, but it 'always supposes taste' (1813: 1: 30). In privileging the sublime as the highest exertion of art, Blair treats it as an emotion shared by creator and audience. It is 'an emotion which can never be long protracted' and the most we can expect of the genius is that 'this fire of the imagination would sometimes flash upon us like lightning from heaven, and then disappear' (1813: 1: 54).

Blair resists Burke's attempts to sever sublimity from moral feelings and make it consist in forms of terror. He particularly emphasizes the 'moral or sentimental sublime' as a feeling arising

> from certain exertions of the human mind; from certain affections, and actions, of our fellow-creatures. These will be found to be all, or chiefly, of that class which comes under the name of magnanimity, or heroism; and they produce an effect extremely similar to what is produced by

the view of grand objects in nature; filling the mind with admiration, and elevating it above itself.

(Blair 1813: 1: 37)

The innate capacity for benevolence and pity is of particularly vital importance to the experience of tragedy. Drawing on the ideas of other theorists, Blair propounds the century's most central explanation of how the pleasure of tragedy is derived from the social feelings:

> Wherever man takes a strong interest in the concerns of his fellow-creatures, an internal satisfaction is made to accompany the feeling. By the wise and gracious constitution of our nature, the exercise of all the social passions is attended by pleasure. Wherever man takes a strong interest in the concerns of his fellow-creatures, an internal satisfaction is made to accompany the feeling. Pity, or compassion, in particular, is for wise ends, appointed to be one of the strongest instincts of our frame, and is attended with a peculiarly attractive power. It is an affection which cannot but be productive of some distress, on account of the sympathy with the sufferers, which it necessarily involves. But, as it includes benevolence and friendship, it partakes, at the same time, of the agreeable and pleasing nature of those affections. The heart is warmed by kindness and humanity, at the same moment at which it is afflicted by the distresses of those with whom it sympathises; and the pleasure arising from these kind emotions, prevails so in the mixture, and so far counterbalances the pain, as to render the state of mind, upon the whole, agreeable.

The experience derives 'an addition from the approbation of our own minds', since we 'are pleased with ourselves, for feeling as we ought, and for entering with proper sorrow, into the concerns of the afflicted' (Blair 1813: 2: 349–50). This unembarrassed acknowledgement of a reflexive complacency characterizes the high-water mark of sensibility. Previous critics had interpreted such pleasure as selfish, attacking the claim of disinterested altruism. Subsequent critics attacked the passiveness of self-pleasing sympathy, urging a more active and costly response to human suffering. In many works of sensibility the authorial persona, Cowper, Harley, Yorick, or some other 'sentimental' traveller, provokes criticism of their indulgent, passive reaction to misery. Blair's spectatorial position is, of course, enforced, and the more legitimate exploitations of this response to tragedy frequently use a similar enforced passivity as events are narrated in retrospect. Wordsworth evokes this validation of feeling in *The Ruined Cottage* where he emphasizes the bond of feeling between the Poet and Margaret, and the response which venerates the feelings displayed by the sufferer and those of the contemplator as shared human values.

In Blair's aesthetic development of the ideas of sensibility there is a direct contradiction of the limitations of sympathy as enunciated by Hume and Smith. Sympathy is not principally the vicarious enjoyment of another's advantages, nor is it restricted in its social range: 'In every rank of life, the relations of father, husband, son, brother, lover, or friend, lay the foundation of those affecting situations, which make man's heart feel for man' (Blair 1813: 2: 355). While these domestic and close relationships focus the most intense images of sympathy, the imagination and feelings can be interested in figures of remote times and places. Indeed the artist must possess in a high degree the capacity to identify himself with the characters that he presents, however remote they may be from his own circumstances. To write tragedy requires 'strong and ardent sensibility of mind. It requires the author to have the power of entering deeply into the characters which he draws, of becoming for a moment the very person which he exhibits, and of assuming all his feelings' (1813: 2: 359). The similarity between the ideas of Blair and Wordsworth has often been remarked,[3] but it is important to note that these ideas are a development of the Shaftesbury/Hutcheson line of sensibility, rather than the conservatism of the Hume/Smith line which was so triumphant in the 1790s.

2

TOWARDS REVOLUTION

The ideas of sensibility were not radical in themselves but they were capable of being applied in a radical way. Hume and Smith aligned the feelings of men with the prevailing state of society, whatever injustice is incorporated with it, and placed men under the guidance of habit and custom, just as in matters of taste they looked for standards based on past testimony, length of duration, and continuance of esteem. The ideas of Shaftesbury, however, could hardly fail to promote liberal views, especially when divorced from the restricted social milieu in which they originated. Shaftesbury wrote in an innovatory, rhapsodic style; he attacked government coercion of opinion and ridiculed customary notions of religion. Of course, his virtuoso was a highly cultivated individual and he argued only for the 'Liberty of *the Club*, and that sort of Freedom which is taken amongst *Gentlemen* and *Friends*, who know one another perfectly well' (*Char*: 2: 44–5). His aesthetic standards, though 'natural', were of the variety which, like Pope's, saw the Ancients as exemplifying nature. But his ideas flourished in a less classically dominated age, and Joseph Wharton's Shaftesburyan 'Enthusiast' of the mid-century preferred the untaught warblings of Shakespeare to the labours of Art, despised the pomp of Versailles, and looked for liberty to America. In declaring against custom, habit, and the artificial distinctions of society, Shaftesbury sounded the note which rang through the primitivism of the century:

> Marks are set upon Men: Distinctions form'd: Opinions decreed, under the severest Penaltys: Antipathys instilled, and Aversions rais'd in Men against the generality of their own Species. So that 'tis hard to find in any Region a

human Society which has *human* Laws. No wonder if in such Societys 'tis so hard to find a Man who lives NATURALLY, and as a MAN.

(*Char*: 2: 96-7)

He descanted on the simple needs of human nature:

Who is there that knows not how small a Portion of worldly Matters is sufficient for a Man's single Use and Convenience and how much his Occasions and Wants might be contracted and reduc'd, if a just Frugality were study'd, and Temperance and a natural Life came once to be pursu'd with half that Application, Industry and Art, which is bestowed on Sumptuousness and Luxury.

(*Char*: 2: 155-6)

It was an extension of Shaftesbury's ideas that art appealed to 'natural' social passions evident in every gradation of society, just as it appealed to a beauty evident in every aspect of the grand system of nature. The system of nature could be unreservedly accepted as an object of feeling. From its most magnificent phenomena to the meanest flower or animal it showed the goodness of the creator and awoke proper responses of love, awe, and gratitude in the spectator. The great system of society could also be revered, but with more discriminating emotions, since the good of the whole was preserved for many writers by the limitations of the social feelings, and even by selfishness and antisocial feelings. The symmetry between the world of 'nature' and the world of man was upheld by a 'best of all possible worlds' argument that could be either optimistic, as Hartley and Priestley saw parallel progress in each dimension, or a matter for gloom and resignation, as Johnson found in life much to be endured, little to be enjoyed, and less that could be amended. For many writers the 'best of all possible worlds' also included the British Constitution which, though not perfect, represented the best compromise between liberty and order possible in our fallen state. Sensibility, itself a new movement in the progress of nations towards perfection, looked to the development of man's affective nature as a source of improvement beyond the accepted limits of a fallen nature, and in the political sphere was given immense impetus by the American Revolution and American rhetoric. Comparisons with other constitutions and conceptions of civic virtue were now not limited to the ancient world. The writings of Franklin, Crêvecoeur, and Paine gave an account of the dynamic new establishment of democracy, while travel-books gave glowing pictures of a nature more various and sublime than that of Europe.

The American Revolution was one of the factors which led to the liberalization of sensibility. Another was the writings of Rousseau with their condemnation of the inequalities and artificialities of polished societies and praise of the life of natural virtue and natural society in alpine simplicity or the small republic ruled by the general will. Rousseau had an immense influence on all those writers who supported the more liberal interpretation of sensibility, yet his primitivistic leanings conflicted with the idea of progress dominant in the British tradition. His influence can especially be seen in the more urgent demands of individual passion in its struggles with social restrictions, the growing independence of sentimental religion from specific doctrinal tenets, and in idylls of pastoral and communal life reminiscent of those in *La Nouvelle Héloïse*. An admiration for these last features was heavily qualified by those who looked for more than uneducated and often brutalized rural characters and distrusted the heavily organized and minutely supervised virtue of Wolmar's estate. Here, as in his political theory, Rousseau, the citizen of Geneva with his perpetual 'Si j'étais roi', showed the taint of that French longing for an impossible virtuous despot. Generally the points of issue debated into the 1790s were those which arose from the British tradition, the points at which the benevolist and liberal trend of sensibility conflicted with ideas based on selfishness or those which aligned sensibility with the forms of traditional society. The association with Rousseau, however, served to alert conservative thinkers to the dangers of a liberal sensibility and began that process of polarization which reached its height in the 1790s.

This conservative sensibility, often taken as the legitimate line of development of the concept in the eighteenth century, departs in vital respects from the ideas of the primary sources of the concept. Shaftesbury and Hutcheson had both stressed the necessity of keeping the partial affections like those to kindred under the direction of universal benevolence which sought the good of the widest system of which man was a part. They had also insisted on the role which the reason and understanding had to play in analysing the tendencies of actions and finding what actions really tend to the public good. They had argued for individual freedom of judgment – though in a limited context – and established what for many was the key characteristic of sensibility, the naturalness of fellow-feeling, sociability, and benevolence. Their arguments against those who explained human behaviour in terms of selfishness were developed in the work of Butler, Hume, Godwin, and Hazlitt, and are still used by modern philosophers of altruism. One of the most intricately argued points about benevolism was its 'selfishness'. Although strict benevolists regarded altruistic actions done for the sake of self-congratulatory complacency as selfish, they maintained that the pleasure one feels at another's happiness is not selfish, since the good and happiness of the other is an absolute prerequisite of the agent's pleasure and is merely another way of defining benevolence – satisfaction with the happiness of another. Many remained unconvinced, and liked to think of benevolence as a passion like any other and thus by definition selfish, an uneasiness in the mind which sought relief in benevolent action. Shaftesbury often talked of the moral sense in terms of the heart and affections, but Hutcheson, locating the moral sense more firmly in the reflective faculties, made it a kind of intuitive apprehension of moral qualities, equivalent in this function to Butler's Conscience or Price's Understanding, yet the overtones of *sense* in the term still gave rise to suspicion.

In the literature associated with sensibility up to the 1780s, there are few unequivocal examples of the Shaftesbury/Hutcheson variety of sensibility. Fielding paid much attention to Shaftesbury's ideas, and Tom Jones is perhaps the best example of the hero who demonstrates spontaneous benevolence and love – in all senses. Yet while his excesses need restraint, the Shaftesbury/Hutcheson restraint would be the development of the reason and the consideration of ministering to the widest happiness, rather than Allworthy's advocacy of the self-regarding virtue of prudence and religion, a sanction backed by eternal punishment. Only in the *Miscellanies* does Fielding envisage a benevolence that is not secured by such sanctions. There Fielding views good nature as an amiable sympathy which is drawn to benevolence 'without the Allurements or Terrors of Religion' (Fielding 1972: 1: 158). In *Amelia* the hero is convinced by his experience that people cannot feel anything for others who are in a widely removed sphere of life. This might agree with Hume's limitations of sympathy, but it is a direct contradiction of God's loving plan of the universe. Booth has to be cured of this impious supposition by a course of Isaac Barrow's sermons, and the arguments for benevolent behaviour in the book are all based on following God's will and avoiding the torments of Hell! Sterne is far too ironic to be taken as representing any one variety of sensibility, though he was widely criticized for his predominantly self-centred epicurism of emotion. Goldsmith's Burchill seems to have been afflicted in his youth by the uneasy desire of benevolent indulgence which, being disappointed, led to a somewhat cynical maturity. His good-natured man, Honywell, adds to this indulgence something of Smith's desire to be loved and not to offend. Mackenzie's Harley is perhaps nearest in his ever-ready benevolence, but Mackenzie's attitude to him is deeply ironic, and he answers to Smith's description of the man of humanity who is an exception in a naughty world, a heart-warming phenomenon, but condemned to victimization.

Mackenzie's man of feeling is a conservative construction, the picture of one who does not recognize that in this divinely ordered world there are certain inevitable evils which must be accepted for the stability and perfection of the whole. Harley uselessly wears himself out reacting emotionally against an order which he cannot change, which does not need to be changed, and which, in fact, he has no real idea of changing. One chapter or 'fragment' of the novel presents Harley's attack on the inhumane rapacity of the East India Company, a cause taken up by most followers of sensibility, but it is entitled 'The Man of Feeling talks of what he does not understand'. Later Mackenzie seemed to regard Burke as a similarly misled man of feeling. In his *Letters of Brutus* he reproached Burke for the 'blind humanity' with which he attacked 'those who have successfully served their country' and 'saved the British possessions in both Indies from . . . ruin and disgrace' and mistakenly championed 'the cheats of St. Eustacia and the blackguards of Bengal'.[1] In the one instance in which Harley's endeavours achieve some result, in uniting the seduced Emily with her father, nothing but fresh misery ensues. The father can only wish her dead, rather than dead to honour, and, though Harley does agree that the world's notions of the case are hard, he can only counsel him to look to the hereafter. Social attitudes can only be accepted, never fought against, and, if transcended, only in the prospect of divine mercy. Many of the novels of sensibility carry a similar message. The subject of distress, invariably a woman, is submitted to various modes of hardship and oppression, many of them arising from society, yet the focus is not on the social criticism which this might provoke, but on the virtuous resignation of the Griselda-like heroine as she displays the Christian and specifically female virtue of passive fortitude. One has to look to the minor fiction, and especially to the novels of the 1780s and 1790s, to find convincing examples of the man of active benevolence and the woman of active courage.

After the Americans, and then the French, had strongly proposed a doubt that British society was divinely ordered and the British Constitution the best means of ensuring freedom under law, the attitude towards the typical female victim-heroine of earlier literature changes. We find direct contradictions of the image, like Holcroft's Anna St Ives or Wollstonecraft's Maria, who refused to 'sentimentalize herself to stone' under her oppression (Wollstonecraft 1976: 154). We also find parodies, like Bage's Miss Campinet and Charlotte Smith's Geraldine. Godwin noted the ambiguous response now possible to previous works, here Rowe's *Fair Penitent*:

> The moral deduced from this admirable poem by one set of readers will be, the mischievous tendency of unlawful love, and the duty incumbent upon the softer sex to devote themselves in all things to the will of their fathers and husbands. Other readers may perhaps regard it as a powerful satire upon the institutions at present existing in society relative to the female sex, and the wretched consequences of that mode of thinking, by means of which, in woman, 'one false step entirely damns her fame'.
>
> (Godwin 1797: 136-7)

Many writers attacked conventions of sentimental fiction which upheld the conservative principles which Smith and Burke placed at the heart of a stable society. Godwin attacked the servility of gratitude and the partial affections, those family loyalties which narrowed the range of benevolence and perpetuated inequality. Wollstonecraft attacked the specifically feminine interpretation of sentimental virtues like modesty, delicacy, passive fortitude, and honour. Bage attacked nearly all the shibboleths of sentimentalized femininity, and familial, religious, and social reverence. Charlotte Smith parodied the conventions of the conservative sentimental novel, modelling her heroes and heroines on conventional figures and then involving them in the most unconventional activities. Helen Maria Williams, a product of provincial sentimental culture, after writing on the slave-trade and colonialist oppression, moved her salon and her family to Paris during the Revolution. There she became one of the most important sources of information to British radicals through her *Letters from France,* dealing with violent events which sensibility, especially feminine sensibility, had not hitherto touched. Many of these writers produced work in the 1790s which is continuous in theme with their contributions to the 1780s, and they show a growing tendency to criticize the limitations of conservative sensibility.

The 'aristocracy of feeling' which sensibility tended to create was often equated with wealth, which provided leisure for the cultivation of finer feelings. Allied to this was the widely held notion that the imagination revolted from pictures of mean and therefore 'disgusting' occupations. Mary Wollstonecraft admits that 'there is something disgusting in the distresses of poverty, at which the imagination revolts' (Wollstonecraft 1790: 144) and she gives a very unprepossessing picture of the peasant: 'a being scarcely above the brutes over which he tyrannised; a broken spirit, worn-out body, and all those gross vices which the example of the rich, rudely copied could produce' (1790: 151). This limitation of the imagination is seen most crudely in the Aikins' famous enquiry into 'the Kinds of Distress which excite Agreeable sensations', which warns an author 'never to attempt to raise pity by anything mean or disgusting' (Aikin and Barbauld 1792: 200). Deformity 'is always disgusting', and poverty, 'if truly represented, shocks our nicer feelings' (1792: 202). It was this seeming limitation of imaginative sympathy, along with many more examples of the constrictions of conservative sensibility, that Wordsworth set out to counter in *Lyrical Ballads.* Hazlitt, only half convinced of Wordsworth's success, described the imagination as the tool of despotism and conservative sensibility in his famous 'Coriolanus' article, and disillusionment with the imagination, hailed in his early work as the agent of benevolence, was one of the main themes of his writing. He takes up a stance very like that of Wollstonecraft when discussing this issue in the *Life of Napoleon*: first the poor are brutalized, then they are held up as brutes who deserve no better treatment (Howe: 13: 16-18). The reactions of sensibility and imagination are not to be trusted to look into the causes of things and the means of reforming them. The Aikins come to a similar conclusion: novels and plays 'do not improve our humanity, [because] they lead us to require a certain elegance of manners and delicacy of virtue which is not often found with poverty, ignorance and meanness' (Aikin and Barbauld 1792: 212). Bage has a fling at this kind of exclusive sensibility when, in a conversation with a lady novelist, it is taken for granted that no one can feel the true passion of love on less than £1,000 a year. Helen Maria Williams in *Julia* (1790) introduces a lady who complains: 'I cannot understand what right people have to the indulgence of so much sensibility, who are in poverty. People in affluence may indulge the delicacy of their feelings; and mine, I own, are so affected by the company of unfortunate persons, that I am obliged, in regard to my health, to avoid them carefully' (Williams 1790: 2: 102). It is Julia's mission to seek out and comfort the abused relative of whom this remark is made.

Charlotte Smith confronts the issue in *Ethelinde* (1789) with a fine awareness of the convention which had prevented Burney from showing her heroines doing the washing, and a defiant invocation of Rousseau. Both Ethelinde and Montgomery are impoverished (though gently born) and both see the imprudence of marriage in these circumstances. Ethelinde cannot 'bear to see Montgomery, the descendant of so many heroes - himself the worthiest, the most truly noble of his name - degraded for my sake to the abject condition of labouring for bread, or humbling himself to the drudgery of a mechanic' (Smith 1789: 3: 132-3). Montgomery's mother admonishes him: 'Could you, Charles, endure to see your wife, the lovely, delicate, and graceful Ethelinde, employed in the occupations of a laundress or a domestic?' (1789: 4: 86). Their circumspection is put into contrast with the behaviour of Ethelinde's brother, who marries his poor bride from debtors' prison, and there is something splendid as well as incautious in this integrity of passion. Montgomery makes a powerful bid to shake off the prejudices of gentility in the picturesque setting of the Lake District:

> as I lay by the scanty embers of the shepherd's fire . . . how did I wish that we had been both been born to a destiny as

humble as his and that even now you could learn to prefer the quiet comfortable cottage on the border of Grasmere Water, to long long years of separate misery, terminated perhaps by death, perhaps by affluence, for which we may find too late that happiness and health have been sacrificed.

(1789: 4: 269)

This shakes Ethelinde's resolution, and he follows up in French: 'Soyons heureux et pauvres; . . . J'ai des bras, je suis robuste, le pain gagné par mon travail' (1789: 4: 270). He is quoting the plea of Saint-Preux in *La Nouvelle Héloïse* after which Julie determines to consummate their relationship, despite the disparity in their social status and her father's wishes. In the face of this, Ethelinde gives way, yet only on condition that Mrs Montgomery, who must look to him for support, recovers funds which are then in jeopardy. Needless to say, she does not grant anything further, but within the conventions of a sentimental relationship Smith raised a powerful suggestion of sexual passion, and the threat which Rousseau posed to traditional social patterns.

Despite this extension of sympathy, granting to the lowly their rights of sensibility, there is still often an irritating sense of élitism among some predominantly liberal writers. The claim that only readers who know such feelings can appreciate their appeals to sensibility falls on sceptical ears today. One can become alienated by Mary Wollstonecraft's distinction between the common female sensibility, capable only of delusive daydreams, and that of herself and other superior beings who create sublime visions. The common mode of sentimental poetry also stresses the capacity of feeling in the poet at the expense of the characters contemplated. The poet revisiting childhood scenes, contemplating the joyous activity of nature, or the hardships of animal or rustic life, bathes these subjects in a sentimental glow of feeling, yet they are patently only the occasion for the display of emotion, and the subjects themselves are often complacently described as lacking the capacity for such feelings. Cowper's hardy peasants are scarcely more humanized than Burns's mouse. Hutcheson himself had counselled his benevolent readers against thinking of lower-class characters as having the same sensibility of their hardships as the sympathizing middle-class onlooker. Their minds and bodies are 'soon fitted to their state' and this should 'support a compassionate Heart, too deeply touched with apprehended Miseries, of which the *Sufferers* are themselves insensible' (Hutcheson 1969: 185). Godwin and others wrote against this kind of attitude, especially when the argument was applied to slaves, and Wordsworth's early poetry shows a struggle against this detached, genteel persona.

The prevalent male character of sensibility was another focus of criticism. This was not the Harley type, but the Tom Jones model, the man of lovable impetuosity. His natural spontaneity leads to incautious acts of benevolence and of love; his chivalrous feelings render him loyal and honourable. Yet he tends to consider only himself in his passions, especially those provoked by honour, and lacks a compassionate awareness of others and any conception of the good of society. He is also prone to violence, particularly duelling, and also to gambling, not from mercenary motives (he is usually rather bad at it) but for its excitements. These traits are seen in characters from Prévost's Des Grieux to Mrs Radcliffe's Valmont. Among its many dramatic avatars the last prominent one to be viewed as a hero is Cumberland's West Indian. In the anti-Jacobin novels he is presented less charitably. Maria Edgeworth's creole, Vincent, in *Belinda*, is clearly a riposte to Cumberland's, and such figures as Willoughby in *Sense and Sensibility* become the villains of later works with their impressive but uncontrolled feelings, or, like Scott's Waverley, the subjects of an education which will discipline their romantic enthusiasms to conform to traditional social responsibilities. Yet the figure was also criticized by radical writers. Bage's Sir George Paradyne in *Man as He Is* (1792) shows all the impulsive benevolence of the model, and his affections are nobly bestowed on the daughter of a ruined merchant. In a reversal of the common 'test for marriage' topos it is the woman who insists that the man show himself worthy. She urges him to cultivate powers which contribute to the good of mankind, recommending the company of French leaders of thought like Mirabeau and Lafayette. She herself, employed as a hand-painter by Wedgwood, apparently enjoys the enlightened conversation of the Lunar Society. Sir George, caught up in the aristocratic dissipations of Continental spas, succeeds very ill in this test, and it seems to be the intensity of his remorse which leads Miss Colerain to accept him – this and Bage's ironic consciousness of his fair readers' tastes. The features of the man of sensibility are also emphasized in Godwin's *St Leon*, whose passions, formed by the aristocratic milieu of fifteenth-century France, are as little conducive to domestic happiness as his ideology, coloured by the displacement of chivalric by commercial values, is capable of bringing peace to war-torn Hungary. Though he is presented sympathetically as a creature of misguided benevolence, the heavy irony of the introductory pages in which he shows the corruption of his values inhibits any reading which would cast him as a hero. Charlotte Smith also criticized the man of sensibility in *Emmeline*, in which Delamere seems to be a direct counterpart to Burney's Delvile. The latter's impulsive violence, which leaves Cecilia at one point abandoned and dreading his death in a duel, is exaggerated in the love-crazed firebrand Delamere. He forcibly abducts Emmeline in an aborted trip to Scotland, and, after challenging any apparent rival, eventually dies violently in a quarrel over his sister. Though Emmeline is attracted to this flamboyant figure, she soon realizes his defects and marries instead Godolphin, a naval captain rather improbably endowed with cultivation and benevolence.

If the male figure of sensibility was to be purged of the defects of aristocratic honour and invested with compassion and a sense of responsibility to the interests of a progressive society, the transformation of the female character was more subtle and often confusing. Conservative sensibility derived woman's suppression of self from a direct translation of the unconditional obedience demanded by fathers, husbands, and societal sexual codes into affectual terms. As the instruments of society's self-reproduction they were not to interfere in society's values. The self-control or self-subordination of conservative sensibility was increasingly described as natural to woman's constitution and in tune with all her feelings. 'Feminine' virtues such as modesty and delicacy could all be reduced to the overriding principle of propriety. To replace this sort of control with a more independent sense of public interest and a more active compassion and benevolence did not necessarily alter the virtue, but only its interpretation as a duty incumbent on male and female alike, accepted as a self-imposed value, not as imposed by authority or custom. Burney displays the construction of female sensibility in her heroines, with their overpowering anxiety to conform to the codes of behaviour sanctioned by fathers, husbands, and society. At one point Evelina, confronted by a kneeling Lord Orville offering marriage, can only say 'I hardly know myself to whom I most belong' (Burney 1968: 353), as she is at that time unaware of who has the power to dispose of her. Her licentious aristocratic father has left her abandoned and unacknowledged. When acknowledged, however, Evelina subsides into tears and a proper reverence and obedience towards the man who now occupies the position that entitles him to this homage of affection. Burney's novels also display the tensions of the conservative construction, especially in the early part of *Evelina*, where the heroine is at once amused and horrified at the etiquette of the ball-room which represents the larger man-made construction of propriety. In *Cecilia* the heroine is actually weaned away from unconditional obedience to guardians appointed by her father, but Burney's contribution to the revolutionary decade was the thoroughly conservative *Camilla*. This is not particularly surprising, since she was marrying a French émigré soldier, a follower of Lafayette, who had actually guarded the Tuilleries when the French royal family were virtual prisoners there. Leaving a royalist father and hopeful of a pension for her service to Queen Charlotte, her book is a sort of plea in mitigation, a monumental testimony to her freedom from 'French principles'. It includes a sermon delivered by Camilla's father to the heroine, later published separately, which inculcates at length the duty of suppressing personal feelings in a loving obedience to father and husband.

Charlotte Smith, who did not hesitate to call the ball-room a cattle-market (Smith 1795: 1: 81), allowed her heroines more independence, and the duties prescribed by conservative sensibility often took second place to benevolence and compassion. Emmeline, however, is rather a contrived heroine with many contradictions. While a will which vindicates her parentage is being proved, she puts Godolphin off with an echo of *Evelina*: she will not listen to him 'while my very name is in some degree doubtful' (Smith 1971: 453). This temporizing also stems from a fear of the rampaging Delamere. Where it suits her she can parrot the usual clichés of duty to confirm her own obedience to Lord Montraville as her guardian in resisting Delamere. She also urges Delamere's obedience to him as a father, calling this one of the first duties. But when Lord Montraville presses her to marry someone else she violently rejects 'the basest of all actions, that of selling her person and her happiness for a subsistence' (1971: 109). Though she condemns the violent passions of Delamere, she is compassionate to the adulterous Adelina, and even attends her in a concealed childbirth where she meets Adelina's brother, the Grandisonian Godolphin. It requires all her efforts to prevent him challenging Adelina's lover, Fitzherbert, and even Fitzherbert has to be restrained from 'that sense of honour which impelled him to give Godolphin imaginary reparation, by allowing him an opportunity of putting an end to *his* existence or losing his own' (1971: 292). Eventually Emmeline persuades Godolphin to accept the repentant Adelina and Fitzherbert into the family and to introduce them into society, something which Hannah More in the following decade regarded as impossible in such cases.

Mary Wollstonecraft objected to the treatment of Adelina, as she did to the general tendency of all sentimental novels to provide exhibitions of violent emotions, preposterous sentiments, and wild scenes which debauched the minds of female readers, rendering them discontented with 'moderate and rational prospects of life' (Wollstonecraft 1989: 7: 26). The theatrical contrition of Adelina, she thought, might make her more admirable to such readers than the companion portrait of Mrs Stafford who, when similarly disappointed in a wastrel husband, turned to her children (which, incidentally, was what Charlotte Smith herself had done). Considering the demands of Wollstonecraft's own sensibility and the behaviour of her heroine in *The Wrongs of Woman*, one might think that she was preaching to herself as well. Yet she was making a serious point about the instability of the language of sensibility. In the *Vindication of the Rights of Woman* she takes Rousseau as a prime example of its dangers. The imagination can:

> depict love with celestial charms, and dote on the grand ideal object – it can imagine a degree of mutual affection that shall refine the soul, and not expire when it has served as a 'scale to heavenly'; and, like devotion, make it absorb every meaner affection and desire ... alas, Rousseau, respectable visionary! thy paradise would soon be violated by the entrance of some unexpected guest.
>
> (Wollstonecraft 1975: 168–9)

Such pictures afford a 'plausible excuse to the voluptuary, who disguises sheer sensuality under a sentimental veil', and by confusing virtue with beauty 'exalted her on a quicksand'. Wollstonecraft shows that the customary language of sensibility degrades women to objects of male appetite. Novels such as Cumberland's *Arundel* present situations of provocative sensuality in a dress of sensibility:

> Throughout, sensation is termed sensibility; and vice, or rather sensuality, varnished over with a gloss, which the author seems to think virtue. He rambled into the country of chimeras for phantoms, whose like never were clothed with flesh, though all its infirmities are ascribed to them.
> (Wollstonecraft 1989: 7: 68)

The greater number of her criticisms of this fault are applied to women writers: 'after talking of the soul of sentiment – double-refined delicacy – how can they, without blushing, own that they have allowed the imagination to revel in *sensual* love scenes? – for we cannot help calling them so, though the gauze veil of artificial sentiments is drawn over them' (1989: 7: 191). Her attitude to Rousseau is mixed: his venture into the land of chimeras, which is how he describes his composition of *La Nouvelle Héloïse* in the *Confessions*, is a 'respectable' vision of an ideal relationship which can find embodiment only in the mind; the attempts of less refined imaginations to imitate it merely elevate the sensual. This attack is part of her criticism of Burke's theory of the beautiful. The sublime provokes fear, respect, and reverence, by evoking forces which threaten the ego, whereas beauty is subservient to our appetites. Burke's main illustration of the beautiful is woman, described in the language of conservative sensibility which stresses her weakness, delicacy, and dependence. As in his political writings, Burke tended to demystify relationships by displaying their basis in power, yet seemed to uphold the use of 'moral drapery' to disguise this fact. Wollstonecraft rebelled against the idea that woman was born merely to serve men's appetites, and claimed more sublime and active virtues.

Her novel *Mary* (1789) is aggressively subtitled 'A Fiction'. Only a fiction, she ironically claimed, could present a heroine who had any strength of thought or feeling. Many have been disappointed with Wollstonecraft's first novel because of its relatively mild complaints against woman's social disadvantages and the widely shared view that Mary seems to be just as much a prey to a debilitating sensibility as other female heroines. Yet within the spectrum of sensibility her variety clearly conflicts with conservative modes. There is a background of philosophical debate in the novel, as Wollstonecraft conducts a campaign not only against Burke but also against Adam Smith. One passage is unintelligible without a reference to Smith. Frankly explaining her estrangement from her husband, Mary affirms the value of true earthly affection as a 'scale to heavenly', virtually confesses her love for Henry, and proclaims her willingness to affront the conventions of society:

> My conscience does not smite me, and that Being who is greater than the internal monitor, may approve of what the world condemns; sensible that in Him I live, could I brave His presence, or hope in solitude to find peace, if I acted contrary to conviction, that the world might approve of my conduct – what could the world give to compensate for my own esteem? it is ever hostile and armed against the feeling heart!
> (Wollstonecraft 1976: 41)

Smith's 'internal monitor' is here opposed to conscience and divine approval, an opposition which is produced by Smith's idea of the internal monitor as the internalized 'impartial spectator', representing the views of society. The religious feelings which sanctioned individual conviction as the only moral ground of action perhaps owe as much to Rousseau as to Radical Dissent, but they contrast strongly with the implanted senses approving of correct behaviour which Smith had endowed with supernatural authority.

Though Wollstonecraft hints at the dangers of solitary ideal meditations, Mary's development of a religious sensibility in her reactions to nature is obviously designed to show her appreciation of the sublime, just as she recognizes the sublime genius of Henry's artistic gifts. Her active benevolence, especially towards one of an inferior class, is seen in her dedication to Ann and in her exertions in a storm at sea. The richness of this novel arises from Wollstonecraft's willingness to explore the complexities and possible contradictions within the character of sensibility she has created, features highlighted by the artless (or ruthless) selection of episodes for dramatic presentation. She does not mask Mary's disappointment that Ann's illness is partially due to her feelings for a man, both a demeaning weakness in her and an irritating demonstration of the rivalry of sexual love to Mary's exalted friendship. She acknowledges the dangers of unreserved sympathy in her own exhaustion: does not such benevolence subject one too much to others? The disappointment which arises from her own sentimental superiority to the 'vulgar' is seen when the recipients of her benevolence become less sensible of her goodness when she has less money to dispense. Sexual feelings, however, are not one of her weaknesses. Her platonic friendship with the terminally ill Henry is potentially adulterous and there are echoes of *La Nouvelle Héloïse* in some scenes. But Henry is a frail vessel of genius, a Saint-Preux unable to till the land, and Wollstonecraft is fantasizing an ideal relationship of elective affinity uncontaminated by power and appetite.

Both famous models of such a passion, produced by men, had broken down under the pressure of desire. Julie 'yielded' one night of consummation to Saint-Preux, only to subsequently marry Wolmar, her father's choice. Yet her eventual breakdown and death suggest that she could not maintain the equilibrium established between the three, whereas Saint-Preux survives his more graphically described despair. Werther, on the other hand, cannot sustain his spiritual relationship with the enigmatic Lotte in the face of Albert's physical presence as her husband. Their transports of passion, even when sublimated in an impassioned reading of Ossian, end in a desperate physical embrace. Helen Maria Williams's *Julia* and the novels of Charlotte Smith continually reconstruct the triangular situation in which the male is the weaker party. Williams's Frederic Seymour actually dies as a result of his unfortunate passion; Smith's Sir Edward Newenden takes his wounded heart to the Continent at the end of *Ethelinde*. The heroines of these novels have a restraint over their feelings that, while sometimes precarious, never relaxes. Wollstonecraft complained that Julie was so secure that her struggles against passion were unconvincing. For Williams, however, the interesting point about Julia's strength was the operation of sensibility. For her, sensibility added resolve to her desire not to hurt Frederic's wife. Sensibility 'is not merely the ally of weakness, or the slave of guilt, but serves to give a stronger impulse to virtue' (Williams 1790: 1: 178). The Rousseauistic point stressed by both writers is that passion is not controlled by propriety, but by considerations of personal integrity and avoiding harm to other people. Hannah More noted with horror that Rousseau's Julie lapsed from honour from principle, not weakness: Rousseau 'exhibits a virtuous woman, the victim not of temptation, but of reason - not of vice, but of sentiment - not of passion, but of conviction; and strikes at the root of honour, by elevating a crime into a principle' (More 1801: 7: 34–5).

Smith's *Ethelinde* escaped Wollstonecraft's usual strictures on sensibility, though it contains scenes of relatively undisguised sexual feeling and seems to make a point of flouting propriety. The transcendent quality of Ethelinde's sensibility allows her to walk through fire without scorching. Ethelinde pays the first visit to Montgomery, who has impressed her with the heroic proportions of his figure while saving her from drowning. They walk unescorted and meet in an isolated bower where Ethelinde declares her love for him. They spend nights in a London hotel unchaperoned and others alone in the shepherd's hut where Ethelinde recovers in bed from a fall. The situation of the Newenden household, with Sir Edward mooning after Ethelinde and Lady Newenden being courted by Lord Danesfort, presents a scandalous spectacle, as many characters point out. Ethelinde emerges uncompromised, subject only to the lightest of authorial irony. In many places one is reminded of *Sense and Sensibility* and the contrasting treatment Marianne receives. Ethelinde, like Marianne, makes her own feelings the standard of propriety: 'In a few moments she had argued herself into the most perfect conviction of the propriety of what she was desirous to do' (Smith 1789: 1: 99). Her feelings for Montgomery seem to dominate her life, since he is so 'replete with natural taste and poetical enthusiasm . . . so much in unison with her own feelings, that the universe seemed to hold nothing else worthy of her attention' (1789: 1: 107). When he kisses her hand on departing, Ethelinde, 'heart-struck, and feeling lost to the rest of the world, retired to her own room; and sent an excuse to avoid joining the company, among whom she was unfitted to appear' (1789: 1: 191). Such reclusive passion is condemned by Austen, but Smith shows such feeling for a worthy object to be part of that sensibility which also moves Ethelinde to benevolent actions like nursing Sir Edward's fever-stricken children at the risk of her own health, and comforting her father and brother in their debtors' prison. Many critics of sensibility objected to the predominance of love as a theme, urging the more social attachments to country and cause. Practitioners tended to reject a Freudian economic model of the emotions, viewing the intensity of personal attachments as an index of the capacity for more extended benevolence. Ethelinde is introduced as an exception among eighteen-year-old girls, since her family circumstances had 'taught her to think and to feel' (1789: 1: 8). Like Wollstonecraft, Smith presents females designed to equal or even excel men in their sublime virtues. Mrs Montgomery is the main exemplar, especially in the episode where she is depicted searching the battlefield of Minden for her husband amid scenes of carnage and the looting of bodies. She also manages the family's finances and seems to dominate her son in their choice of life. Smith's tormented but resourceful mothers may be idealized self-portraits, but they play an integral role in the organized polemic of her novels.

One of the connections between the fictional worlds of novels and systems of ideas, especially if they are reformist ideas, is the sort of communities which are represented. For the writers of the eighteenth century the predominant image of social life was the country estate, its inhabitants dependent upon the owner for their welfare, their justice, and their representation in parliament. Only towards the end of the century did the idea of a whole society unified by national regulations superseding local proprietors gain some following, and even then, for many, it incorporated the largely autonomous estates or generalized customs common on such estates. The fervour with which Paine prophesied the benefits of government providing marriage and death benefits, pensions, and even employment, and the practical examples of large-scale centralization in France found little response in Britain. The large-scale reforms contemplated by Continental 'benevolent despots' were too much identified with the absolutism from which the Whig Revolution had freed Britain. The restricted, local model of society qualifies the universalist basis of reformist ideas, but there are differences in the estates presented in novels which point to new values. Judith Stanton is overstating the prevalence of the traditional order when she finds an ominously atavistic note in the conclusion of Smith's *Old Manor House* when the hero and heroine take over the old Rayland estate. She views it as the assumption of 'a tenuous new patriarchal order which we can barely trust because of its nominal and local similarities to the old' (Stanton 1989: 23). True, such uneasiness is often felt at the accession of characters, who have won through against the grain of traditional society, to vast traditional estates where they propose to diffuse benevolence over their dependants, and the device became less used as its anomalies were appreciated. Holcroft agreed with similar criticisms of his conclusion to *Hugh Trevor*. In the case of the Rayland estate, however, the contrast between old and new is particularly marked. The rigid hierarchical forms of the old estate which chimed in with Mrs Rayland's notions of the priority of birth and the patriarchal authority of princes is abandoned. The Rayland pride, which even sundered the family, gives way to a benevolence which takes in not only the family but the worthy characters from humble life whose virtues recommend them. The repentant Mrs Roker is given a place, as is a sailor's widow, and the old soldier Hugh March, who is given the independence of a life-tenancy of the lodge. The fate of the adjoining estate is also a pointer to a better lifestyle as the castle and its pleasure grounds which once ministered to the pride of birth and then to the pride of riches are converted into farms.

The old hierarchical community can be seen as an object of sentimental regard in many of the novels of the period, in which the lord of the manor dispenses benevolence to assembled rustics and glories in his patriarchal responsibility of judging the 'desert' of his flock. Brooke's *History of Lady Julia Mandeville* features an estate similar to that of Lady Raynal. Lord Belmont's estate 'conveys the strongest idea of the patriarchal government; he seems a beneficent father surrounded by his children, over whom reverence, gratitude, and love, give him absolute authority' (Brooke 1769: 1: 16). The catastrophe of this novel is caused by the patriarchal basis of power. It concerns the love of Harry Mandeville for Julia, the daughter of Lord Belmont, apparently fruitless because of Belmont's avowed intention to marry Julia to the affluent son of a friend and heir to an earldom. Unknown to Harry, by the complications of a will, he is that intended spouse, but the intentions of the fathers are concealed until he has been killed in a duel with a supposed rival. The traditional patriarchal estates are notable for pictures of contented, ignorant peasants, well aware of their dependence on the proprietor. Mrs Rayland gives annual feasts to her tenantry which follow strict rules of precedence and decorum until she retires, when they degenerate into violent and bawdy saturnalia. Lord Belmont sponsors dancing in a 'rural assembly', and even Mackenzie's haughty aristocrat Montauban cavorts with the peasants during the wine-pressing. *Julia de Roubigné*, however, revolves around the gloomy pride which leads Montaubon to poison his wife on suspicion of infidelity. In all these manifestations of conservative sensibility the forms of society which are presented as 'free' are free only in appearance and are securely based on traditional authority; there is rarely any suggestion that this freedom can be improved upon. In Mackenzie's *Julia* the hero, Savillon, frees slaves in the West Indies only to put them under the authority of their hereditary chief who gets more work out of them! Pratt, who valued himself on his liberal opinions, wrote against slavery in his poem *Humanity*, but he called only for slaves to be admitted to the protection of the laws which bound the 'chain' of society together. He realized that the condition of many servants was just as bad, but it was their status, not their condition, he wished to change. He would not even commit himself so far as to press for an abolition of the trade.

In more liberal models of the country estate the proprietor indeed rescues the unfortunate with a display of largesse, yet tries to establish them in positions of some independence. Commercial enterprises are not excluded from these liberal establishments. Janet Todd is right in suggesting that the benevolent woman of sensibility and means will not employ her money to 'increase wealth' in the sense of making a personal profit, but surely wrong in suggesting that she will hold herself aloof from economic realities and merely 'spend it to gratify others' (Todd 1986: 119). Certainly Burney's Cecilia, guided by the somewhat unhinged Albany, tends to indulge her feelings by surrounding herself with grateful dependants, including a 'lady's companion', but Wollstonecraft's Mary 'established manufacturies' and 'threw the estate into small farms' (Wollstonecraft 1976: 67). The establishment of farmers with some security of tenure and prospects of independence on the large estates was a practical step towards the diffusion of liberty, and Wollstonecraft noted the presence of small farms as an encouraging feature of the landscape of Norway. In her *Vindication of the Rights of Men* (1790) she condemned the landowner who improved his estates merely for the 'prospect': if 'the heart was allowed to beat true to nature, decent farms would be scattered over the estate, and plenty smile around . . . It is not by squandering alms that the poor can be relieved, or improved – it is the fostering sun of kindness, the wisdom that finds them employments calculated to give them habits of virtue, that meliorates their condition' (Wollstonecraft 1790: 145–6). In her *Historical and Moral View of the Origin and Progress of the French Revolution* (1794) she calls charity 'the most specious system of slavery' and looks forward to the time when 'humanity will take place of charity, and all the ostentatious virtues of an universal aristocracy' (Wollstonecraft 1794: 71).

The liberally administered estate is best represented by Bage's *Mount Henneth*, written in response to Pratt's *Shenstone-Green; or the New Paradise Lost, Being a History of Human Nature* (1779). The narrator of Pratt's engaging work is Sir Benjamin Beauchamp, a man of transcendent sensibility who even fears lest an abrupt exhalation will destroy airborne animalculae. His tale is a warning to 'projectors on poetical principles' that the attempt to establish a utopian community will founder on the rock of obdurate human nature:

> It is to you, ye gentle beings, whose bosoms are fraught with foreign woes; whose weeping eyes and milky tempers render you the slaves rather than the friends of virtue; to you I address the sentiments and the adventures of a man who was arrogant enough to suppose he could make human nature live FOR rather than UPON one another.
> (Pratt 1779: 1: 3).

His benevolent foundation grants houses and pensions to those abject and plausible enough to impose upon him. The consequence of such wealth and leisure is the introduction of corresponding vices. The ladies must have a playhouse and masquerades; a race-course is laid out, cock-fights are held, 'sporting ladies' are introduced, and the town is stricken with venereal disease. Eventually Beauchamp is persuaded by a friend that

> Good and gentle characters, require no other impulse to virtue than the dictate of the heart, which is their unerring rule of right; but the majority, being neither gentle nor

good; it is necessary to prevent the force of bad habit or bad nature, by the interposition of wholesome laws.

(1779: 3: 56–7).

This friend, a philanthropist in a disguise of poverty, has been touring the countryside with no thought of altering the state of the poor but rewarding their behaviour with small monetary gifts. Beauchamp generalizes the result of his experiment to validate the legal system of the entire empire, since good order among men can only be secured where 'there is a regular code of laws, which pervades the empire, and provides equably reward and punishment to guard the privileges of one man from the violations of another' (1779: 3: 191). Sir Benjamin had consulted Sarah Scott's *Millenium Hall* in planning his town, but did not like all its regulations. *Millenium Hall* is indeed a strange work, full of the tensions created by the position of woman. The stories of five of its inmates cover most of the situations in which women suffer the tyranny of men, unequal laws, or an unequal moral code. Surviving their ordeals, they devote their wealth, often provided by the deaths of their oppressors, to founding an asylum for similarly oppressed women. Here the standard of morality is a strongly asserted Christianity which upholds the feminine virtues of submission and the rigid distinctions of society which had been responsible for their own plights. In its incorporation of commercial enterprise into the charitable community it foreshadows the practicality of Bage's co-operative vision.

Mount Henneth was Bage's first novel, published in 1781 after an iron foundry venture had failed in the depression caused by the American War. The novel returns repeatedly to criticism of the unjustifiable claims of Britain on America, which are compared to the more successful plundering of India. The projector of a benevolent community is James Foston who, in the words of his friend, the cautious Scottish doctor Sinden:

> conceiving it would be for the good of the species, if it could be taught to *associate* rather than to *herd* . . . hath determined, after the example of Sir Benjamin Beauchamp, to build himself a green, to be called the Green of Association.
>
> But he hath not, like Sir Benjamin, determined to people the social green with vice and folly, to the utter exclusion of common sense.
>
> (Bage 1824: 244)

Their purpose, Sinden tells his friend, is 'to sow the seed of happiness on our own ground, and to diffuse the plant around us', but the point is 'to go about it like workmen' (1824: 238). They establish a ship-building enterprise, a glass-works, and an improved system of agriculture designed to profit the tenants, while the women of the main community also work in 'plantations'.

One of the minor beneficiaries of Foston's benevolence is a bereaved mother whose distress is conveyed through gesture in the best traditions of sensibility:

> The poor woman turned her head at Julia's entrance, glanced upon a coat hanging on the opposite side of the room, cast a piteous look upon the children on the floor, kissed the infant she held in her arms, and with a deep sigh fixed her eyes again upon the grave.
>
> (Bage 1824: 170)

She is set up as a dairymaid 'but not in the common way': the cottage and grazing for eight cows is provided rent free for one year, Foston guaranteeing to take the produce at a market rate. That perennial of benevolent communities, the broken soldier, is another admitted into 'Henneth Castle, the chosen abode of love, friendship and benevolence' (1824: 192). Sensibility works hand-in-hand with practicality in relieving distress and 'fostering' independence.

The principal characters of *Mount Henneth* display a universal benevolence verging on the quixotic, but their feelings are rarely demonstrative and their letters are often witty and satirical. Shaftesbury's influence, perhaps noticeable in the remark about herding and associating, encouraged not only effusive sympathy but also the wit and humour which he recommended should be directed against false principles and customs of society. Bage's work demonstrates both tendencies, though the wit becomes more prominent and is more relished today. Foston's own story contains the improbably cosmopolitan figure of Duverda, a Persian living in India, whose Jewish friend is the victim of a corrupt government. Duverda marries his friend's wife according to Jewish ritual. Foston, serving in the East India Company, falls in love with his daughter just after they have been attacked, pillaged, and the daughter raped by the

Company's soldiery. Six days are enough to convince Duverda of his integrity and fitness to inherit his vast fortune: 'Six days I have noted the currency of his thoughts, have seen his eye kindled by the imaginary tale of honour, his brow scowling contempt at baseness, his bosom heaving with the story of distress' (Bage 1824: 160). But, while sensibility reigns in this passage, it is reason that is appealed to in Foston's reaction to the fact that Cara has been raped, a reaction in which Bage shows that laxness in his attitude to female chastity for which he was criticized by Scott. Cara has learned from English books that all women who suffer rape or seduction 'must die or be immured for ever; ever after they are totally useless to all the purposes of society; it is the foundation of a hundred fabulous things called novels, which are said to paint exactly the reigning manners and opinions: all crimes but this may be expiated.' Foston's brisk response is that 'things like this, which cannot stand the test of reason, seldom take strong hold of the minds of the people. It is to be found in books, sir, and I hope, for the honour of the human intellect, little of it will be found anywhere else' (1824: 161). Bage could be called one of the major feminists of the period in his satiric analyses of the dominant constructions of femininity. Kames had sentimentalized chastity as a branch of the moral sense, implanted particularly in women to ensure complete commitment to the monogamous connection. Infidelity in a wife testified to the complete subversion of all her affections away from the husband, while the husband, not being troubled so much by the bothersome principle, could lapse without the alienation of his affections. Bage demystified the double standard in a crisp exchange in *Hermsprong* in which the hero affirms equality as far as personal morality applies, but points to heredity as the social justification for the distinction.

The amount of sensibility in Bage's novels declines towards the 1790s as he focuses his satire on the degenerate aspects of the cult. The hero of *James Wallace* (1788) is a man of sensibility, but a weak one, who fails as a lawyer by underestimating the rapacity of his fellow-men and failing to secure a legal document against the cunning of an exploiter of innocence. He shows an active benevolence, attempting to reform a libertine companion, succeeding in preventing a duel, and urging his mistress to benevolence, but his over-sententious and trusting humanity is put into contrast with the more combative characters of Paracelsus Holman and the merchant Paul Lamounde. Holman's version of filial piety to a father unreasonably attached to Filmerian notions is to give him a good thrashing. Paul Lamounde answers James's sentimental exhortations with tirades against: 'the cant of benevolence; books are full of it; it fills our mouths, and sometimes gets as far as the eye, but never reaches the heart' (Bage 1788: 2: 38). He urges James to become a merchant, a point which most commentators have thought worthy of notice, but this is not an injunction to cast aside his sensibility and look out for number one, but an exhortation towards the active life of a wider benevolence. James's father counsels him: 'you may be a gentleman with an independent fortune. I should rather advise you to be a merchant and increase it; but do not regard the gain of the profession as your sole inducement. You are affluent; every day presents a benevolent merchant opportunity to benefit some worthy man' (1788: 2: 271). The praise of the manufacturing and trading interests is usually associated with Paine and the dissenting connection. Paine's motto in *Common Sense* had been that kings make war, republics make trade, and he viewed trade as a pacific process, unifying people and nations by appealing to their interests. Though he often invoked humanitarian and democratic sentiment, he had no dealings with the elevated concept of benevolence or of 'theoretical reformation': 'The most effectual process is that of improving the condition of man by means of his interest; and it is on this ground that I take my stand' (Paine 1969: 234).

Bage never loses contact with the benevolence of sensibility or its basis in a 'naive' response of personal feeling, despite his attacks on conservative and degenerate sensibility. Hermsprong attacks Caroline Campinet's overstretched feelings of filial loyalty by referring to Wollstonecraft's idea of the reciprocal duties which must validate such feelings. Bage exposes the instability of the terms of sensibility by using one of its key terms of personal appreciation, 'merit', to describe the housekeeper/companion of Lord Grondale, whose merit obviously derives from sexual services rendered. The doubleness of the language of sensibility is consummately employed by Miss Fluart to both entice and deflect the lascivious Grondale, whose artistic taste seems to be confined to the appreciation of unclothed female classical deities. Yet the narrator of the novel is the man of feeling, Gregory Glen, who comes to share the more assertive virtues of the hero. The benevolent efforts of Hermsprong and Caroline among villagers struck by a storm are made the occasion of exposing the inhumanity of Grondale and his ecclesiastical toady Dr Blick, who condemn such 'charitable ebullitions' as not flowing from 'Christian benevolence' (Bage 1985: 76). The novel includes the plan for another benevolent community, this time in America, as Hermsprong despairs of finding justice in England. This echoes the contemporaneous pantisocratic scheme of Coleridge and Southey which was also motivated by reaction against English corruption. In Bage's novels reason and sensibility are combined in a way characteristic of the earlier period but show the increasing strains of ideological polarization as sensibility becomes identified with a conservative conformism or passivity.

3

SENSIBILITY IN REVOLUTION: GODWIN AND WOLLSTONECRAFT

Burke's *Reflections on the Revolution in France*, published in late 1790, together with his persistent attacks on the French Revolution and its supporters during 1791, was the major factor which polarized the conservative and radical aspects of sensibility. His appeal to the loyalties of Nation and Church were based firmly on the model of the family and the feelings associated with it, creating the image of one great British family stretching back into the past, securing its identity, property, and liberties by the principle of heredity. Many commentators have noted the ways in which his theories of the sublime and the beautiful are employed to create the majestic and awe-inspiring edifice of the British Constitution, the product of ages of experience and foresight in which all the natural feelings of man find an embodiment. Marie-Antoinette is graced with the weakness, beauty, and domestic piety that call for masculine defence.[1] The sublime potential of the Revolution of the masses is dissipated in attacks on individuals and cabals. Horror, rather than sublime terror, is provoked by pictures of mob violence and de-natured women whose aggression stirs deep sexual anxieties. The sublime of power is evoked in the collective response to the Gordon riots. The 'low' language which brings home both the threat of revolution and the need for strong repression might well have licensed the ten thousand cudgels (rather than rapiers) that leapt to the defence of property, home, and womanhood in the Church and King mobs for which Burke pointed out victims.

There are points in the *Reflections* at which Burke does admit the possibility of progress, concessions later admired by Matthew Arnold. In fact if Burke genuinely believed that the Constitution was the product of historical wisdom progressively adapting principles to changing situations, then development, if not progress, must be its distinctive feature. But however much his theory hinted at change, his model was a static society preserving an inherited balance of constitutional powers. Even the cautious Millar was aware of the shifts in the balance of power that necessitated new formulations of traditional rights, but for Burke the 1689 settlement, itself based on past practice, was an indissoluble contract which alienated natural rights.

Two aspects of Burke's strategy had significant consequences for subsequent writers. Firstly, he laid claim to the values of feeling and sensibility in the name of traditional values and stigmatized his opponents as metaphysicians whose reasonings dealt with only the superficial aspects of human nature. Secondly, he implicated all who answered him in a defence of the French Revolution. Burke made much of the violence of the crowd in the march on Versailles and it did not require much percipience to foresee more, though Burke's commonplace of eighteenth-century historiography that democratic licence led to anarchy and the rise of dictatorship was spectacularly vindicated. In the House he continually attacked the opposition with accusations of democratic sentiments, taunts which Fox and Sheridan parried with some discomfort.

In 1790–1 Burke, despite his often breathtaking claims to be speaking for the majority, was not representative of contemporary opinion as literary London flocked to Paris to congratulate the French on a revolution against monarchic absolutism comparable with their own. Irreproachable figures in the movement of sensibility enthused openly. Cowper, Hayley, Seward, even Mackenzie, supported the early phases of the Revolution and thought Burke unnecessarily alarmist. The most prominent violence of 1791 was perpetrated under the red flag of authority, such as the massacres of the Champs de Mars. The violence recollected by Wordsworth in *Descriptive Sketches* was associated with the 'red banner'. But the event which had encouraged more radical hopes and had probably alerted Burke to the dangers of the Revolution was that celebrated in red ink in Godwin's Diary on 19 June 1790: 'Titles of nobility abolished by national assembly'. This was a symbolic act, in no way comparable in practical significance with the wholesale renunciation of feudal dues which marked the session of 1789, yet it showed how much the French aristocracy were still willing to surrender to maintain a footing in the new alignment of forces. In Britain, aristocracy was triumphant. Little threat came from popular movements, and the king seemed powerless or disinclined to continue the power-struggle on the lines laid down by Millar by encouraging the People as a weapon against the nobles. The spectacle of an aristocracy divesting itself not only of powers and immunities but of the names which linked it to the illustrious family of memory was fraught with danger to the comfortable accommodations of established power in Britain.

The 1780s had been a crucial decade in British Constitutional politics and had revealed the close relationship between Crown and aristocracy to those who supported the popular cause. Godwin, like Millar and Burke, had supported the Rockingham Whigs in their efforts to counter the influence of the Crown and mitigate anti-American policies. The defeat of the first Rockingham administration and that of the Fox/North coalition which succeeded the second showed the prevailing power of the monarchy and its unholy alliance with aristocratic interests. The later illness of the king and the Regency crisis highlighted the unseemly wranglings of aristocratic factions. Burke, dependent on aristocratic patronage, could hardly be accounted a neutral when linking monarchy and aristocracy in his appeal to chivalric ideals. For those like Godwin, the French declaration and its implications for Britain focused a growing antagonism towards aristocracy and a disillusionment with the famed balanced Constitution.

Godwin's *Letters of Mucius* show his allegiance to constitutional politics up to 1790. Like Millar, he was confident that the power of the Commons to grant taxation was the safeguard of popular rights. In the preface to *Political Justice* he ascribed his conversion to a simpler political organization to ideas arising from the French Revolution. This was not a sudden inebriation of the intellect or ingestation of the ideas of Paine and other activists. It was the French declaration against aristocracy which crystallized his experience of British politics over the previous decade, encouraged by the welcome given by public opinion to a nation which had not only determined to restrict monarchical power but had as its first measure destroyed the royal prison which had incarcerated the victims of aristocratic oppression. The evidence for this lies in his unpublished 'Letter of Mucius' to Sheridan of April 1791,[2] the substance of which found a place in

Political Justice. In this letter he urges Sheridan to lay aside all temporizing and make a stand on the 'great points of government'. He must go further in opposition to 'hereditary honours and hereditary power' than objecting to their introduction in Quebec, as Fox had done, and must imitate the French: 'Does truth alter its nature by crossing the straits and become falsehood? Are men entitled to perfect equality in France, & is it just to deprive them of it in England? Did the French do well in extinguishing nobility there, & is it right that we should preserve hereditary honours?' He admits that a few years previously it would have been thought 'bold and paradoxical' to propose the abolition of 'all distinctions of rank and hereditary greatness' but in this period of revolutions 'Truth has gone so far, that it must go farther'. A brief section on limited monarchy encapsulates the experience of the 1780s. Such a monarch, Godwin asserts, 'ought to be a pageant or a statue' and his ministers should be solely responsible for measures. But if the king may choose ministers he will infallibly choose measures too, as few ministers will sacrifice their places to their virtue:

> The king wants at first but little. Only a bishopric for a pimp, or a judge's gown for the venal instrument of corruption. Only immunity for this villain, & proscription for that man of illustrious talents or uncomplying virtue. And the minister that gives him these will hardly scruple in the sequel an unjust war or the coercion of men animated by the love of freedom.

Courts become places of 'cabal, faction and intrigue' where the sycophant and time-server flourish and the 'man of generous virtue' is sure of discouragement. 'What sort of character', he asks in the spirit of *Political Justice,* 'will this circumstance diffuse through every recess and corner of the land?' The House of Commons is a painful scene to an honest mind, where 'men obtain their admission by bribery, by riot & vice, & where hundreds, brought in by some titled patron, dare not vote & dare not think but as he directs'.

His attack on a 'nobility trampling upon the minds & exterminating the virtues of mankind' is obviously inspired by a love of equality, but even in this most optimistic period, when he forecasts the imminent collapse of the Constitution, he realizes that a corrupted populace are not ready for political responsibility. A passage scored out in the manuscript acknowledges this:

> Are the lower classes animated with that independence, the fearless intrepidity, that conscious equality, which true liberty must infallibly inspire? No. On the contrary, their most intimate persuasion is that it would be folly in them to trouble themselves about political government & political truth, that government is not influenced by the sentiments of them, or such as they, but is wholly at the disposal of the higher ranks of the community. Where the people are degraded & corrupt, their superiors never fail to be contemptible.

Uncertainties about the practicalities of introducing equality are put aside in 1791 in the general attack on aristocracy and inequality.

In *Political Justice* the attack on aristocracy becomes an assault on the exclusivity of the partial affections and Godwin slipped neatly into the niche Burke had prepared for those who undertook to criticize the 'natural feelings' of conservative sensibility. He became the caricature of the unfeeling rationalist, the coldest-blooded metaphysician of the age in anti-Jacobin satire, and a misleader of youth in Wordsworth's self-exculpatory 1805 *Prelude*. The majority of commentators have also concentrated on his criticism of the passions and have neglected the affiliation of his dominating idea of universal benevolence with the Hutchesonian brand of moral sense.

Mark Philp, in his study of *Political Justice*, asserts that the first edition is built on the premises of Rational Dissent, specifically the doctrines of Richard Price. The object is to improve men's reason, their apprehension of social reality, and the faith is that the enlightened reason will apprehend the duty of justice and virtue. Philp goes on to assert that in subsequent editions Godwin replaced the Rationalist framework with one based on the benevolist premises of what Philp calls the 'British Moralists' (Philp 1986: 101). Dugald Stewart made a more specific attribution in 1814 when he identified Godwin's system as that of Hutcheson, with the mischievous addition of the obligation of justice to the promptings of the moral sense (Stewart 1854). Godwin certainly studied Hutcheson at Hoxton, and his proposal for a seminary at Epsom in 1783 uses the language and ideas of a Hutchesonian cast which we associate with his work after 1793. Here he posits an intuitive moral faculty which operates through sympathy and imagination:

> Our enquiry . . . is respecting the time at which that intuitive faculty is generally awakened, by which we decide upon the differences of virtue and vice, and are impelled to applaud the one, and condemn the other . . .
>
> The æra of foresight is the æra of imagination, and imagination is the grand instrument of virtue. The mind is the seat of pleasure and pain. It is not by what we see, but what we infer and suppose, that we are taught, that any being is the object of commiseration . . . The sentiment that the persons about us have life and feeling as well as ourselves, cannot be of very late introduction . . . From thence to the feelings of right and wrong, of compassion and generosity, there is but one step.
>
> It has, I think, been fully demonstrated by that very elegant philosopher, Mr Hutcheson, that self-love is not the source of all our passions, but that disinterested benevolence has its seat in the human heart.
>
> (Godwin 1966: 194–7)

The turn to Hutcheson was then a *return*, if, indeed, he had fundamentally turned at all.

It seems to me that Godwin constructed the first edition of *Political Justice* with purposeful ambiguity about its philosophical affiliations. A great number of eighteenth-century philosophical ideas are invoked where they aid his system, yet in ways which often subtly contradict their original contexts. Smith's impartial spectator makes an appearance, Hartley's theory of association is praised but relieved of its physiological basis, even Sterne's Conscience garbed as a constitutional British judge is hauled in. References to the immutability of truth invoke Price and the Rational Moralists; the stress on universal benevolence is Hutchesonian, though shared by Price; similarly, the stress on the right of private judgment is most closely associated with the Dissenters but is also one of the natural rights claimed by Hutcheson. It was designed to appeal to all who recognized their own keywords. Rigorous critics, however, were dissatisfied. Thomas Belsham, a Hartleyan tutor at Hackney Dissenting Academy, saw the lack of sanction or obligation to justice: what makes us choose the course of justice? The answer for a Hartleyan should be 'pleasure', but though Godwin does expatiate on the pleasures of benevolence, Belsham recognized that he referred it to an operation of the mind, 'reflection', which confirms our choice of benevolent actions. Altogether, there is just too much stress, even in the first edition, on the 'great and inexpressible operations of reflection' (*PJ*93: 1: 58) to content a Hartleyan. In the revisions the Hutchesonian basis becomes much clearer. 'Virtue' in the first edition is regularly replaced by 'benevolence', a key point of identification, since Hutcheson was notorious for reducing the concept of virtue to the approval of benevolence. Even in 1793 virtue is defined not as the product of reason but of desire: 'a desire to promote the benefit of intelligent beings in general, the quantity of virtue being as the quantity of desire' (*PJ*93: 1: 254), and Godwin produces a formulation close to his later statements about justice being a criterion, and emotion the exciting cause of action: 'Virtue, is nothing else but the pursuit of general good. Justice, is the standard which discriminates the advantage of the many and of the few, of the whole and a part' (*PJ*93: 2: 468). Godwin's standard of justice is notoriously discriminating, judging the worth of individuals by their virtue. Yet, here as well, virtue is equivalent to benevolence, the capacity to spread happiness and enlightenment to others. In what Lamb called the 'famous fire cause, Archbishop Fénelon versus my mother', Godwin later complained that people had misunderstood him to imply that the saving of Fénelon would proceed from calculation, whereas the saving of the mother would be provoked by passion. No noble action, he maintained, could be performed without passion, and in other sections the reader can be in no doubt that Godwin is praising the most ardent passion of heroic benevolence in the Roman heroes who sacrificed private consideration and even their lives for their country.

The difficulty arises because in the Fénelon passage Godwin is attacking the partial affections which had been exaggerated into unthinking principles of action by conservative sensibility. In his attack on family affections he is attacking the exclusivity and self-aggrandizement of the great aristocratic families who monopolized the wealth and power of Britain. His suggestion for the abolition of surnames continues this assault. The injustice of inequalities perpetuated by aristocratic institutions leads him to question the values which had been celebrated in the literature of conservative sensibility. Most notoriously he attacks gratitude, the slavish dependence, bred of unequal institutions, which makes men the objects of demeaning and ostentatious charity rather than fellow-beings who may claim a just right to the means of life. Gratitude, he comments, 'a principle which has so often been the theme of the moralist and the poet, is no part of either justice or virtue' (*PJ*93: 1: 84). Godwin blamed the unequal institutions of society for producing all the bad passions of envy, jealousy, and malice, but he also saw a similar generation of factitiously exaggerated 'amiable' passions which prevented the progress of society to a state of greater equality. His later acknowledgement of the value of family affections and the mutual good offices which spring from them was embarrassing, but perhaps less of a shock if we realize the polemic nature of his initial attack upon them. Even in his retractions he restated the familiar benevolist line that, though the partial affections were a source of good, they should be restrained. Hutcheson, in the Preface to *An Essay on the Nature and Conduct of the Passions and Affections*, had defined 'Perfection of Virtue' as 'having the *universal calm Benevolence*, the prevalent Affection of the mind, so as to limit and counteract not only the *selfish Passions*, but even the *particular kind Affections*' (Hutcheson 1969). Even in his denial of the obligations of gratitude, Godwin could have found a source in Adam Ferguson, whose primitive tribes, living in natural sociability, had similarly denied them.

In categorizing Godwin as a rationalist who softened into sensibility, critics may be over-valuing the diaries and journals which he kept from 1789 onwards. A man of thirty-three might be suspected of having formed some previous opinions, and the course of rationalist reading which he undertook to produce *Political Justice* could indicate a new emphasis to be incorporated with previous opinions, not the complete furnishing of the mind that some critics seem to imagine. Central to his system are the idea of natural benevolence, extending to the widest communal good, and the idea that the passions, including the partial passions, can be regulated by the individual, rather than by the coercion of institutions, the observance of social customs, or a subservience to general moral rules. Equally essential to his scheme is the recognition that there are 'higher' pleasures above the sensual which involve man in realizing his fundamentally social, benevolent nature. In holding that benevolence is the source of the highest happiness and a mark of the highest human development, Godwin is not only following the ideas developed in aesthetic theory, but echoing Hutcheson. Godwin's scale of happiness (*PJ*98: 1: 445-8), where he offers to our contemplation the gradations of human development possible in contemporary society, from the labourer, 'happier than a stone', to the wealthy and cultivated aristocrat, and finds their satisfactions unfulfilling beside the model of the man of benevolence, greatly resembles Hutcheson's strategy. In his *Short Introduction to the Principles of Morals* Hutcheson asks us to

> imagine with ourselves a person possessed of every ornament and elegance of life, along with all the means of bodily pleasures . . . and that he were employed in the noblest contemplations with uninterrupted leisure, and yet void of all social affection, neither loving any nor beloved, without any opportunities of friendly offices . . . Is there any man so divested of humanity as to wish for such a lot to himself, or think it desirable?
>
> (Hutcheson 1753: 1: 46)

For Godwin the disposition towards benevolence is as natural to the mind as it is for Shaftesbury and Hutcheson. In a crucial passage he uses Hutcheson's term 'reflection' for the internal sense which naturally validates benevolent actions. We may form habits like miserliness from a mistaken idea of their connection with the ultimate end of happiness, but:

> When ever we have entered into so auspicious a path as that of disinterestedness, reflection confirms our choice, in a sense in which it never can confirm any of the factitious passions we have named. We find by observation that we are surrounded by beings of the same nature with ourselves. They have the same senses, are susceptible of the same pleasures and pains, capable of being raised to the same excellence and employed in the same usefulness. We are able in imagination to go out of ourselves, and become impartial spectators of the system of which we are a part. We can then make an estimate of our intrinsic and absolute value; and detect the imposition of that self-regard which

would represent our own interest as of as much value as that of all the world beside.

(*PJ*98: 1: 427)

A complex series of echoes here reminds us not only of Hutcheson, but of Smith's impartial spectator, here raised to a more disinterested plane, and the imagination with which Smith, in pointed contradiction to Hume, maintains that we can sympathize with a victim on the rack. Also in the background is Hume's reason, unassisted by moral feelings, which could prefer the destruction of the world to any personal inconvenience, and Hume's argument for sympathy by an appeal to the similarities of men's senses and internal constitutions which enable them to share another's feelings. Wordsworth almost paraphrases this passage in 'The Old Cumberland Beggar', where, in the practice of traditional charities,

> habit does the work
> Of reason, yet prepares that after joy
> Which reason cherishes

and raises the mind from the 'inevitable charities' of kindred to the true satisfaction of universal benevolence, a benevolence which is valued

> for this single cause,
> That we have all of us one human heart.

(*OA*: 52-3)

The benevolist principle that man naturally approves of what is good for humanity is also used by Godwin to deliver him from a pessimistic conclusion in his examination of necessity. If the assassin cannot help the murder he commits any more than the knife, a depressing picture of inevitable corruption and crimes fostered by the injustice of society is in prospect. But Godwin's model for this necessity is Hume, not Hartley. The pre-eminence of moral motives leads Godwin to hope that even a criminal whose experience had convinced him that society was a state of lawless war could be reformed by offering him ideas of human benevolence which could not fail to find an echo in his heart. Godwin exploits the metaphors drawn from the 'subtle fluids' of electricity and magnetism common to writers of sensibility to convey man's susceptibility to more than merely physical influences. A man differs from an object as an iron candlestick differs from a brass one. Iron will be drawn by magnetism and man will be convinced by arguments appealing to his better nature. In *Caleb Williams* the 'philosophical' outlaw Raymond is convinced by Caleb's rather priggish admonitions but is unable to return to legality because the law would execute him for his previous unenlightened conduct.

In the first, less systematic, version of *Political Justice* Godwin optimistically sees all error 'hastening to its own detection' (*PJ*93: 1: 31) as men are drawn towards moral truth. Only the influence of government inhibits this progress. But even the errors and passions fostered by imperfect systems of society cannot resist the evidence of man's own natural reaction to virtue:

> The man, who is enslaved by shame, superstition or deceit, will be perpetually exposed to an internal war of opinions, disapproving by an involuntary censure the conduct he has been most persuaded to adopt. No mind can be so far alienated from truth, as not in the midst of its degeneracy to have incessant returns of a better principle. No system of society can be so thoroughly pervaded with mistake, as not frequently to suggest to us sentiments of virtue, liberty and justice.
>
> (*PJ*93: 1: 29)

This passage from the section on 'Causes of Moral Improvement' might well have contributed to Wordsworth's view of nature, including the world of man, as fundamentally attuned to moral good, capable of inspiring the virtuous and awakening the conscience of the vicious. One of the reasons Wordsworth disliked the third edition might have been the omission of this section and the more systematic development of the idea that a society *can* be thoroughly pervaded with error. By 1797 Godwin viewed the 'spirit of government' as so insidious as to leave no aspect of social life free from its despotism. The evidence which could recall the mind to natural principles of virtue had then to be sought in history and in treatises like his own, which could teach man that 'real knowledge' is 'benevolent, not cruel and retaliating' (*PJ*98: 1: 461).

Godwin's stress on reason in *Political Justice* is the product of a radicalism which saw benevolist ideas as a potentially revolutionary force if the limitations proposed by Hume and Smith were counteracted. In Hutcheson's benevolism, the limit to our capacity for benevolent action is the limit of our reason, the faculty which directs benevolence to the highest ends. If we admit that our actions are motivated by a calculation of consequences and a desire for those consequences, then it follows that the greater our power to envisage those consequences, the greater is our power to originate actions which promote the desired object with least contradictory effect. If it is contended that we can have no trust in a personal estimate of consequences, then the individual is no longer capable of virtuous action, but only of following law, custom, or general rules. If we contend that the individual is capable of appreciating what is desirable, but is incapable of consistently acting in such a way as to promote that end, then we are in Godwin's view either asserting that motive plays no part in action, in which case all observed consistency in human behaviour would be fallacious and men would be uneducable as well as ungovernable, or that reason is not yet as strong or consistent as Godwin thinks it can be made. And here Godwin would agree. All actions are the result of real preferences, made on a calculation of the pleasure to arise from them, but this opinion 'may be exceedingly fugitive; it may have been preceded by aversion and followed by remorse, but it was unquestionably the opinion of the mind at the instant in which the action commenced' (*PJ*98: 1: 58). It follows that an improved calculation of the consequences, and a more deeply impressed desire for 'the good' would enable the individual to avoid such actions. The difficulties raised by such arguments take us back to the similarities in the work of Godwin and Hutcheson. Both tend to conflate the passions that impel man to benevolent actions and the power that regulates and directs them. Hutcheson tended to conflate them under the terminology of affection, Godwin under the terminology of reason and understanding. Even after he had revised *Political Justice* to acknowledge Hume's distinction more clearly, the conflation is still confusing and has led to some misunderstanding of the strongly affective nature of Godwin's 'reason'. 'Passion', he states,

> is so far from being incompatible with reason, that it is inseparable from it. Virtue, sincerity, justice and all those principles which are begotten and cherished in us by a due

exercise of the reason will never be very strenuously espoused till they are ardently loved; that is, till their value is clearly perceived and adequately understood. In this sense nothing is necessary but to show us that a thing is worthy and to be desired, in order to excite in us a passion for its attainment.

(*PJ*98: 1: 81)

The two powers of passion and reason are at work in the act of convincing the understanding of the truth of a moral proposition. Truth is 'not merely to be exhibited but adequately communicated; that is . . . distinctly apprehended by the person to whom it is addressed' (*PJ*98: 1: 87). A generally brave man, temporarily inclined to cowardice by a rainy day or toothache, would soon recollect himself if he responded adequately to 'the ideas of the benefits to arise from his valour, safety to his family and children, defeat to an unjust and formidable assailant, and freedom and felicity to be secured to his country' (*PJ*98: 1: 78). Conduct is sure to be affected by 'the point, of which I have been intimately convinced and have had a lively and profound impression', and there is 'no conduct which can be shown to be reasonable, the reasons of which may not sooner or later be made impressive, irresistible, and matter of habitual recollection' (*PJ*98: 1: 80). If truth can be 'brought home to the conviction of the individual', it obviously amounts to more than an acquiescence in the accuracy of a matter of fact, since Godwin compares it to fanatical religious faith and the heroism of figures of antiquity who endured torture and death for their ideals. 'Are all good stories of our nature false?' Godwin exclaims:

Did no man ever resist temptation? On the contrary, have not all the considerations which have power over our hopes, our fears, over our weaknesses, been, in competition with a firm and manly virtue, employed in vain? But what has been done may be done again. What has been done by individuals cannot be impossible, in a widely different state of society, to be done by the whole species.

(*PJ*98: 1: 74)

But the appeal to outstanding and exceptional examples and the reference to a widely different future state of society show how far

Godwin was from believing men presently capable of controlling their conduct by such exalted principles.

A major emphasis of *Political Justice* is the difficulty of adequately communicating the ideas of virtue in an unjust society where unjust opinions inevitably influence the educator and where realities contradict his benevolent doctrines in the eyes of his pupil. The 'perfectibility' of our reason does not assert that it is now, or indeed ever will be, *completely* capable of forecasting all consequences, or infallibly capable of withstanding the force of habit, the temptations of sensuality, or the unthinking preferences of the partial passions, but it does assert that it is capable of being improved in that direction to produce more consistent conduct in pursuit of benevolent ends.

It is only when the narrower affections come into conflict with universal benevolence that they become harmful, and Godwin does not retreat from that position. The values which promote a good family life are same as those which promote the good of the community: truthfulness, sincerity, and equality of consideration. An eloquent passage of Godwin's *Thoughts Occasioned* (1801) asserts the natural compatibility of interests in a society dedicated to progress:

> We shall be astonished to see in how many instances interests, supposed incompatible, perfectly coincide; shall find that what is good for you, is advantageous to me; that, while I educate my child judiciously for himself, I am rendering him a valuable acquisition to society; and that, by contributing to the improvement of my countrymen, I am preparing for my child a society in which it will be desirable for him to live.
>
> (Godwin 1968: 337)

In *St Leon* Godwin showed that the aristocratic and materialistic faults of his 'hero' equally unfit him for public and private happiness and usefulness. The experience of an idyllic marriage, like the experience of an enthusiastic chivalric engagement in the service of society, remains only a torturing memory of transcendent pleasure which St Leon, in the weakness of his 'reason', cannot impress upon his mind sufficiently to maintain the virtuous conduct that would ensure its continuance.

The improvement of reason is also necessary to combat the power of custom and habit in moral thinking. Godwin's quarrel with Hume here shows interesting similarities as well as differences. Hume developed Hutcheson's idea of the primacy of the passions in moral judgments, which are only discoverable by a reflex sense, not reason. You can never arrive at a moral judgment 'till you turn your reflexion into your own breast, and find a sentiment of disapprobation, which arises in you, towards this action. Here is a matter of fact; but 'tis the object of feeling, not of reason' (*Treatise*: 468-9). Hume also acknowledged that 'reflexions on the tendencies of actions have by far the greatest influence' on moral judgments (*Treatise*: 590). Therefore, since it is the reason that influences our conduct, when it discovers the 'connexion of causes and effects, so as to afford us means of exerting any passion' (*Treatise*: 459), surely reason, in analysing the tendencies and consequences of actions, should play as large a part in moral action in Hume's theory as it does in Godwin's. But Hume's scepticism will not allow him to use reason, even in this sense, with any guarantee of certainty, since causes and effects are discoverable not by reason but by experience. It is experience, and not any knowledge of the qualities of matter, that allows us to predict the direction in which a billiard ball will travel when hit, and Hume emphasizes this ignorance of the basis of cause and effect more particularly in moral reasoning: 'The most perfect philosophy of the natural kind only staves off our ignorance a little longer: as perhaps the most perfect philosophy of the moral or metaphysical kind serves only to discover larger portions of it' (*Enquiries*: 31). Godwin, after referring to this passage, is more optimistic, and, while allowing all Hume's sceptical doubts, asserts that 'it is impossible that this species of foresight should not be converted into a general foundation of inference and reasoning' (*PJ*98: 1: 369).

Hume, after seemingly divorcing reason from experience, can only found belief in causation on custom and habit. In maintaining that 'all inferences from experience . . . are the effects of custom, not of reasoning', Hume does not distinguish between good or bad customs, yet he clearly has an idea of the conflict between 'custom' and reason and experience in arriving at opinions: 'I am persuaded, that upon examination, we shall find more than one half of those opinions, that prevail among mankind, to be owing to education, and that the principles, which are then implicitly embrac'd, over-ballance those, which are owing either to abstract reasoning or experience' (*Treatise*:

117). Godwin agrees that 'perhaps no action of a man arrived at years of maturity is . . . perfectly voluntary', that is, the result of a reasoned pursuit of a desired end. We are all liable to find 'resting-places' in general lines of conduct which have been beneficial in the past. But Godwin asserts that we should be able to counteract this tyranny of habit by revising our opinions in the light of experience and 'be on all occasions prepared to give a reason for our actions' (*PJ*98: 1: 68). It could be affirmed that Godwin extended to moral thinking the more positive features of that reason based upon experience and experiment which Hume used in cognitive thinking.

In the *Inquiry* Hume modified his position considerably towards the benevolist point of view, though the ground occupied by benevolist sentiment is continually undermined by the appeal to 'utility'. The main lines of his argument are often sufficiently close to Godwin's as to suggest a direct influence, or as direct as Godwin's habitual quarrelling with his 'sources' can be. Here Hume uses arguments drawn from our responses to literature, appealing to 'any one who wears a human heart' and declaring against the 'cold sensibility or narrow selfishness of temper' which could be indifferent to images of human happiness and misery (*Enquiries*: 225-6). The 'benevolent principle of our frames' engage us on the side of social virtues, the public good, and 'the promoting of peace, harmony, and order in society' (*Enquiries*: 231). This sentiment lies behind our adherence to justice, since its utility in promoting these ends is obvious. The necessity of justice arose from scarcity and competition for goods, and he looks back to a golden age of abundance which had no need of the 'cautious, jealous virtue of justice' (*Enquiries*: 184). He even gives a modern version of the utopian, primitive paradise in a benevolist dream, supposing that men had, even in present circumstances, retained that original benevolence. Justice, he sees, would be 'suspended by such an extensive benevolence, nor would the divisions and barriers of property and obligation have ever been thought of'. Promises would be vain:

> Why should I bind another, by a deed or a promise, to do me any good office, when I know that he is already prompted, by the strongest inclination, to seek my happiness, and would, of himself, perform the desired service?
>
> (*Enquiries*: 185)

Godwin himself could wish for no more except that this natural beneficence be directed to the greatest good of the widest community. But Hume's idea of utility, or 'general usefulness', is relative to the prevailing ideas of society. While Godwin's justice is perceived as the direct outcome of natural human propensities, Hume's justice is still an 'artificial' construct, even if Hume no longer uses the term, since it sanctions the 'order, peace and harmony' of widely differing societies and stages of social evolution.

Godwin appreciated that the natural sociability of man made conservative social pressures inevitable as each man was framed insensibly to concur with his fellows by a sort of social contagion, and he used the terms of Smith, Hume, and Burke to describe the mechanism of this acquiescence. He sometimes gave way to a pessimism that saw 'all in man' as 'association and habit' (Godwin 1797: 312), and he well understood the difficulty of standing out against social hostility, as he saw former friends deserting him during the 1790s. One of the major points of discussion in *Political Justice* is the due balance between 'individuality and concert'. We are formed for society, but to live unthinkingly immersed in the ways of society is itself a dereliction of social duty. Society cannot be benefited by such conduct. The progressive rational powers are stunted by enforced co-operation in communal activities and even by marriage. Yet our means of communication and progress, language, is a vital species of co-operation, and Godwin admits his conjectures on the progress of individual freedom to be mere speculations. There is even a way in which the insensible communication of ideas by social means can be a progressive force, like the dissemination of the influence of Shakespeare and Milton. Godwin continually stressed the gradualness of progress to the young and impatient Shelley, and his insistence that new ideas were percolating through society in an unnoticeable way could have contributed to Shelley's idea of the progressive yet virtually unconscious spirit of the age which can find expression through the artist.

In espousing the principles of the French Revolution, radical sensibility politicized ideas which had previously been points of debate within the same tradition and took to extremes ideas which had been firmly restricted by prevailing practice. So it is that during the 1790s the idea of the domestic affections is so strongly charged with conservative force, and universal philanthropy considered a dangerously radical propensity, that the ability to regulate passion assumes a high profile in radical writers, often uneasily coupled with a plea for a more accommodating public morality, and that the moral and social tendency of art and imagination is challenged. The concept of the 'genius' comes under scrutiny, and the exercise of pity and compassion can be scanned for its ideological leanings. The Burkean denunciation of philosophers and rationalists had other targets: the selfish reason of the followers of Hobbes, and the 'demonstrative' reason of a Paine or Bentham that worked up a plan for society from first principles. But it was equally directed against, and more destructive of, that Godwinian reason that was the organ of benevolence, based on the same appeal to experience as that of Burke and Hume, but capable of correcting prejudice in the light of experience and guided by social goals whose attraction had been brought home to the individual imagination and feelings.

In response to conservative attacks on sensibility and its growing instability as a term, many writers turned at some point to Godwinian ideas, usually to strengthen their assertion that the passions were not naturally selfish and inordinate but controlled to benevolent ends by an educable faculty within the individual. Their stress on the education of this faculty, on the mutual dependence of reason and passion, and on a faculty of imagination which could envisage a more satisfying state of society, contributed to the imbalance of the Romantic era. Creative artists were still described by terms such as 'sensibility', 'originality', and 'genius', yet their works were most often devoted to a reconciliation of the visionary world with the world of experience, and judged by fierce standards of conformity to social norms. Utopian, impractical, and naive as their hopes had been, the proponents of radical sensibility had asserted the capacity of man to originate, from his innate propensities, a form of social life which would satisfy his emotional needs and provide a framework for genuine moral behaviour. The necessity for basing the moral and even the religious life on the authentic experience of the individual was echoed in otherwise conservative systems of thought. Evangelicalism, with its strong stress on inner experience, became a dominant force at the turn of the century. Later, Newman distinguished 'real assent' as a totally individual experience. Coleridge, whose later conservative writings retain a vestigial Godwinism, was insistent that, like poetry, morality and religion had to come from within, and could not be achieved by observing external rules. Coleridge wrote to Godwin in 1811, praising him for daring to 'reveal at full that most important of all important Truths, that Morality might be built up on it's own foundation, like a Castle built *from* the rock & *on* the rock' (*CL:* 3: 313-14). The metaphor of a rock was a questionable one for ideas which had their basis only in the individual imagination. In the 1790s, while assuring Godwin that most were in favour of the theory of progressiveness in their hearts, Coleridge admitted to Thomas Wedgwood that it required 'a sort of heroism in believing the progressiveness of all nature, during the present melancholy state of Humanity' (*CL:* 1: 558).

The prospect of wandering in an ideal world was an ever-present possibility to Mary Wollstonecraft, whose radical sensibility owed as much to Rousseau as to the Rational Dissenters. In fact the idealization of the object of passion above the possibilities of this imperfect world is for her an ennobling thing, testifying to the true home of the soul in the hereafter, and essential for personal development and education. If we had no illusions about the objects of our ambitions, fostered by the imagination and the passions, we should remain passive vegetables. On the face of it, this is a rather pessimistic philosophy and ill-adapted to a reforming creed. The cold, true, objective view of the world is of a fundamentally unsatisfying place. Superiority of mind 'leads to the creation of ideal beauty, when life, surveyed with a penetrating eye, appears a tragi-comedy, in which little can be seen to satisfy the heart without the help of fancy' (Wollstonecraft 1975: 309). Now the creation of an ideal realm and consequently being unable to do justice to the world of reality is a fault of which she accuses Rousseau and Burke, and a similar criticism is made of those females not of a superior mind whose imaginations dwell in the dream-world of sentimental novels. The factor which legitimizes and controls the workings of passion and infuses a reformist capability is the reason. Her theory is not set out very clearly in the works which are most readily available, and some rather extensive quotation from the *Vindication of the Rights of Men* will yield more clarity. Here her commitment to passion is most strongly expressed and the dependent but essential role of the reason is expounded. 'Sacred be the feelings of the heart!' she proclaims:

> concentred in a glowing flame, they become the sun of life; and without his invigorating impregnation, reason would probably lie in helpless inactivity, and never bring forth her only legitimate offspring – virtue. But to prove that virtue is really an acquisition of the individual, and not the blind impulse of unerring instinct, the bastard vice has often been begotten by the same father.
> (Wollstonecraft 1790: 70)

Further distinguishing between the bastard offspring of feeling and instinct and the legitimate progeny of feeling and reason, she warns us to beware 'of confounding mechanical instinctive sensations with emotions that reason deepens, and justly terms the feelings of *humanity*' (1790: 137). When reason deepens an emotion it seems to become a laudable passion: 'Why is passion or heroism the child of reflection, the consequence of dwelling with intent contemplation on one object?' she asks rhetorically. To introduce a phrase from the *Short Residence*, 'We reason deeply, when we forcibly feel' (Wollstonecraft 1989: 6: 325). But the imagination works as well: 'My passions pursue objects that the imagination enlarges, till they become only a sublime idea that shrinks from the enquiry of sense, and mocks the experimental philosophers who would confine this spiritual phlogiston in their material crucibles' (Wollstonecraft 1790: 76–7). The trouble with Burke and Rousseau is that the working of the imagination has dominated the work of the reason: to both she applies the comment that their reflection inflames the imagination instead of enlightening the understanding (1790: 6; 1976: 189). This is an unusual linking of Burke with Rousseau, and the link is not solely produced by Wollstonecraft's feminist objections to their attitudes to women. Godwin had linked them in their defects of sensibility in his *Letters of Mucius* in 1785.

The attack on sensibility in the *Vindication of the Rights of Men* is managed better than in the later *Vindication of the Rights of Woman*, since she defines sensibility as an instinct 'supposed to reside in the soul, that instantaneously discovers truth without the tedious labour of ratiocination' (Wollstonecraft 1790: 68).

This is closer to the most current definitions than Johnson's and shows its links with the Shaftesbury/Hutcheson line of Moral Sense. She herself was not averse to claiming an intuitive faculty of judgment, especially in the aesthetic sphere, but here she is quarrelling with Burke's idea that instinctual feelings are an ultimate court of appeal and have a different authority from that of reason. The guides of Burke's sensibility, she argues, are not instincts but habits, and habits 'with which the reason of others shackled them . . . Affection for parents, reverence for superiors or antiquity, notions of honour, or that worldly self-interest that shrewdly shows them that honesty is the best policy: all proceed from the reason for which they serve as substitutes; – but it is reason at second-hand' (1790: 71-2). Among these so-called instincts she includes the family affections: such affections 'may be included in the sordid calculations of blind self-love' (1790: 44). Yet she refers to 'natural' affections with respect when criticizing primogeniture: 'it is the spurious offspring of overweening pride – and not that first source of civilization, natural parental affection, that makes no difference between child and child, but what reason justifies by pointing out superior merit' (1790: 46). Here we have a typical example of the struggle between conservative and liberal/radical interpretations of the same terms. Both Burke and Wollstonecraft appeal to natural family feelings, but what is natural is defined within a political context. What makes Wollstonecraft radical in the same way as Godwin is her attack on the distinctions among men flowing from the inequalities of property, and her antagonism to the gothic constitution which perpetuates such inequality. It has, as Smith and Burke demonstrate, affected habits of sympathy, whereby the rich and powerful are thought more worthy of attention. Burke's heart opens for a distressed queen, whereas he accepts with equanimity the impressment of an ordinary mortal. 'Only metaphysical sophists and cold mathematicians', she comments, 'can discern this unsubstantial form' (1790: 26). It is the same point which Paine makes in his comment about pitying the plumage and forgetting the dying bird, but it raised questions about the moral status of the imagination which exercised radicals into the next century.

Godwin and Wollstonecraft were both involved in issues which were debated within the movement of sensibility, and frequently use its terms, though redefined in more liberal or radical ways. Wollstonecraft's *Vindication of the Rights of Woman* is a sustained attempt to redefine the terms of conservative sensibility, like delicacy, chastity, and modesty, in ways which suggest equality, self-respect, and independence, rather than following the code of feminine propriety, and in ways which are applicable to men as well. Real modesty, in her definition, can be attributed to the heroine of *La Nouvelle Héloïse*. It can also be applied to Christ, Milton, and Washington! Sometimes her habit of redefining all the terms of feeling by asserting that the true and valuable version of the term comes from reason can be unconvincing: true voluptuousness too apparently comes from reason. Sometimes the battle for the terms of sensibility can lead to downright confusion. In one passage from *The Wrongs of Woman* the heroine comments on her lack of response to the overtures of other quite prepossessing men when she was totally alienated from her husband:

> My reserve was then the consequence of delicacy. Freedom of conduct has emancipated many women's minds; but my conduct has most rigidly been governed by my principles, till the improvement of my understanding has enabled me to discern the fallacy of prejudices at war with nature and reason.
>
> (Wollstonecraft 1976: 156)

'Delicacy' here is the conservative principle of female delicacy, bound up with propriety and decorum, one of the principles which reason has disabused her of. When later she is ready to consummate her relationship with Darnford and is pressured to return to her husband, Darnford comments: 'In her case, to talk of duty, was a farce, excepting what was due to herself. Delicacy, as well as reason, forbade her ever to think of returning to her husband' (1976: 187). This is a delightfully iconoclastic use of the term. To conservative sensibility, the spectacle of a strayed woman returning penitently to her husband would be eminently proper and show evidence of delicacy. Yet again we have to register the almost sacramental terms in which Wollstonecraft describes Maria's sexual union with Darnford: 'As her husband she now received him' (1976: 188). That delicacy which prescribes exclusive loyalty to a 'husband' is seen as the natural concomitant of a union based on feeling. Wollstonecraft looks forward to a society where marriage might be more sacred, instead of wishing to abolish it, as Godwin did. She is enmeshed in disputes within the terms of sensibility, rather than wishing to break entirely with traditional social forms.

4
SENSIBILITY IN REACTION

Godwin and Mary Wollstonecraft were not the only radicals at the beginning of the 1790s using the language of universal benevolence, but few opposed it so fearlessly to the partial affections. Price had examined patriotism critically but saw no antagonism between a love of one's country and a desire to improve its institutions by the light of the best available models. Roe cites many examples of the doctrine amongst Coleridge's Cambridge fraternity where it was developed in a specifically Christian context. Coleridge's own formulations of the idea may, as Roe suggests, owe as much to these and to Hartleyan ideas as to Godwin (Roe 1988: 115-17). Thelwall's adoption of Godwinnian texts for his political lectures seems to have provoked Coleridge's attack on Godwin in his Bristol lectures, where Godwin's criticism of the domestic affections is the starting-point for a wider assault on the moral tendency of his philosophy. Nevertheless, Coleridge's ideas on property and the stunting effect of inequality on the poorer classes show a Godwinian influence which lasted into his later years and *On the Constitution of Church and State*, which replaces notions of individual property with the categories 'propriety' and 'nationalty'. Even in the late 1790s, when Coleridge was distancing himself from organized radicalism, Thelwall testified to the violence of his views on property. Coleridge's anger at the publication of Lloyd's *Edmund Oliver* in 1798 was probably provoked as much by its revelation of how much his mind was still occupied with the abolition of property as by its lurid reworkings of his youthful escapades. A poem of 1799 congratulates Georgiana, Countess of Devonshire, a rather unlikely heroine for a strict moralist, on her sensitivity to the plight of the poor, so unexpected in one born to the enjoyment of riches. A more characteristic product of aristocratic inspiration would have been tales of 'rustic happiness', anodyne celebrations of contented poverty which Coleridge attacks:

> Pernicious tales! insidious strains!
>   That steel the rich man's breast
>   And mock the lot unblest,
> The sordid vices and the abject pains,
> Which evermore must be
> The doom of ignorance and penury!
>
> (Coleridge 1974: 243)

The Godwinian influence in these lines is qualified by the point which Coleridge often made against him, that he saw a conflict between the domestic affections and the wider love of society. For Coleridge, in his Hartleyan period, love of mankind developed harmoniously from the primary familial affections. Georgiana had nicely expressed this idea in her 'The Passage of the Mountain of St Gothard', which describes how Tell had 'first preserv'd his child' and then killed the tyrant. Typically Coleridge attributes her sensitivity to the sublimity of William Tell's heroism to the development of the domestic affections.

Of those who recanted their radical opinions under the pressure of conservative reaction, it is significant how many chose to highlight the valuation of domestic or parental affections to mark their return to the fold, just as the works immediately directed at Godwin, such as those by Proby and Green, concentrated their fire on Godwin's 'stoicism' or 'barbarity' on this point. Mackintosh in 1791 had reproached those whose sensibility was of the squeamish variety which shrank from revolutionary violence as from the surgeon's knife. In 1798 he proclaimed that the welfare of society rested on the sanctity of family affections, and that anyone who was willing to suspend their priority for universal interests was dead to public and private virtue. Southey, the former pantisocrat who had given up the pursuit of universal benevolence in the persuasion that virtue was only to be found in domestic life, was only one of those who provoked Coleridge's suggestion that Wordsworth write a poem admonishing such a dereliction of social responsibility, a task typically wished on another by the deeply divided Coleridge. The preoccupations of the early 1790s with universal issues was superseded by a discourse of virtue which limited itself to the domestic setting as a model for patriotic unity, and set itself against the libertarian, Enlightenment values of the Revolution. It renewed its connections with traditional religious conservatism of the Johnsonian variety yet maintained an urgency of social criticism. The prominent Evangelical voice proposed individual and family reform and thrived on the separation of the enlightened few and an unregenerate 'society'. In a parallel development the ideals of education, once envisaged as the means of elevating the mass of society to self-regulated, progressive, communal virtue, were restricted to the promotion of rational pursuits which would ensure usefulness and happiness in a domestic paternalistic regime which had to be insulated from 'society'.

Parr's *Spital Sermon* of 1800 (published 1801) is a particularly interesting document in this process. Parr was a Whig and made no secret of his allegiance to the Constitution, but Godwin had been a welcome visitor in 1797 and an amicable corresondent, and it was his attack which stung Godwin into writing his *Thoughts Occasioned* (1801), both a defence and a valedictory survey of the fate of radical ideas in the revolutionary decade. It rankled because Parr had adapted his sermon to the prejudices of his audience and had cloaked a Godwinite exhortation to universal benevolence in a framework of anti-Godwinite rhetoric. Parr's sermon was preached to the commissioners of the Christ Church charity foundation and his text seemed to restrict charity to 'those of the household faith'. In a fairly direct attack on Godwin, he rhetorically asks 'what would become of society, which parental affection, which friendship, which gratitude, which compassion, which patriotism do now uphold?' (Parr 1801: 10). He links attacks on these feelings with criticisms of charity institutions from a suitably execrable French source, Turgot, though the charges of offering a prize for idleness and throwing the burden of the unemployed on to the industrious could have been ascribed to Smith or Kames. Yet the purpose of his sermon is actually to widen the scope of benevolence in extending charity to the former criminal. Here he is at one with Godwin in an optimistic faith in personal reformation and even more in unison in attacking the inequalities of society which drive even good men to crime: we '*virtually*, I do not say intentionally, compel to the crime, and then punish the criminal'

(Parr 1801: 23). Godwin noted the duplicity whereby the text of the sermon abounds in fervent praise of the domestic affections, while the criterion of virtue which should govern the exercise of the affections and direct them to more universal objects is relegated to the footnotes. Here Parr even pays a warm tribute to Hutcheson as an author too much neglected. The sermon shows a literal submergence of the universalist ideas of liberal benevolence beneath the discourse of conservative sensibility.

It was not just universal benevolence or 'philanthropy' that was branded with radicalism but all the aspects of sensibility which demonstrated a confidence in human nature and the capacity of individuals for moral and beneficent action independent of traditional authority. Shaftesbury and Hutcheson had envisaged universal benevolence as a discipline for the passions, a naturally evolving consciousness that the satisfaction of an immediate or partial passion may be followed by disappointment of that fundamental human impulse towards a kinship with the wider family of humanity and the universe it inhabits. This sense of wider allegiance was undermined as a self-justifying creation of the mind, capable of being the apology of Terror. Theories of progress temporalized the idea of the plenum and virtually destroyed its practical value, since the good of the whole, the harmony which it asserted as the divine plan, was now located in the future as a benign result of the discords evident in contemporary society. Such temporalization was not new. Pope's *Moral Essays* on the 'Use of Riches' had envisaged the succession of miser and profligate as a 'balance' affecting the dependants of an estate, and Adam Smith's 'hidden hand' was trusted to equalize the balance of trade, though each process produced hardship in their negative phases to dependants and operatives. What was new in the revolutionary temporalization of the plenum theory was that the providential outcome was problematic, the triumph of a 'good' that could only dimly be seen in contemporary society, grasped only by theory and selective evidence. The French had adopted theories of benevolence and public virtue as progressive and egalitarian characteristics, but the triumph of these required state action in the name of the people or general will, in exterminating those considered obstructive and regimenting individuals in the service of the State which embodied their claim to individual rights. This regimentation was necessary in the face of international hostility. The fact that so many were willing to dedicate themselves to the cause of their country in the armies that won Valmy left tears in Wordsworth's eyes which survived even to the 1850 *Prelude.*

In Britain the response is well named 'reaction'. Burke had sought to define the goals of benevolence in terms of established family values and historical precedent. Virtue was seen as the product of social conditioning, and individualism (except in the economic field) was discouraged. The noble savage and the original genius were distrusted as dangerously unconditioned and unreliable. Even Burns, who had provided comforting pictures of the cotters' domestic happiness and celebrated a stalwart peasantry ready to perish in faint huzzas for royal George, could make disparaging remarks about belted earls and be suspected of redirecting confiscated cannons to the French and of joining in the singing of the *ça ira.*

Burke's attack on the atheistic literary cabal responsible for popularizing the ideas of revolution led to a suspicion of literature, especially in the school-room. The spate of anti-Jacobin works in which characters were corrupted by their reading of Godwin or Mary Wollstonecraft pointed to dangers which far exceeded the eccentricities satirized in the 'Quixote' format. The danger was greater because of the acknowledged power of the writing. Robert Bissett, one of the most virulent anti-Jacobins, did not hesitate to ascribe genius to both these vilified writers. Coleridge's distinction between the commanding genius and the absolute genius (Coleridge 1983: 1: 31-2) was symptomatic of the asssociation of 'genius' with the threatening force of individual energetic thought and action subverting the traditional order of society. Here the history of ideas has to acknowledge the contamination of its serene intellectual continuities by raw historical fact, the fêted heroes of the Revolution, and the world-historical individual. Within a decade the sentimental idea of the genius as a child of nature bearing new insights into the harmony of the natural world and the brotherhood of man was converted into the bugbear of the nursery. The determination with which British war heroes were socialized and disinfected of any taint of Napoleonic glamour can be seen in Wordsworth's picture of the Happy Warrior, a model family man and conscientious self-abnegating servant of society, a picture supposedly inspired by Nelson! Coleridge's distinction seeks to rescue the imaginative genius at the expense of the active genius, and it is a strategy shared with Wordsworth. The redirection of the urge to remodel society into the effort to revolutionize ways of thought, the apocalypse of political society replaced by the apocalypse of the imagination, is the theme of Abrams's *Natural Supernaturalism*. One of the disappointments of Nicholas Roe's investigations into the radical years of Wordsworth and Coleridge is his failure to take this idea much further and, in showing their probable affiliations with extreme radical groups, he presents an even more embarrassing apostasy. Much in the way of extenuation can be advanced in emphasizing the power of conservative reaction, the employment of a system of spies, prosecutions of publishers and booksellers, and the activation of tests of loyalty as the condition of Church, State, and university employment. Sheer force, however, can do little unless supported by public opinion – witness the failure of the 1794 Treason Trials – but in time of war the government was able to marshal public opinion behind its measures and by the end of the century Jacobinism was dead. In the swiftly changing intellectual climate of the 1790s radical resistance had to combat the new forces that were emerging as collaborators with reaction, such as Evangelicalism, and it is this resistance that can be traced in the work of Wordsworth and Coleridge.

Evangelicalism adopted many of the reformist aims of moral and humanitarian sensibility, yet fostered a dependence on constituted authority. Milton had explained that the dominance of man over man was a product of the Fall, and Paine and Price agreed that government was created by our vices. Government was built on the ruins of the bowers of Paradise and justified by the ineradicable depravity of man. For Evangelicals, it provided the conditions for repentance and self-reconstitution in order to merit eternal life. Despite this fundamental anti-humanism, the Evangelical viewpoint coincided in some respects with ideals of sensibility. Evangelicals were certainly not hostile to the feelings: Wilberforce asserts that 'it is the religion of the Affections which God particularly requires' (Wilberforce 1805: 89). In a new twist of the usual criticism of sensibility, Wilberforce accepts that the 'ideal presence' of fictitious distress provokes more sympathy than a dry account of a real battle. The necessity for such imaginative 'contact' with a situation is, he thinks, less discreditable to humanity than Adam Smith's explanations of man's natural insensitivity to public misfortune (1805: 111).

Christianity, which proposes 'not to extinguish our natural desires, but to bring them under just control, and direct them to their true objects' (1805: 225), would seek to utilize the imagination by presenting religion, and especially the Redeemer, with all the adjuncts of affecting fiction in its particularity and 'pathetic contemplation'. Religion is similarly no foe to the pursuits of taste, learning, and science, but they must know their 'just *subordination*' to religious truth (1805: 184). Wilberforce's Christian benevolence is the successor to Godwinian universal benevolence in remonstrating against an established 'system of *decent selfishness*' and 'sober settled plan of domestic dissipation' (1805: 176-7). His attacks on the code of honour and on a sensibility which is barren of practical benevolence are also continuous with those of radical sensibility. But his benevolence has no wish to change the organization of society or to relieve its God-appointed inequalities and hardships, nor can merely human feelings and human benevolence avail to conquer the radical depravity of the fallen creature. If he seems liberal in his acceptance of all the powers of natural man and his wish to see them acting in harmony, this harmony is imposed by an imperative subordination to religious ends: it is Christianity's 'peculiar glory, and her main office, to bring all the faculties of our nature into their just subordination and dependence; that so the whole man, complete in all his functions, may be restored to the true ends of his being, and be devoted, entire and harmonious, to the service and glory of God' (1805: 88-9). Other writers influenced by Evangelicalism show the less liberal implications of the creed.

Hannah More would devastate libraries, cleansing them of that 'unsuspected mass of mischief, which, by assuming the plausible names of Science, of Philosophy, of Arts, of Belles Lettres, is gradually administering death' to their readers (More 1801: 7: 33). The arts might refine a barbarous age but in a modern civilization they 'enervate and deprave' (1801: 7: 91) by exciting the imagination and stimulating the passions. She would not lure children into learning by using the pleasures of imagination, since education should be an initiation to 'that state of toil and labour to which we are born and to which sin has made us liable' (1801: 7: 202). The imagination must be restrained by a stress on facts. The facts of history will give a 'clearer insight into the corruption of human nature' and a 'truly Christian commentator' will trace 'the *plan* of Providence in the direction of events, and in the use of unworthy instruments' (1801: 7: 227). While More attacks sensibility and imagination in secular education she encourages its use in religious instruction. The 'ardent and ever-active power, the imagination ... is a lion, which though worldly prudence indeed may *chain,* so as to prevent outward mischief, yet the malignity remains within: but when sanctified by Christianity, it is a lion *tamed*' (1801: 7: 299). More does not want to lose the qualities of sensibility which she had hymned in her poem of 1785. She still claims for feminine sensibility 'that delicacy and quickness of perception, and that nice discernment between the beautiful and the defective which comes under the denomination of taste' and an 'intuitive penetration into character' (1801: 8: 29-30). True sensibility for her is still linked with active universal concern 'flowing out in active charity, and affording assistance, protection, or consolation to every kind of distress within its reach' (1801: 8: 138). Yet this is charity, not benevolence, a Christian charity working with the plan of Providence which established the inequalities of society and gave each class appropriate virtuous feelings to exercise:

> the generosity, kindness, and forbearance of the superior; and the patience, resignation, and gratitude of the inferior: and thus, while we were vindicating the *ways* of Providence, we should be accomplishing his *plan,* by bringing into action those virtues of both classes, which would have had little exercise had there been no inequality in station and fortune.
>
> (1801: 7: 141)

Pity could not be if God did not make somebody poor!

In More's religiously chastened sensibility there are still echoes of the more liberal variety. Even in corrupt humanity the flame of disinterested generosity, enthusiasm, and even sentimental love still burns to warm and illuminate the virtuous home and neighbourhood, when properly trimmed. On the other hand the Edgeworths' *Practical Education* (M. and R. L. Edgeworth 1801) makes no such assumptions about humanity's capacity for benevolence. Though it is the product of a secular rationalism, it shares many of the characteristics of Evangelicalism, just as Maria Edgeworth's *Belinda* (1801) at many points echoes More's 1799 *Strictures on the Modern System of Female Education* (More

1801). Proposing to erect a system which will produce happiness in the present state of society, their ideas of happiness centre on home life and the satisfactions of learning. More than any other educational system of the century, except perhaps Robert Owen's, they regard the child as a tabula rasa, with no innate principles which can be appealed to as a ground of morality. Children's characters are to be formed, and the method of forming them is association. The one assumption carried over from eighteenth-century sentimental doctrines is the human need for sympathy and affection, which can be made the motive power of teaching. Let the child associate pleasure with obedience, and affection with achievement. But the further ramifications of Adam Smith's theory of sympathy as the root of all moral and social virtues are dismissed in terms which seem to derive from political radicalism. Smith's man of feeling

> would be a nuisance to the world; his pity would stop the hand, and overturn the balance of justice . . . his gratitude would exalt his benefactor at the expense of the whole human race; his sympathy with the rich, the prosperous, the great, and the fortunate, would be so sudden, and so violent, as to leave him no time for reflection upon the consequences of tyranny, or the miseries occasioned by monopoly.
> (M. and R. L. Edgeworth 1801: 2: 3)

The sympathy of other schemes of sensibility is also rejected as a dependable moral principle. The 'quickness of sympathy with present objects of distress' is a virtue 'frequently found in persons of abandoned character' (1801: 2: 4), a contention which is clinched by citing Rousseau and Sterne, and a desire for sympathy is seen as the motive of great crimes as well as virtuous actions.

The Edgeworths present the task of the educator as one of transmitting to the child the 'treasure of accumulated facts' which must be 'crammed speedily into his pupil's memory' (1801: 1: 178). In this utilitarian process poetry is useless, since the poet does not deal in knowledge 'detailed or clearly explained' but in appeals to the imagination and passions: 'in proportion as his language is sublime or pathetic, witty or satirical, it must be unfit for children' (1801: 2: 167). The Edgeworths are clearly aware of the eighteenth-century connection between literature and the noble and generous passions, but such passions should not be cultivated in those whom they would educate for a practicable happiness in a world which gives scant encouragement to enthusiastic idealism. The qualities they would cultivate are diligence, patience, prudence, and economy, and they use the phrase 'men of genius' ironically to signify those who trust to intuitive and innate propensities rather than to steady perseverance. To their model pupil, impelled solely by the prospect of personal pleasure and the praise and affection of his parents/educators, the practice of benevolence is alien. It may be true that 'the most benevolent and generous persons act from the hope of receiving pleasure, and their enjoyment is more exquisite than that of the most refined selfishness' (1801: 1: 407), but it is essential to our ideas of generosity that no such reasoning motivates the generous action:

> [W]e know that the feelings of generosity are associated with a number of enthusiastic ideas; we can sympathise with the virtuous insanity of the man who forgets himself whilst he thinks of others; we do not so readily sympathise with the cold strength of mind of the person who, deliberately preferring *the greatest possible share of happiness*, is benevolent by rule and measure.
>
> (1801: 1: 408)

Yet the only motive their system offers is to encourage their pupil to 'add this item of pleasure to the credit side of his account' (1801: 1: 409). It is powerless to raise the enthusiastic feelings of true benevolence. The nearest their pupil can come to benevolent actions motivated by feeling is to associate generous actions with the praise and affection of its educators. A comparable impasse is reached when considering the inspirational value of literature. After referring to Burke, and the propensity of the imagination to be drawn to elevated rather than to mean objects, one can appreciate a reluctance to cultivate 'that temporary suspension of the reasoning faculties, which is often essential to our taste for the sublime' (1801: 3: 140), but while they are concerned to mitigate the extravagant enthusiasm raised by Burkean oratory, they also cut themselves off from the enthusiastic imaginative inspiration which is the essence of genius and heroism. The enthusiasm of the man of genius 'borders upon insanity', and heroes 'endure all the real miseries of life, and brave the terrors of death, under the invigorating influence of an extravagant imagination. Cure them of their enthusiasm, and they are no longer heroes' (1801: 3: 163–5). The Edgeworths hope that by a 'due mixture and alternation of eloquence and reasoning, we may cultivate a taste for the moral sublime, and yet preserve the character from any tincture of extravagant enthusiasm' (1801: 3: 144).

The 'moral sublime' is a phrase from Blair, whose lectures are recommended when the pupil is ready for them; but other recommendations show a certain inconsistency. They would cross Hutcheson off a book-list but include Hume and Smith, even though Smith's theory has been roundly condemned. They would recommend Plutarch's *Lives*, since it had influenced many noble characters such as Rousseau, Gibbon, and Mme Roland, yet they acknowledge its influence to be dangerous. It kindled a republican 'enthusiasm' in Mme Roland which gave her a 'partial view of affairs'. They imply that her famous last words 'Oh Liberty, how many crimes are committed in thy name' were a recantation of her republican views (M. and R. L. Edgeworth 1801: 3: 182–3). An able preceptor would have corrected these enthusiastic feelings in her youth. In the Edgeworths' system this preceptor is always at the pupil's shoulder, interpreting the facts of history, making sure that no inflammatory reading matter like *Robinson Crusoe* enters the nursery, and flourishing the scissors and paste with which to excise and obscure the noxious parts of books. Theirs is emphatically a fugitive and cloistered virtue, secured by eternal vigilance from knowledge of vice and from the interference of strangers and relatives. The 'unbroken course of experience, which is necessary for the success of a regular course of education' (1801: 1: 210) outlaws any gifts, praise, or sympathy other than the carefully economized affection of the parent/educator. The Edgeworths' scheme has sometimes been considered to be in the tradition of Rousseau, but there is a great difference in the role of the preceptor. Rousseau's much criticized charades by which 'nature' and 'circumstance' seem to teach the pupil the natural result of his actions had as their end a conformation of educational experience to experience in the world, even if the circumstances were pre-arranged. The Edgeworths, in a fine show of honesty, deconstruct Rousseau's practice into a mechanism of enforcing obedience to the supervisor, and determine to acknowledge to the pupil that what is required is obedience to their will, from which no appeal to 'nature' or universal practice is valid. Their own mechanism for enforcing obedience, sympathy and affection, places a great strain on family feelings and isolates the nuclear family as a forcing ground for intellect and virtue. While they maintain that their system is directed to happiness in the present world, their aim is not happiness as defined by 'society'; but equally their 'happiness' is not connected with wider social goals. In their peroration they affirm that they 'have endeavoured to substitute the words *domestic happiness* instead of the present term, "success in the world – fortunate establishments" etc.' (1801: 3: 311).

While the work was attacked for neglecting religion, its dynamic was aligned with that of Evangelicalism in opposing aristocratic dissipation and 'honour', and in fostering domestic virtues. Both systems cultivate a particular kind of intellectual discipline, either the pursuit of personal salvation by the study of religious truth or the amassing of useful knowledge. Maria Edgeworth's *Belinda* and More's *Coelebs in Search of a Wife* are very similar in their representation of a 'benevolent community' centred on the nuclear family, featuring children and education as central themes. Parents exert an inquisitorial dominance, seconded in More's case by the local clergyman. The influence of More's *Strictures* on *Belinda* is evident in many verbal parallels as well as in the general theme. The intellectually gifted and witty Lady Delacour, the victim of a fashionable marriage in which she has been not mated but joined, rebels against the dominance of her dull and usually drunken husband. She takes up with a virago, one of the new breed of heroines castigated by More, who seeks to rival males in their freedom, and is appropriately called Freke. This hubris is punished by the frailty of female anatomy. In discharging a pistol, Lady Delacour damages her breast. This provokes a progressive decline near to death, during which Belinda has the opportunity to reconcile her with the limitations of her sex and with her husband, who drinks a little less when supported by true wifely attentions. The emphasis on female anatomical limitations as conclusive evidence of inferior status seems to echo the cruel anti-Jacobin triumphs over Mary Wollstonecraft's death in childbirth. The taming of wit and ridicule is a further attack on a doctrine which both Edgeworth and More recognize as derived from Shaftesbury.

The prominence of this debate can be judged by the tensions of *Pride and Prejudice*. Even when admonished by the female incapacity to take any initiative in deciding her marital fate, and convinced of the irresponsibility of her father's unfeeling wit, Elizabeth Bennet still cannot be trusted not to laugh at Darcy's complacent pomposity. The constriction of Edgeworth's view of education and knowledge is apparent in comparison to More's. Whereas More's community is actively proselytizing a religious and moral doctrine which purveys generally prudent advice to the estate's dependants, the serious intellectual concerns of Edgeworth's moral family are ideologically neutral and involve such riveting topics as the communication of fish underwater.

Both of these developments spelled the death of sensibility in either its extreme radical or its conservative forms, except in so far as the particular formulations of feminine conservative sensibility fitted the aspirations of those women who, inured to their inferiority, were sustained by the hope that they were contributing to the moralizing of the infant who would later do battle on the fields of commerce, and were establishing in the home the humanity and morality that were sadly lacking in public, male-dominated life.

It was to this area of apparently neutral subjects, like education, literature, and the 'lesser morality' of domestic life, that both Godwin and Wordsworth turned during the 1790s in seeking a discourse which would not immediately arouse political prejudice yet bear strongly on ideological conflicts.

Godwin now tried to create the persona of the Enquirer, the man exploring the different ways in which a social practice could be viewed, appealing to those whose minds were open to various perspectives. He was willing to represent his conclusions as provisional and pragmatic rather than doctrinaire and adversarial, 'not as *dicta*, but as the materials of thinking'. Yet he could still be seen as continuing the programme of *Political Justice*. He had there argued that the true means of reform were publication and discussion, and *The Enquirer* was the result of discussions, for the most part flowing from points in the earlier book. We can even speculate with varying degrees of likelihood on the participants in these discussions. Wordsworth, Thomas Wedgwood, Mary Wollstonecraft, and Mary Hays are likely opponents in specific essays, and the reader is envisaged as a third party to these discussions, liable to respond to either participant.

Whereas *Political Justice* had often presented opposing views within inverted commas as if holding them up to ridicule, *The Enquirer* attempts to give even prejudice fair play in seeking a position above polarized dogmatism. The emphasis is not on presenting logically irrefutable argument, but on using feeling to prompt thought, the literature recommended is imaginative and poetic, and the important principle of sensibility, of putting oneself in the position of others, is invoked not only as a principle of morality but to urge an understanding of opposing viewpoints, even prejudices. One of the lessons which Godwin learned from the triumph of conservatism was the force of resistance to new ideas, a resistance born of education and the social sympathy which unifies public opinion. Such pertinacity in false ideas is, he recognizes, 'closely interwoven with the nature of man; and, instead of conceiving . . . that the persons in whom it betrays itself fall below the standard of humanity, we ought, on the contrary, to regard those who conquer it as having lifted themselves above the level of almost the whole mass of their species' (Godwin 1797: 308).

The introduction of some of these ideas from the complex of sensibility seems to put rather a damper on hopes of reform. If '[n]ot only the passions of men, but their very judgments, are to a great degree the creatures of sympathy' (Godwin 1797: 58), and such is the force of this 'magnetism of sentiment' that '[i]t is scarcely possible for a man to adhere to an opinion, or a body of opinions, which all other men agree to condemn', then what chance is there of rising above social prejudices? Yet that is what Godwin proposes as the purpose of his educational programme: the production of genius, defined as the capacity to confront the insensible growth of tyranny, and to 'analyse the machine of human society, to demonstrate how the parts are connected together, to explain the immense chain of events and consequences, to point out the defects and the remedy' (1797: 10). Such a genius would be 'one of the long-looked-for saviours of the human race' (1797: 11). The situation is made more complicated by Godwin's contention that the social sympathies motivate all activity of mind and are the root of all morality. What Godwin calls 'those expansive affections, that open the human soul, and cause one man to identify himself with the pleasure and pain of his fellows' are the springs of an active benevolence and efforts to reform society.

In *Political Justice* Godwin had obscured this social dimension of his philosophy by his overemphasis on the individual reason, the means of reform, though one can find many passages that do stress that individuality is only valuable as a means to public benefit. *The Enquirer* redresses this balance perhaps too fully, since society seems both to provide the impulse towards reform and to exert its magnetic force of sentiment against individuality and change. The problem again is the due medium between individuality and concert. The influence of Rousseau encouraged a beleaguered or élitist individual sensibility which considered society corrupt and artificial. Godwin resisted this polarization. No society, he thought, could be so corrupt as not to exhibit some aspects of virtue and justice. His idea of progress was to some extent derived from Scottish social historians such as Ferguson, Kames, and Millar. He quotes Logan, whose *Elements of the Philosophy of History* (1781) gives a succinct account of their main ideas. Godwin did not, however, agree with their tendency to see individuals as borne along by the current of social and historical forces. Godwin believed that historical progress was subject to flux and reflux, as institutions which had been valuable in one stage of human progress remain in situations of greater potential as positive inhibitors of progress and perverters of progressive human values. *The Enquirer* asserts that competitive materialism and the desire for extensive dominion are two of the major survivals of barbarism which threaten the progress of society towards the further realization of human potential. The individual has a vital role in investigating these inhibitions and perversions and in moving public opinion. The Rousseauistic appeals to individual natural feeling are balanced by an effort to translate the responses of individual sensibility into social practice. Gradualism is essential to this model of the dynamic interaction of the individual and society. Society, like the individual, resists abrupt change, yet is continually changing as ideas permeate practice. The force of public sentiment is actually a strong force for change. The ideas of great artists and thinkers gradually filter into every rank of society so that even the peasant shares in the heritage of Shakespeare and Milton. Conversely, every thinker and artist is permeated by the ideas and attitudes of his age. This progressive notion of the spirit of the age re-surfaces, like many of Godwin's ideas, in Shelley's *Defence of Poetry*, where Shelley affirms that even those artists who seem to oppose progress are in fact imbued with its spirit. Shelley is even willing to deconstruct himself into a part of speech as long as he can be the vehicle of this spirit.

Shelley also echoes Godwin's praise of imaginative writers, yet Godwin, while praising their inspirational qualities, their ability to move the sympathetic imagination and to expand the faculties, is also anxious to demystify the notion of genius. Though he gives a passably organic description of the construction of a work of the imagination, Godwin refuses to see genius as of comparable organic growth. Genius for him is the product of natural and common powers of observation, investigation, and sympathetic imagination, which, exceptionally, have met with the chance of cultivation. He uses the terms genius and talent interchangeably and laments that society stifles it in the majority, especially in the poor. In these discussions, which also have reference to the educational plan of Tom Wedgwood, involving Wordsworth and Coleridge, Godwin shows the same attitude to genius as Wordsworth when the 'Preface' insinuates that organic sensibility is not as unusual as is thought. Godwin combats the emerging quietistic idea of genius as a mysterious inner quality – a 'supererogatory and prodigious gift of heaven' (Godwin 1797: 360) – which is most evident in thought and literature rather than in action, a sphere in which its influence might be feared, like the active genius of Robespierre and other Revolutionary energumens. He contradicts arguments which present talent as leading to 'bold, bad deeds' (1797: 7) and champions the man of genius whose irregularities are seized upon by detractors, instancing Fox as one of these.

The concept of genius was another site of ideological tension, espoused by radicals and attacked by conservatives. The terrain of this debate of the 1790s is, however, obscured by the development of the term. The false opposition between lawless genius and rule-bound art which Young's famous essay propagated was attacked first by associationist thinkers in Britain. They stressed the connection between feeling and thinking, and the habits of association which enabled the 'genius' to perceive analogies and discriminations with an apparently intuitive immediacy.[1] When such habits had been fostered by the powerful impression of (or pleasure associated with) important human values, then the genius was one for whom, like Wordsworth's Poet, the connection of subsequent impressions from experience with the grand, elementary principles of our being could be described as mechanical. The later adoption of organic theories from Germany explained the same process, but in a way which described the activity of genius as specialized, almost mystical in its intuition of the natural laws which were the principle of its growth and production, and tended towards a conservative identification of these natural laws with those underpinning the social structure. For associationists the unity of a work was produced by conscious organization, the fruit of extensive experience. Godwin even uses an 'organic' metaphor when describing such unity:

> What a comprehensive view must I take of my subject? How accurately ought I to perceive the parts, or branches, as they extend themselves from the trunk, each constituting a well arranged and beautiful whole of itself, yet each depending, for its existence and its form, upon the root by which the entire mass is sustained? From how many sciences ought my illustrations to be drawn? There is scarcely any one branch of knowledge, however apparently remote, from which my work might not be improved, and my ignorance of which will not be apparent to a discerning eye.
> (Godwin 1797: 362)

Style is also the product of meditated experience, not 'elaborated by any effort to be exerted at the moment, as by a long train of previous considerations, which have familiarised to the mind beauties the most uncommon and exquisite'. Such order arises from what Kames called following the customary order of experience. The 'customary order' of a man of genius's experience is marked by a more intense sense of human values and a more extensive range, but it answers to universally accepted rules of grammar and logic. Organic theories tend to exalt the unconscious operations of genius and the autonomous order of the work of art, obedient to its own laws (which are at the same time intuitively grasped laws of the universe). Coleridge demonstrates this shift in *Biographia Literaria* when he first appeals to the laws of 'grammar, logic, psychology', and the taste and '*good sense*' which is knowledge 'rendered instinctive by habit', the 'reward of our past conscious reasonings, insights, and conclusions' (Coleridge 1983: 2: 81), and then invokes 'the prerogative of poetic genius' and its 'parental instinct' for distinguishing the true from the false in style (1983: 2: 83). For associationists, the 'mysterious' and exclusive characteristics of genius are its strong organic sensibility, which is partly a gift and partly the product of auspicious early circumstances, and the inspirational properties of sympathy and the sublime, qualities associated with 'sensibility', the birthright of all men in different degrees. When Godwin pays his tribute to imaginative writers like Shakespeare and Milton he praises this ability to extend human sympathy and provide inspiring images of human perfection, just as Shelley did later, not any arcane gift of imagination that implied a privileged ordering of experience. In *The Enquirer* he extols those authors who

> Pour their whole souls into mine, and raise me as it were to the seventh heaven; . . . who raise my ambition, expand my faculties, invigorate my resolutions, and seem to double my existence . . . I can guess very nearly what I should have been, if Epictetus had not bequeathed to us his Morals, or Seneca his Consolations. But I cannot tell what I should have been, if Shakespeare or Milton had not written. The poorest peasant in the remotest corner of England, is probably a different man from what he would have been but for those authors. Every man who is changed from what he was by the perusal of their works, communicates a portion of that inspiration all around him. It passes from man to man, till it influences the whole mass.
> (Godwin 1797: 140)

Thomas Wedgwood's plan for an educational institution dedicated to the production of genius outlines a minutely supervised regime of progressive exposure to sensory stimuli. It has been seen as the catalyst which prompted Wordsworth to examine his own ideas of the education of nature (Gill 1990: 131), and eventually resulted in the attack on systematic education in Book V of the 1805 *Prelude*. One thing which makes this unlikely is that the genius which Wedgwood and Godwin hoped to foster could hardly be the 'worshipper of worldly seemliness' (v. 298) depicted by Wordsworth. They look to produce a reformer of the world, capable of effecting a 'general revolution of sentiment'.[2] Apart from the rather ludicrously exaggerated supervision, Wedgwood's educational ideas are remarkably close to those of Wordsworth and Godwin. Godwin's *Enquirer* essays were produced during his period of correspondence with Wedgwood and share the same theoretical basis.

Wedgwood sees the rudiments of genius in the acquisition of 'distinct vivid primary & conseq[uently], *distinct vivid* second[ary] ideas with *high degrees of Pleasure* associated'. The care over the reception of ideas stems from the fear that if they came too densely the attention would be too saturated to focus on detail and develop emotional response. This sensory overload is what Wordsworth condemns in London in *The Prelude* and in city life, sensational entertainments, and news stories of war in the Preface to *Lyrical Ballads*. The 'savage torpor' produced by such outrageous stimulation destroys the active response which is of primary importance to Wordsworth, as it is to Godwin and Wedgwood. In the Preface Wordsworth fulminates against those who consider a 'taste' for poetry as the same as a taste for wine, and in 1815 he recognized the way in which the term 'taste' had, in describing the response to the sublime and the beautiful, taken on an essentially active sense, extending the capacity for experience. In the Preface he maintains the more Hartleyan approach common to Wedgwood, in seeing such active response as in some way a mechanical result of association.

Like the Edgeworths, Wedgwood relies on the pleasure which the preceptor can give his pupils by a winning manner and 'a little acting, in the improvement of our dull natures', but he stresses the importance of 'connecting their chief pleasures with rational objects'. This association of pleasure with valuable objects is of the utmost importance in fostering 'strong Desires' for similar objects. To sustain and reinforce these desires 'it seems necessary that a series of resembling impressions should have been system[atically] administered, so that the view or idea of any object may, where desire urges, instantly suggest a thousand analogies'. Regular exposure to impressions connected with valuable objects might give pupils 'the desirable habit of independent exertion, forethought, activity & invention'. Wedgwood had formulated his ideas independently of Hartley, and was mortified when Godwin directed him to this source. Wordsworth had become acquainted with Hartleyan association through Coleridge, whose theological, Priestleyan interpretation had credited a divinely animated Nature with the capacity to direct association into the healthy and progressive habits which Wedgwood ascribed to a rational education. The precise religious orthodoxy of Nature was a moot point between Wordsworth and Coleridge. For Wordsworth Nature, the nature of the rural community, subject to regular seasonal successions and cyclic familial occasions of loss and renewal, provided just such a regular education in basic values as Wedgwood posited, and in the Preface he linked the importance of such impressions with their regularity as representing the permanently important conditions of life.

It is unlikely that Wedgwood gave Wordsworth furiously to think, since I hope to show that Wordsworth was by this time accustomed to transforming the demands of reason into the influences of Nature, and in this Wedgwood might well have confirmed him. Wedgwood's letter, written mostly in pencil in one of those erratic seizures of inspiration which mark his manuscripts, is hardly consistent in itself. The genius envisaged in the first part of the letter is a philosopher capable of interpreting experience in terms of permanent 'rational' value, but the conclusion of the letter looks on the desired genius not as a philosopher but as a communicator. We already possess a 'large stock of truth' but its circulation is very limited and the inspiring teacher should above all appeal to the feelings: 'the tones of his voice, his gesture should be such as irresistibly to win esteem & affection, whilst his reasoning impresses conviction; his manner should be full of tenderness, consideration & sympathy: It should be impossible to look on him without love and admiration.' This is very much in tune with Godwin's investigation in *The Enquirer* into the means by which a progressive philosophy might be recommended to a recalcitrant age, the tone and personal image which could appeal above party rancour to a common humanity. In other speculations in his manuscripts Thomas Wedgwood is close to Wordsworth and Godwin in characterizing the genius. Here the genius is not moulded by any special circumstances but by a development of common powers of observation and discrimination:

> The business of early life is to observe and familiarize ourselves with the great & obvious relations of things . . . Genius consists chiefly in refining as much as possible on the early observation; in ascertaining scrupulously how far objects resemble and differ which can be effected only by an unwearied search after the nicest shades of distinction. This

persevered in begets a general habit of delicate discrimination which, the moment any object is presented to it with the rapidity of intuition immedeately analyses it with its ingredient parts which it assorts, and recompounds.[3]

If there is any mystery in genius it is for Wedgwood, as for Blair, in the gift of sensitive organs of perception, not only for accurate perception but in connecting perception with strong feeling. In another fragment Wedgwood cites Rousseau as one of those 'whose senses are originally so acute, or in other words, whose sensations are so lively & attended with so much feeling, whether pleasure or pain that without the aid of instruction, a character of high sensibility will result. The plea[sant] feelings of these sensitive beings constitute the genuine standard of beauty.'[4] Less gifted beings can only be 'drilled into admiration' by 'teaching them to feel what the others have felt untaught'.

Godwin thought that this connection of genius with 'a certain state of nervous sensibility originally existing in the frame' was a 'gratuitous assumption' (Godwin 1797: 13), and pointed to the children of peasants to demonstrate the far more widespread promise of genius which the adverse circumstances of society rendered barren: 'Nothing is more common than to find in them a promise of understanding, a quickness of observation, an ingenuousness of character, and a delicacy of tact, at the age of seven years, the very traces of which are obliterated at the age of fourteen' (1797: 16).

The assertion that original sensibility was a universal gift and the foundation of genius, coupled with the linking of genius and imagination with egalitarian social progress, heavily compromised these terms in an age of reaction. Wordsworth retained many of the features of radical sensibility in his conception of imagination, but identified his social goals with a restricted, nostalgic model of society. Coleridge developed a concept of imagination which emphasized its ordering power as it coerced all elements of a poem into unity. The order of an imaginative work for Coleridge mirrored the ideal order within the individual, each faculty exercising its powers, but subordinated to the highest spiritual and moral principles. There is an obvious parallel between this hierarchical inner order presided over by the Coleridgean faculties of Reason and Imagination and the hierarchical society which he accepted in his social criticism and reconstructed in the ideal form of his *Constitution of Church and State*. Yet his conservatism differs from similar identifications of the order of imagination with a traditional, accepted order, such as that of Kames. Coleridge looked to self-discipline to enfranchise man from external coercion. As he said in his Bristol lectures: 'If we would have no Nero without, we must place a Caesar within us, and that Caesar must be religion' (*Lect*: 229). Authority is not prescriptively granted to traditional forms but is located within the individual. Coleridge's position is very similar to Evangelical attitudes which reinterpret social relations of power in terms of positive spiritual and moral influence, yet his abiding objection to the property basis of society often provoked more radical social criticism.

Shelley's conception of imagination is a direct legacy of radical sensibility. Natural man is healthily well adjusted. Passions and affections need no external control but are naturally directed to social ends. The characteristics of beauty are themselves the self-begotten principles of natural society, expressing a co-operative rather than an authoritarian spirit:

> The social sympathies, or those laws from which as from its elements society results, begin to develop themselves from the moment that two human beings coexist; the future is contained within the present as the plant within the seed; and equality, diversity, unity, contrast, mutual dependence, become the principles alone capable of affording the motives according to which the will of a social being is determined to action, inasmuch as he is social; and constitute pleasure in sensation, virtue in sentiment, beauty in art, truth in reasoning, and love in the intercourse of kind.
> (Shelley 1977: 481)

As he expands on the implications of these terms in the *Defence of Poetry* their kinship with the radicalism of the 1790s becomes more apparent as he confines the attribute of 'poetry' to the expression of these social principles. Traces of the conflicts of sensibility in the 1790s can be seen in the contrast between his radical, empirical, Platonic imagination and the conservative, Germanic imagination of Coleridge.

In *The Enquirer* Godwin's aim was the production of genius, the capacity to reform the world, and as his end was social so were his means. The motives to learning are primarily social ones: 'a liberal satisfaction in communicated and reciprocal pleasure', self-esteem, and the esteem of one's peers (Godwin 1797: 57). The most powerful engine of education is the sympathy between the teacher and the pupil: 'There is, as it were, a magnetical virtue that fills the space between them: the communication is palpable, the means of communication too subtle and minute to be detected' (1797: 124). In the parallel task of engaging a reader's attention, an emotional sympathy must be produced: 'He must sympathise with my passions, melt with my regrets, and swell with my enthusiasm.' The reader must be turned into a co-operator, for proper reading is an active process. Similarly the child must be impelled to active rather than passive learning. Whenever study is without desire, it is useless. But Godwin uncompromisingly asserts that 'All education is coercion' and he feelingly describes a child's frustration under normal teaching conditions and the way in which his slavery rouses the antagonistic passions. Godwin's ideal is a pupil-led education where the teacher is a companion of study, his role being restricted to discussion and providing materials. He must even be content for chance stimuli outside his control to have more effect than his own advice – the playground and the pub are often the most effective educational institutions. *Political Justice* had started by stressing the potentially beneficial power of government, and had then proceeded to demonstrate that all government is an evil; *The Enquirer* begins by affirming the power of education to mould character, and progressively reveals that any attempt by the teacher to exercise authority in this moulding is worse than useless. If a parent or teacher wishes to *enforce* an opinion it should be made known that there is no appeal to reason allowed. Better an open than a disguised tyranny. Parents who present a choice between Lyswen Farm and Kilve by the sea as an open question when they are determined to enforce their own choice breed liars or mutinous sophists like Basil Montague. The relationship in which the forms of intimacy and openness are preserved while one partner insensibly assumes dominance is one of the evils of co-habitation. The teacher is not even allowed to stipulate a course of reading. Any attempt to bowdlerize or restrict the child's reading will have dire effects on the child's natural curiosity, and curiosity is the first indication of genius. The locked bookcase, like Falkland's locked iron chest, will turn this curiosity into a demon determined to circumvent arbitrary regulation.

Although not an education of nature in the full Wordsworthian sense, in that external nature plays little part, Godwin's scheme is fully natural in following, not prompting, the natural processes of maturation. Wordsworth's ideas on education are often thought to be derived from Hartley, but *The Enquirer* might be a more immediate source. In many sections Godwin makes the same contrast as Wordsworth between the natural and the artificial child, and the progress from the pleasures of the eye to those of the mind. Godwin thought that the attributes of childhood were too soon resigned under the pressure to conform to adult behaviour or the 'crimping house of oppression'. He thought that some of the natural hilarity of youth ought to be preserved into adulthood and that even this hilarity had an appreciation of serious values. Where they parted company was in their estimation of conscious knowledge and the benefit of books. For Godwin the mute Miltons of rustic life had been deprived of their rights of education and self-improvement and were the brutified victims of society; for Wordsworth even an idiot boy could show the inarticulate signs of a creative poetic mind.

In its faith in the unspoiled nature of the child and confidence that the natural social sympathies would develop from exposure to the widest range of experience, *The Enquirer* offered the most liberal educational ideas of the age. It was at the furthest pole from those doctrines becoming fashionable which counselled ceaseless vigilance and control and, in Evangelical versions, breaking the spirit of unregenerate nature. Kames had earlier warned against allowing children to mix with servants; the Edgeworths went on to advise parents to construct their houses in such a way as to prevent such contact. This was symptomatic of a general increase in the exclusiveness of rank as Revolutionary ideas brought a new consciousness of class. The promiscuous social gatherings depicted by Fanny Burney were becoming a thing of the past; Vauxhall was declining; difference of class was becoming marked by characteristics of less easy acquisition than dress, above all by manners and education. One could claim, in Wildean phrase, that the playing fields of Eton were won on the battlefield of Waterloo.

The moral dangers of mixed national public education

worried Mary Wollstonecraft, and it was in deference to her opinion that Godwin ended his essay on public education with a nod in the direction of day schools as combining the advantages of the public and the domestic. Generally Godwin felt that a private and highly supervised education was more liable to break the spirit of the child, and he valued the rebellious independence that revolted against supervision. Such independence was more likely to be found in a public institution, where the condition of being equally oppressed tended to produce virtues which were based on equality.

The teacher, reduced to rational persuasion and exhortation in his efforts to influence the child, must rely on what Godwin calls the 'intrinsic' values of the studies which he recommends. Godwin holds that there are certain studies, certain social practices, certain actions and feelings, which minister to the highest and most general human happiness, and which have an intrinsic attraction. This seems again to be based on the Hutchesonian moral sense, since Godwin asserts that man is naturally drawn to approve of those actions and feelings which fulfil the social nature of man, in sympathy, commiseration, and benevolence. Truth, sincerity, scientific and literary culture, are only satisfying in so far as they fulfil the purposes of benevolence. The educator can appeal to this natural benevolence when recommending particular studies. Opposing theories of education were based on contrivance and an appeal to selfishness, by the manipulation of extrinsic motives: rewards and punishments. Rousseau had disfigured his system with such deceptions, and the Edgeworths' system of manipulating the child by its desire for parental approval is criticized as a perversion of the genuine social passions.

Godwin perpetually stresses that sensibility, the benevolent social feeling, is the source of all efforts to better the lot of mankind, both individually and in the mass: 'The form may be wrong', he comments, 'but the substance ought to remain . . . wherever civilisation exists, sensibility will be its attendant, a sensibility, which cannot be satisfied without much kindness, nor without a kindness of that condescending nature, that considers the whole chain of our feelings, and is desirous, out of petty materials, to compose the sum of our happiness' (Godwin 1797: 334-5). Such is Godwin's stress on sensibility that it seems likely that many elements of Wordsworth's work which have been seen as anti-Godwinian might actually have stemmed from his reading of *The Enquirer* or from the conversations on which it was based. True politeness (as distinguished from cold formality) lies, says Godwin, in the practice of the 'lesser morality'. We may not often be called upon to save Fénelon from the burning palace, but every day gives opportunities for kindness, sympathy, and 'attentions too minute for calculation' (1797: 329). These actions 'the heart can record, but the tongue is rarely competent to relate'; they include minute sympathetic gestures so nuanced that they are indeed 'nameless kindnesses'. These quotations take us well on the way to Wordsworth's 'best portion of a good man's life; / His little, nameless, unremembered acts / Of kindness and of love' (*OA*: 132).

When Legouis (1939: 10) made a kind of recantation of earlier attacks on Godwin in *La Jeunesse de Wordsworth*, he pointed to a passage of *Political Justice* which seemed to him to be near in spirit to 'Simon Lee'. In this Godwin asks us to observe the pauper, speechless with gratitude at the charity he has received. It was a common trait of radical sensibility to attack notions of charity that bred servility and dependence, and reinforced the inequalities of society. Certainly Hazlitt read Wordsworth's concluding line as an indictment of the society in which such aid is necessary, and so unusual as to prompt such servile gratitude: 'Alas, the gratitude of man has oftner left me mourning!'[5] A more likely influence on Wordsworth is Godwin's more complex treatment of the beggar in *The Enquirer*. Here the beggar 'seems to look up to his petty benefactor, . . . as to a height that it makes the eyes ache to contemplate. He pours forth his blessings and prayers for you in so copious a stream, that the powers of speech seem to labour beneath the vastness of his gratitude' (Godwin 1797: 191–2). After the poet's petty act of assistance to Simon Lee, 'The tears into his eyes were brought, / And thanks and praises seemed to run / So fast out of his heart, I thought / They never would have done' (*OA*: 88). The two cases are not strictly parallel, since Godwin is describing a common beggar, while Simon Lee does not even ask for assistance. Godwin, however, like Wordsworth, considers this abject being in two ways, as a symptom of social malaise, but also as a fellow-being, however stunted or even depraved, to be treated with humanity. While the doctrinaire might withhold charity from professional beggars, Godwin affirms that the 'man of feeling and humanity' will 'dispense with general maxims, and, for no possible calculation of distant evils, . . . turn a deaf ear to the cries of humanity'. Godwin certainly would not 'incarcerate them in the house of correction', though he may allow himself to 'expostulate' with them.

The *Enquirer* essay most directly concerned with Godwin's social criticism is deliberately constructed as a 'literary' work. 'Avarice and Profusion' situates itself in the tradition of Pope's *Moral Essays* on the 'Use of Riches' with sketches of the contrasting characters of debtor, miser, and magnifico. It is also confessedly a 'paradoxical' essay, a *jeu d'esprit*, in recommending the example of the miser. But despite its slight attempts to entertain, its serious point is thoroughly established. It engages with the theories of political economy and tries to correct the public approval of those who use their wealth to provide employment. True wealth, he asserts, is the leisure and means to further one's own self-improvement; economic wealth is most commonly the power to deprive others of this true wealth by multiplying the hours to be spent labouring to earn enough to survive. Too much of this employment produces little of any real value, but merely ministers to luxury and vanity. The factory of his friend Wedgwood employs vegetating human drudges, and those who construct elaborate gardens are similarly 'adding to the weight of oppression, and the vast accumulation of labour, by which [the labourers] are already sunk beneath the level of the brutes' (Godwin 1797: 178). Labour is the measure not so much of the value of a product as of its cost in human terms. This reaction against the arguments of *The Wealth of Nations* is echoed in Wordsworth's *Prelude* and *Excursion*.

In his own works of imagination, Godwin sought to explore the genesis of such perversions. *St Leon* demonstrates the fallibility of economic explanations of motivation as his 'hero' tries to impose materialistic happiness upon war-torn Hungary, only to find his efforts defeated by man's desire for freedom, independence, and true companionship. Individual happiness can only be attained by refinements of political science, a science which his hero dismisses in the first two pages as outmoded, replaced by the dream of material wealth. Here Godwin is expanding on his refutation of the narrow Micawber definition of happiness and also considering the phenomenon of Burke. By focusing on an aristocratic anti-hero in the time of the historic 'death of chivalry' and its supersession by economists and calculators of self-interest, he is trying to show how an élitist paternalism which had ideals of public service could develop into an individualistic pursuit of private gain, just as Burke's rhetoric of aristocratic responsibility coexisted with his laissez-faire economic ideas. The explanation is sought in the psychology of St Leon, and in the aristocratic society which had warped that psychology by its habits of profusion, and the love of a distinction based on rank and not on personal qualities. Godwin generally, like Shelley, preferred to focus on the more positive elements of the age of chivalry, notably the elements of public service, increased respect for women, and the growth of personal and familial emotional bonds rather than power relationships. These elements demonstrated human progress and provided, in the literature celebrating such values, a permanent record of human achievement that could not be obliterated by an epoch of narrow selfishness.

The Enquirer was predominantly well received, and though it made an almost obligatory appearance in Gillray's 'New Morality', there were few expressions of political outrage. The Edgeworths felt that they could praise its remarks on public education, though they decided, on balance, to favour private. In partly a retreat from direct political discussion, Godwin identified the apparently 'neutral' subjects which offered most chance of combating the forces of reaction. In his 'unsystematic' method he anticipated the journalistic techniques of writers such as Hazlitt in insinuating political perspectives in discussions of popular topics. As a record of conversations among those still adhering to the radical cause in the mid-1790s it shows the development of new themes and approaches to the task of reform as new antagonistic trends emerged in economic, educational, and aesthetic thought.

5
HELEN MARIA WILLIAMS: RADICAL CHRONICLER

Helen Maria Williams and Charlotte Smith provide particularly useful examples of the development of radical sensibility during the 1790s. Both had established reputations as poets before the French Revolution and Charlotte Smith had produced her popular first novel *Emmeline*. From 1783 Williams had entertained the literary intelligentsia at her salon in Portman Square. Well established as a poet on such topics as the horrors of war, the iniquities of the slave-trade, and colonialist oppression, no odium attached to her views before the Revolution and the staunch conservative Dr Johnson had kissed her hand.[1] Wordsworth's first publication was the sonnet 'On Seeing Miss Helen Maria Williams Weep at a Tale of Distress' and he linked her with Charlotte Smith in his memories of the Revolutionary decade.[2] Smith provided him with a letter of introduction to Williams when he went to France in 1791 but she was not in Paris. Shelley attempted to make contact in 1815 and was similarly disappointed. Wordsworth, whose knowledge of the contemporary literary scene was fostered by Taylor at Hawkshead, was capable of repeating from memory poems by both writers.

Both writers welcomed the French Revolution and suffered criticism for maintaining their loyalty to its ideals. Anna Seward condemned Williams's break with Bluestocking respectability, privately lamenting her liaison with John Hurford Stone and publicly denouncing her activities in France. Her admonitory letter to Williams of 17 January 1793 (Seward 1811: 3: 202) was published in the *Gentleman's Magazine*. Smith, patronized by the 'Surrey Maecenas' William Hayley in the early years of the decade, gave vent to her disappointment at the falling off of friends in prefaces and through autobiographical characters in her novels. Despite her supposed 'recantation' of her radical views in 1794, she was pilloried with Williams and other 'unsex'd females' such as Wollstonecraft and Hays in the *Anti-Jacobin*. Both writers developed intellectual and personal links with Godwin. After the Napoleonic Wars, Williams in Paris looked back to their association in the early days of the Revolution, planned publishing ventures, and received visits from Mrs Godwin. Smith corresponded regularly with Godwin from 1797 and admitted reading *Political Justice* for the first time in 1798. Godwin and his family visited her at Tilford up to her final illness, when he sent Sir Anthony Carlisle to see her. Carlisle's prognosis of recovery is annotated: 'Poor Mrs Smith died in 3 days. These medical men often mistake.'[3]

When Williams moved her family and her salon to Paris she turned from poetry and the novel to the letter form. She exemplified the radical faith in individual experience reacting to the events of the moment, her letters being based on her own personal involvement and that of her friends with the moving spirits and horrific events of France in the 1790s. As a commentator on historical events she is easy to criticize, partial towards her Girondin friends and naive in her enthusiasms. Most of her acquaintances, including Wollstonecraft, remarked on the excessive affectation of sensibility in her appearance and manner, yet responded to her genuine warmth in the cause of humanity. Her very naivety makes her an outstanding example of the reactions of sensibility to the swift changes of events, and a guide to the analogous reactions of more major figures like Wordsworth. Her letters influenced Wordsworth, Coleridge, and other radicals at the time, and proved a source for later historians such as Hazlitt.

The immediacy of the letter form had many dangers, some of a personal nature. She feared that Barère, when inquisitor-general of the English expatriates under Robespierre, would take exception to the letters in which she described his former close association with her Girondin circle. The main danger of the form, however, was a lack of consistency and an over-optimistic seizing on favourable indications which had to be subsequently retracted. With one exception, her publications coincided with moments when events on the Continent seemed most propitious for universal revolution. Her enthusiasm for the Fête of the

Fédération in 1790 led her to identify with the French cause, yet a subsequent series of letters looks forward to French military defeats as a salutary check to the excesses of the ruling party. After the fall of Robespierre she again saw visions of returning glory, and ended her *Tour in Switzerland* with a eulogy of Napoleon and an anticipation of the benefits which Switzerland might expect from an extension of French influence. These too had to be retracted. Such inconsistencies inevitably draw the criticism of hindsight, yet in the historical context she offered the most vivid and moving pictures of historical events, exercising her sensibility in situations quite foreign to those previously regarded as its province, and presenting a chronicle of the revolutionary period suffused with feeling; indeed her image of the Terror was of 'the tumultuous horrors of this convulsion of the passions'.[4]

Her initial loyalty to the principles of the Revolution was more emotional than reasoned. Though she celebrated it in 1791 as 'surely the work of literature, of philosophy, of the enlarging views of mankind',[5] she later asserted that 'the ancient system was overthrown, not because it was unphilosophical, but because it could be upheld no longer' (Williams 1795: 2: 129). She seemed to be mainly moved by the humanitarian motives associated with the Revolution, especially the abolition of the slave-trade, and by her reaction to the adventures of her former tutor, Augustin Thomas Du Fossé, which she described in her first series of letters. He had offended his father, the Baron, by his marriage to Monique Coquerel and had been pursued into Switzerland and then to Britain, where he had found employment as a French teacher. Inveigled back to France by his father's show of conciliation, he had been imprisoned by means of a *lettre de cachet* for two years before escaping. On the death of the Baron he had returned and, laying aside the principle of primogeniture, shared his fortune with his brothers. These had ungratefully conspired against him and, fearing another *lettre de cachet*, he had fled again to England, returning only after the fall of the Bastille. The account may well have contributed to Wordsworth's presentation of the unhappy loves of Vaudracour and Julia. Williams's emotional reaction to the story provided a complete vindication of the Revolution, as her intuitive sensibility transcended the laborious work of philosophers:

however dull the faculties of my head, I can assure you, that
when a proposition is addressed to my heart, I have some
quickness of perception. I can then decide, in one moment,
points upon which philosophers and legislators have
differed in all ages.

(Williams 1792: 1: 195-6)

Her reaction to Burke had the advantage of meeting him on his own ground within the polarizing aspects of sensibility. Not for her the legalistic arguments of Mackintosh or the factual refutations of Paine. Whereas Burke took his stand on a conservative sensibility that revered feudal bonds of loyalty and hierarchical submission as providing a habituated form for man's emotional needs, Williams concentrated on those aspects of the days of chivalry which favoured a freer, more generous ideal:

living in France at present, appears to me somewhat like
living in a region of romance . . . All the motives which
most powerfully stimulate the mind in its ordinary state,
seem repressed in consideration of the public good, and
every selfish interest is sacrificed with fond alacrity at the
altar of the country. For my part, while I contemplate these
things, I sometimes think that the age of chivalry, instead of
being past for ever, is just returned; not indeed in its
erroneous notions of loyalty, honour and gallantry, which
are as little 'l'ordre du jour' as its dwarfs, giants and
imprisoned damsels; but in its noble contempt of sordid
cares, its spirit of unsullied generosity, and its heroic zeal
for the happiness of others.

(Williams 1792: 2: 4-5)

Godwin later appealed to similar ideals of chivalric disinterestedness in his address to the aristocracy in *Political Justice* and his presentation of the positive aspects of chivalry in *St Leon* and his *Life of Chaucer*. Williams here is not encumbered with Godwin's theories of gradual social progress and the difficulties of distinguishing the progressive and the regressive aspects of the chivalric ideal. In 1791 she could cheerfully assign the dark ages to a remote Gothic night of unreason, and speak of Burke as a mole, hiding his head from the 'philosophic day':

Must feudal governments for ever last?
Those Gothic piles, the work of ages past;

> Nor may obtrusive reason scan,
> Far less reform the rude misshapen plan;
> The winding labyrinths, the hostile towers,
> Whence danger threatens, and where Horror low'rs,
> The jealous draw-bridge, and the moat profound,
> The lonely dungeon in the caverned ground,
> The sullen dome above those central caves,
> Where lives one tyrant, and a host of slaves.
>
> (1792: 2: 12)

Viewing the installation of the French, American, and British flags in the Hall of the Jacobins, she meditated on the different forms of liberty they represented. Speculating on the reforms necessary to a liberty which had been obtained 'in the Gothic darkness of the twelfth century', she hoped that Britain 'may avoid those storms and convulsions which are only necessary to purify the moral, as well as the physical world, from any mighty contagion' (Williams 1792: 2: 114-15). It is ironic that the very real convulsions which she was later to chronicle, the Terror, and the assault upon rational and civilized values, were displaced by novelists into the fictional settings which she derided as antiquated. Ironic, too, is the reappearance of her dome and caves in 'Kubla Khan', another poem about a tyrant haunted by coming convulsions. Coleridge's poem of 1798 presents the origin of poetic imagination as morally ambiguous. The recapturing of a lost Paradise in images which derive from a tyrant's artifice of luxury is ascribed to a mysterious, unhallowed source beyond responsible moral control. In 1798 Williams herself had come to doubt, like Hazlitt after her, the central tenet of aesthetic sensibility, that the imagination was firmly on the side of truth, justice, and all the amiable virtues.

The letters of 1793 are far less optimistic and show her bewilderment at the course of the Revolution. Robespierre and his conspirators had taken over the Jacobin clubs and, in conjunction with the Commune of Paris, 'endeavoured to lead the people to the last degree of moral degradaton, by teaching them that the love of order is the love of despotism, and that the most unequivocal proof of patriotism is to remain in permanent insurrection' (Williams 1793: 3: 23). She was particularly disgusted with the excesses of sansculottism by which 'a person of education is hated for that reason only; any superiority of mind being considered as an aristocratic deviation from the great principles of equality' (1793: 3: 23). Robespierre himself was an awesome enigma:

> fanatical and exaggerated in his avowed principles of liberty, possessing that eloquence which gives him power over the passions, and that cool determined temper which regulates the most ferocious designs with the most calm and temperate prudence. His crimes do not appear to be the result of passion, but of some deep and extraordinary malignity, and he seems formed to subvert and destroy.
> (1793: 3: 7)

This collection of letters includes her most forthright denunciation of French policies. She had no reservation in asserting that when France 'commanded where she promised support, and enslaved where she had offered independence – she became a tyrant in her turn – and the friend of liberty, true to his principles, equally rejoices in her defeat' (Williams 1793: 4: 78). Anna Seward thought that Williams was meditating an escape and had 'sent out this work as her pallinode and harbinger, to smooth her reception here, and apologise for the too confident triumph of her former volumes' (Seward 1811: 3: 335). Whether Wordsworth saw the original publication or later editions, such as that published in Dublin in 1794, there is a strong possibility that Williams's views contributed to his own disillusionment with French policies, which is expressed in similarly idealistic terms. He too had reacted to liberated France as a 'Country of Romance', and echoed Williams's criticism of French imperialism:

> become oppressors in their turn,
> Frenchmen had changed a war of self-defence
> For one of conquest, losing sight of all
> Which they had struggled for.
> (*Prelude*: x.791-4)

De Selincourt has argued persuasively that Wordsworth recognized France's apostasy in late 1794, when the fall of Robespierre failed to herald a return to earlier ideals and French armies were advancing into Italy. F. M. Todd, while maintaining that Wordsworth was still a supporter of the Revolution in 1798, also holds that it was disappointment with the policies of the Directory which impelled him to seek a firmer Godwinian foundation for his radical hopes (Todd 1957: 217-18). Roe and Gill acknowledge that Wordsworth became a Godwinian before the death of Robespierre but seem to accept the traditional view that the actions of the Directory induced a disillusionment far greater than that described in *The Prelude*. Wordsworth specifically states that the Directory's policies 'vex'd' him but did not shake his trust in the French people nor his faith of 'passionate intuition' that France would move on to victories 'Great, universal, irresistible' (*Prelude*: x.586). The account of *The Prelude* may be salvaged by acknowledging that he, like Williams, questioned the integrity of the French leaders and condemned the expedition into Belgium in 1793. While this led him to turn to Godwin, possibly in the same year, for a creed more firmly based on principles of human nature rather than on the example of France, he remained confident in the progress of the Revolution. In 1793, however much Williams deprecated the French 'Quixotic' expeditions to impose liberty on other countries, she could still assert:

> the friends of liberty in France have little cause for dejection at their seeming reverse. It was, indeed, wanting to bring them back to their original system, from which the French have so unhappily strayed. Their minds were yet too young in freedom to appreciate its blessings aright; and they were yet to know that the triumphs of liberty are scarcely ever those of the sword.
>
> (Williams 1793: 4: 117)

The widely read letters about the Terror and her personal experience of imprisonment were written at a distance from events, mostly in Switzerland, whence she and J. H. Stone had escaped until the death of Robespierre. In these, despite their disordered chronology (which allows her periodically to advert to the blissful hopes of the present), a more considered view of Robespierre's reign emerges. The enormities of Robespierre are no longer the inexplicable Satanic actions of a human enigma but the magnified consequences of human passions:

> It is a curious consideration, that the unexampled crimes of this sanguinary usurper, and the consequent miseries which have desolated the finest country of Europe, may

perhaps, if traced to their source, be found to arise from the resentment of a disappointed wit.

(Williams 1795: 1: 228)

She presents him as a man of immense and frustrated ambition, an ambition fostered by winning several literary prizes but frustrated by lack of the oratorical skills needed as a lawyer to plead important causes at Paris. His relegation to an obscure legal practice in Arras, she thought, gave him a profound bitterness against men of genius. A similar effort to humanize the monsters of the Terror is seen in her treatment of Collot d'Herbois and his atrocities at Lyons:

It will scarcely be thought possible, yet it is very generally believed, that Collot was led to this vengeance on the people of Lyons for having hissed him from the stage.

(1795: 1: 166)

He had originally been an actor and was nicknamed Ghengis, since he had played the part, and was accused of 'having taken him as a model, and of having avenged, like him, private injuries' (1795: 1: 60).

Robespierre may be considered to be the historical original of many of the fictional villains of this period, such as Mrs Radcliffe's Schedoni, who similarly unites ambition, resentment, and an icily rational homicidal logic. Writers who wished to maintain a hopeful estimate of man usually tried to demonstrate that these traits were not native to man but explicable as the result of unnatural circumstances. They often followed Williams in using the mechanism of thwarted ambition in their psychological explanations. Godwin produced a long line of misanthropic self-tormentors, culminating in the aptly named Mandeville, and Wordsworth provided a similar explanation for the villany of Rivers in his preface to *The Borderers*.

Coleridge's depiction of Robespierre in *The Fall of Robespierre* and in *Conciones ad Populum* might owe something to Williams's earlier description. In the latter, he writes of Robespierre: 'he possessed a glowing ardor that still remembered the *end*, and a cool ferocity that never overlooked, or scrupled, the *means*'. Coleridge's interest in what might be called the pathology of the benevolent passions leads him to the generalization that '[t]he ardor of undisciplined benevolence seduces us into malignity', but he also ascribes Robespierre's villany to individual characteristics: 'gloom, and suspiciousness, and inordinate vanity' (*Lect*: 35). The contrasting picture of the 'Girondists' as men 'of enlarged views and great literary attainments' may also be influenced by Williams's praise of her friends. Williams also recounts Mme Roland's judgment of Brissot: 'he was formed to live with the wise, and to be the dupe of the wicked ... he was well acquainted with the nature of man, and altogether ignorant of the characters of men' (Williams 1795: 2: 80). Coleridge calls him 'rather a sublime visionary than a quick-eyed politician [whose] excellencies equally with his faults rendered him unfit for the helm, in the stormy hour of Revolution' (*Lect*: 35).

Williams cannot avoid painting a scene of widespread depravity, as if Robespierre had only unleashed the natural cruelty and selfishness of man. She blames the uneducated nature of local functionaries, combined with the temptations of power:

> The greater part of mankind, in all ages, even when accustomed to the most elevated rank, have abused power: how then could it be hoped that unlimited power would not be abused, which was confided to men who were, for the most part, ignorant and unenlightened.
> (Williams 1795: 1: 12)

She hopes that her account may enlighten 'those countries which are destined to labour through revolutions, and who will learn, while they contemplate this terrific chart, how to avoid the rocks on which Liberty has been nearly wrecked' (1795: 2: 213). This hope for peaceful democratic revolutions in other countries sometimes seems like wishful thinking. The violence of revolution is often presented as almost a physical necessity; it is likened to 'the tremendous tempests which sometimes sweep along the western islands', when the devastation is naturally replaced by calm when 'a soft light hovers on the horizon' (1795: 2: 116-17). If it is 'alas! the condition of our uninstructed nature, that nations like individuals should acquire wisdom only in the school of experience' (1795: 1: 256), then she has to look for even such terrible experiences producing an overbalance of good in the distant future: 'Let us hope that this stormy revolution will at least produce some portion of felicity to succeeding generations, who have not like us, felt the tumultuous horrors of this convulsion of the passions' (1795: 1: 117). Like Mary Wollstonecraft, she believed that the education of experience was generally a harsh one and, in extending this model of education from the individual to society, she entered regions where sensibility, especially feminine sensibility, had rarely ventured, in accepting that evil, even the horrors of massacre, was acceptable when balanced against the future good of the whole. In her first letters she had shivered at the sight of the famous lamp-post on which the first opponents of the Revolution had perished, and had many another opportunity for shuddering, including her famous expedition after the killing of the Swiss Guards in the storming of the Tuilleries. But her apparent endorsement of these excesses led to a chorus of disapproval. The *Gentleman's Magazine* condemned her principally for not displaying the correct emotional responses of feminine sensibility. It retailed the story of Boswell striking out the epithet 'amiable' from his description of her in the *Life of Johnson* because she had 'walked, without horror, over the ground at the Thuilleries, when it was strewn with the naked bodies of the faithful Swiss guards', and complained that she 'has not condescended to "heave one sigh, or set apart one tear", to the memory of the ill-fated Queen of France'. A later review asserted that she had 'debased her sex, her heart, her feelings, her talents, in recording such a tissue of horror and villany, and we hesitate not to say, daring to insult a regular government, and a happy people, with such detail'.[6]

Wordsworth's reactions to the Terror show great similarities with those of Williams. Like her, he accepted its necessity as a prelude to future glory. He saw the death of Robespierre as the dawning of a new day: 'Come now ye golden times', was Wordsworth's response, 'as the morning comes out of the bosom of the night' (*Prelude*: x.542-5). Williams had attempted to dissociate the French people as a whole from the policies of the governing party, and in the letters of 1793 Williams had comforted herself and those who shared libertarian ideals with the thought that 'though tyrants and despotism will assuredly vanish before the light of reason, yet freedom and the people will be eternal' (Williams 1793: 4: 75). Wordsworth too, while admitting that official policy was of 'heartless omen', asserted that 'In the people was my trust / And in the virtues which mine eyes had seen' (x.578-89). This trust in his own experience of a whole people's feelings later made Wordsworth into a conservative populist, but in the 1790s his allegiance to the ideals of the Revolution led him to see the excesses of Revolutionary behaviour as in part the result of external pressures and, in more Godwinian terms, as the premature achievement by violence of goals which should more genuinely have come from universal enlightenment. He viewed the horrors of the Terror in Godwinian terms as the product of the old regime, as the unenlightened people incurred the guilt of revenge. It was the product of

> a reservoir of guilt
> And ignorance, fill'd up from age to age,
> That could no longer hold its loathsome charge,
> But burst and spread in deluge through the land.
>
> (x.437-40)

Like Williams, he was unwilling to admit that such guilt attached to the whole nation, and he echoed her assertion that, amidst the Terror, some individuals distinguished themselves by their humanity and their heroism. The 'disastrous period', he affirmed:

> did not want
> Such sprinklings of all human excellence,
> As were a joy to hear of . . .
> those fair examples given
> Of fortitude, and energy, and love,
> And human nature faithful to itself
> Under worst trials.
>
> (x.443-9).

The situations of her fellow-victims of the Terror gave Williams full scope for that favourite topic of sensibility, virtue in distress, and she has been justifiably accused of treating all the victims as resplendently virtuous just because they were victims. She even lamented the death of Danton, and wrote of him 'expatiating on the charms of nature, on the beauties of rural scenery, and the peace of rural shades' in a prison scene which she could not have witnessed (Williams 1795: 2: 28). All her friends die with firmness and sorrow for their country, but it is the heroism of the women that Williams particularly highlights and presents as rivalling that of the men. Like Mary Wollstonecraft, Williams was anxious to bridge the sexist gap between the prevailing image of man as capable of energetic action, heroism, and genius, and that of woman, weak, dependent, and capable only of the passive virtues of sensibility. Her female victims are not the heroines of sentimental novels, languishing in imagined terrors or prey to mental distraction, but strong women facing the guillotine with the firmness of those dying in a great cause. She gives a heroic account of the trial and death of Charlotte Corday, but Mme Roland is her principal heroine. Sensibility and heroism are united as Williams writes of finding her reading Plutarch with a placid resignation which only breaks down when Williams mentions her children. Her actions are scenically described as she appears in white at her trial and takes second place at the guillotine to spare her male fellow-sufferer the agonies of anticipation. She left a name, averred Williams, which 'will be recorded in the annals of history, as one of those illustrious women whose superior attainments seem fitted to exalt her sex in the scale of being' (1795: 1: 201). Williams attributed the fortitude and serenity of the female victims directly to their sensibility, that 'superior sensibility which belongs to the female mind, and which makes it feel that it was less terrible to die, than to survive the objects of its tenderness' (1795: 1: 213). Certainly in their attendance on accused friends they showed themselves superior to fears of accusations of complicity. Williams anticipated Anne Wentworth in claiming that while 'men assume over our sex so many claims to superiority, let them at least bestow on us the palm of constancy, and allow that in the fidelity of our attachments we have the right of pre-eminence' (1795: 1: 40-1).

In her portraits of victims of the Terror Williams is undeniably partial in appealing to radical sensibility. The Girondins are presented as moderates, despite the fact that earlier they, not the Jacobins, had been the most extreme in their anti-monarchical policies and in advocating war against external enemies of liberty. Manon Roland had been a terrorist *avant la lettre*, as violent against internal enemies as Marat. Many of Robespierre's policies are supported, especially those against established religion, and, as the *Gentleman's Magazine* pointedly noticed, she makes no reference to the most notable victims of the guillotine. When she does appeal to outraged domestic feelings she cites three generations of the family of the legal reformer Malesherbes, all slaughtered in a day. When she presents high birth brought low she presents a Polish princess, a representative of a country raped by the Continental Allies, guillotined in spite of representations by Kosciusko. No sigh is heaved for Marie-Antoinette.

In her own imprisonment, Williams found consolation in nature. From her prison it was just possible to glimpse the Luxembourg Gardens:

> It is scarcely possible to contemplate the beauties of nature without that enthusiastic pleasure which swells into devotion; and when such dispositions are excited in the mind, resignation to suffering, which in the sacred words of scripture 'are but for a moment,' becomes a less difficult duty.
>
> (Williams 1795: 1: 17)

The mood is a common, even hackneyed, reaction to nature in the literature of sensibility, yet in such a context the possibility of transcendence is startling. While using the common sentimental technique of alternating situations of joy and sorrow, her object is not merely to intensify emotions by contrast, but, as the mature Wordsworth attempted, to affirm a vital connection between the two. Writing in Switzerland, the scenery reminds her of a tapestry in her prison depicting 'those scenes of beauty and grandeur which have calmed my troubled spirit, and in which I have found a renovation of existence' (1795: 1: 29). Just as the tapestry had transported her into nature, so now the torrent before her eyes bears her into her prison room. One may speculate on the influence of these passages on the Gothic novel. In *The Mysteries of Udolpho* (1794), Emily St Aubin in her imprisonment is led by her contemplation of nature only to tears and memories of Valancour, but in *The Italian* (1797) Mrs Radcliffe provides her imprisoned heroine with a turret-room commanding sublime views, which allows her to achieve similar transcendence and strength to bear her persecution.

Another source of comfort to Williams in prison was the society of those equalized by hardship. Williams depicts a gay round of music, parties, and lectures, with the prisons exhibiting 'of an evening almost as much brilliance and gaiety as the Thuilleries or the Champs Elysee' (Williams 1795: 2: 96). Social life outside the prisons, however, had ceased to exist in the petrifying atmosphere of suspicion: 'Even in his own habitation, and in the bosom of his family, no man dared to utter a complaint but in anxious whispers, lest a servant should overhear the forbidden expostulations of humanity, and denounce him as a counter-revolutionary' (1795: 2: 64-5). Living in fearful anticipation of *les visites domiciliaires*, she had to conceal or destroy any incriminating papers. As she seems to have provided a channel to British publishers, other writers entrusted their papers to her, and Mme Sillery later attempted to claim compensation for documents destroyed in this way. At the time of her release Williams showed how far her social sensibilities had suffered: 'How I envied the peasant in his lonely hut! for I had now almost lost sight of the idea of social happiness. My disturbed imagination divided the communities of men but into two classes, the oppressor and the oppressed; and peace seemed only to exist with solitude' (1795: 2: 4). This de-socialization is very similar to that which Godwin imagined would be the effect of living in a thoroughly unjust society, and Williams's sensibility, like Godwin's, was not usually liable to envy the isolated rural life. The peasant labourer for Godwin was the lowest form of human life, 'happier than a stone', and true benevolence consisted of trying to raise all men to a full enjoyment of all human potentialities, not to complacently praise the negative virtue of harmlessness. On the delights of rural life Williams commented:

> However innocent and pastoral the life of the shepherd and the husbandman has been represented, and however productive of those vices that corrupt and evervate mankind the commercial intercourse between nations might have been found; this communication brings with it an interchange of knowledge and manners which improves and embellishes society, while the permanent habitudes of the former serve to retain him in a state which adds nothing to the common stock of knowledge, and contributes nothing to the progressive improvement of mankind. The negative merit of exemption from vices to which we have never been tempted, may be granted to this intellectual darkness.
> (1795: 1: 117-18)

The sympathy of adherents of radical sensibility for the peasantry was largely a sympathy for the deprived, the stunted, and the oppressed. Although they appreciated the basic human feelings of rustic life celebrated in the work of Goldsmith, Burns, and Cowper, they did not glorify them but wished to rid them of their cramping physical and intellectual restrictions. Wordsworth's major departure from the ways of radical sensibility was his more 'comprehensive' appreciation of the moral and spiritual worth of the feelings and traditions of the countryside. In his early work, these feelings, even among the inarticulate, bore a moral message just as radical as the articulate productions of his colleagues whose radicalism looked to the triumph of reason and education. Godwin's exposure of the limitations of a virtuous education when counteracted by the practical and pervasive 'education' of a corrupt society led Wordsworth to look to those who were outside the influence of this pervasive corruption, 'convinced at heart / How little that to which alone we give / The name of education hath to do / With real feeling and just sense' (*Prelude*: xii.168-71).

One of the remarkable features of this series of letters is the long attack upon David in connection with his designs for the Festival of the Supreme Being. The destruction of the social sympathies was not the only shock given to Williams's faith in the ideals of sensibility by the events of the Terror. The spectacle of an artist lending his genius to the celebration of a sanguinary tyranny appalled her. In her companions in the prisons Williams had found such representatives of the worlds of art, literature, and science that it seemed obvious that Robespierre was making war on those forces which were the natural antagonists of despotism. No vituperation seemed enough for an artist of genius who had severed his art from the values which seemed inseparably connected with its inspiration, who:

> not satisfied with displaying on canvas those scenes of sanguinary guilt which from the horrors they excite furnish fit subjects for the pencil, has contributed to give them in his bleeding country 'a local habitation and a name'; who, instead of cherishing that sacred flame of enlightened liberty which is connected with the sublimer powers of the imagination, was the lacquey of the tyrant Robespierre, and the friend of the man of blood Marat; who, ambitious of recorded disgrace, of immortal ignominy, debased the noblest gift of heaven, genius, and employed his degraded pencil in tracing the hideous features of the monster Marat,

while a groaning people were compelled to bow the knee before the image he had set up.

(Williams 1795: 2: 74-5)

The festival itself is presented as the antithesis of the Fédération which had thrilled her in 1790. Spontaneity is now reduced to obedience, nature to art, while the form of the concerted actions represents those aspects of 'sensibility' which reinforce the patriarchal authoritarian state:

> At this spot, by David's command, the mothers are to embrace their daughters – at that, the fathers are to clasp their sons – here, the old are to bless the young – and there, the young are to kneel to the old – upon this boulevard the people are to sing – upon that, they must dance.
>
> (1795: 2: 86-7)

The decoration of the city seemed to Williams another rape of nature as woods 'had been robbed of their shade, and gardens to an extent of some leagues rifled of their sweets' (1795: 2: 88).

By the time of her next publication she was willing to admit not only that genius can be divorced from the cause of liberty and morality, but that this is invariably the case. The just philosophical estimate of actions is contradicted by poets, who extol 'with frantic rapture those brilliant actions which shrink from the test of moral scrutiny' (Williams 1798: 2: 55). But while marking this conflict, she is praising Bonaparte as equally worthy of the poet's and the philosopher's plaudits. He is:

> the benefactor of his race converting the destructive lightning of the conqueror's sword into the benignant rays of freedom, and presenting to vanquished nations the emblems of liberty and independence entwined with the olive of peace.
>
> (1798: 2: 56)

Later she admitted her mistake in peculiarly revealing terms:

> When I found that he united to a noble simplicity of character, and a generous disdain of applause, a veneration of Ossian, this circumstance filled up the measure of my admiration. I did not know then that Buonaparte valued Ossian only for his description of battles.
>
> (Williams 1815: 1: 9)

The *Tour in Switzerland* (1798) is from one point of view her most satisfactory work. It has consistency of viewpoint and variety of subject, and gives an impressive analysis of the political framework of the cantons. But as a vehicle of sensibility it is limited by its adversarial stance. The landscape draws her whole-hearted response, but Swiss life and manners are heavily criticized. Her efforts are bent to the task of destroying the myths of Switzerland as the land of liberty and independence. Her purpose might be seen as anti-sentimental, as she tries to subvert the complacent versions of Goldsmith, Rousseau, and especially William Coxe, author of the standard guide to Switzerland, whose travels were published first in 1780, later expanded and revised in the light of a subsequent tour in 1786. Williams refers both to the second edition and to the translation of the first by Ramond de Carbonnières.

Williams's purpose could equally be seen as political. She hints of a possible intervention by the French in favour of the Pays de Vaud, and her long-time companion, John Hurford Stone, was travelling as a commissary of the French government. Williams might have been preparing the ground for the intervention of 1798 by publicizing the abuses which needed such intervention. Her declared allegiance, however, was to the original principles of the Revolution, an influence as much moral as political. She uses the common metaphors of sensibility, magnetism, lightning, and electrical discharges, to describe the spreading of this spirit, metaphors also used by Shelley in the *Defence of Poetry* to express the homologous inspiration of poetry and social idealism:

> The governments of Switzerland, placed within reach of the electrical fire of that Revolution, flashing around all of their borders, behold the subtle spark, which finds a conductor in the human heart, escaping beyond its prescribed limits, and feel its strong concussion in every agitated nerve.
>
> (Williams 1798: Preface)

When the French did intervene, she was horrified at their conduct, though she could denounce it as rivalling the rapaciousness of the former oligarchs and bailiffs, rather than seeing it as the destruction of some mythical state of liberty.

The invasion of Switzerland has been likened to the 1956

invasion of Hungary in its effect upon international opinion, and its 'subjugation' was singled out by Wordsworth as a crucial point of transition in public sympathies with the French in his pamphlet on the *Convention of Cintra*. Only after this, 'and not till then', he tells us, 'was the war with France regarded by the body of the people, as indeed both just and necessary' (*Prose*: 1: 226). Wordsworth may be slightly obscuring the chronology to include both the intervention of 1798 and later measures, culminating in Napoleon's imposition of a constitution in 1802. If we are to believe his letter to Losh of 1821, itself owing something to the phraseology of the Cintra pamphlet, it was not until Napoleon's treatment of Switzerland that Wordsworth finally abandoned hope in France. Significantly, the letter stresses the destruction of his trust in the virtue of the French people, as 'the Nation that could submit to being the Instrument of such an outrage' (*LY*: 97). The *Monthly Magazine*, in its half-yearly review of literature, treats the *Tour* at length, and considers that Williams's arguments serve 'not only to justify the invasion of Switzerland by France, but to shew that it was simply the honourable fulfilment of an old engagement in favour of the people'.[7] Wordsworth might well have shared this view, but France at that time was less the focus of his concern than the low morale of the Reform Movement in Britain and his own attempts to modify Godwinian doctrines which no longer satisfied him.

It was not only Wordsworth who found that the critical rational analysis of traditional moral sentiments distanced him from the emotional sources of his own ideals of humanity. In attacking the notion of Swiss liberty, Williams too was divesting the image of liberty of a basis in shared reality and making it a bare idea, a construction of the mind. Williams admits the adverse effect of the 1798 invasion on 'the liberal part of Europe', and tries to argue that the Directory were drawn into it by events in Berne. But the effect, she asserts, was exaggerated by the fact that

> though the original freedom of most of their political institutions had degenerated into coteries of family domination, and personal interest, an habitual reverence for Swiss government, fostered by the complaisance of travellers, prevailed in a greater or less degree throughout Europe.
> (Williams 1801: 1: 22)

Goldsmith's Traveller, to be fair, had given an austere account of the Swiss. He had stressed their equality and content, but it was an equality of hardship and a content of contracted wants. He had drawn attention to their ignorance and their lack of refinement in morals and manners. But the weight of his general attack on luxury, here and in *The Deserted Village*, emphasized a contrast between the healthy, primitive, sterner virtues, which could be compared with those of the ancient world, and the corruption of modern commercial societies. William Coxe was especially fond of drawing parallels between Switzerland, the ancient world, and Britain. The venerable appearance of the mountaineers reminds him of the old patriarchs, Glaris's victory of 1388 over the Austrians is compared with Marathon, Plataea, and the English 1688 Revolution; Lucerne's similar triumphs awaken memories of Greece, Rome, and the Armada. He relishes a freedom which he compares with that of Britain and he approves of the laws by which the cantons preserve a Spartan simplicity and virtue, such as the sumptuary laws, laws against excessive gambling, and the severe legal penalties for adultery. 'Happy people', he apostrophizes, 'the nature of whose country, and the constitution of whose government both equally oppose the strongest barriers against the baneful introduction of luxury' (Coxe 1780: 39).

Wordsworth had taken the French translation of Coxe's book on his own tour of Switzerland, and in *Descriptive Sketches* similar images occur. The wooden construction of the houses of both richer and poorer inhabitants imply a fundamental equality. Independence and contentment are united; there are images of the 'Spartan fife', the 'Marathonian Tale', and the Patriarchs. Wordsworth goes further in his primitivism than Coxe in finding 'traces of primaeval man', guarded by nature in the Alps: 'The native dignity no forms debase, / The eye sublime, and surly lion grace. / The slave of none, of beasts alone the lord' (*DS*: 90). It might seem odd that this poem, which celebrates the Revolution, shares sentimental images with a book that is politically opposed to French principles. Coxe is far enough from Wordsworth's political Rousseauism, but near enough to his Rousseauism of sentiment for ambiguities to arise. His book was published in an earlier period when attitudes towards the more radical expressions of sensibility had not hardened. Coxe frequently refers to Rousseau's account of Switzerland, and actually takes the *Nouvelle Héloïse* out of a local library when visiting Meilleries and Clarens to enthuse over the letters of Saint-Preux which work up the passions of love and despair 'almost to madness'. Coxe felt constrained to add a footnote reprobating the 'pernicious tendency of Rousseau's writing' (Coxe 1780: 265).

Generally Coxe's literary and political tastes are in a firmly conservative mould. In Gessner he finds an artist who affirms, in healthy contrast to Rousseau, those feelings which stem from traditional ties and seem to be of the nature of duties. His idylls

> abound with those nice touches of exquisite sensibility, which discover a mind warmed with the finest sentiments; and love is represented in the chastest colouring of innocence, virtue and benevolence. Nor has he confined his subjects merely to the tender passion: paternal affection, and filial reverence; gratitude, humanity, in short every moral duty is exhibited and inculcated in the most pleasing and affecting manner.
>
> (Coxe 1780: 85)

Coxe's pictures of Swiss happiness have the same appeal to traditional feelings. The interiors of Swiss cottages 'convey the liveliest image of cleanliness, ease and simplicity' and 'cannot but strongly impress upon the observer' the happiness of the inmates (1780: 60-1). An open-air meal with Michel Schuppach, the physician of the Alps, gives him an opportunity for a set-piece celebrating the virtues of domestic harmony, charity, gratitude, and simplicity of manners. Everything, he summed up, 'has the appearance of the pleasing simplicity of former ages' (1780: 380).

Williams's attack on Coxe, Goldsmith, and Rousseau is conducted almost solely in political terms. She argues on a level which cannot match the emotional appeal of her adversaries. She can offer competing accounts of the disaffection of the Pays de Vaud and the revolt of Geneva; she can stress the oppressive exploitation of their subject territories by the 'democratic' cantons, but the tone of her attack is rationalistic, indignant, and satiric. She can no longer appeal to images of reality which associate sensibility with radical ideas. The aspect of sensibility which is dominant is that passionate intuition of the truth of democratic ideals which still showed some signs of motivating universal reform, as 'the human mind, placed within the sphere of the French revolution, has bounded over the ruggedness of slow metaphysical researches, and reached at once, with an incredible effort, the highest possible attainments of political discovery' (Williams 1798: 2: 271). A few touches of personal reaction and experience enliven what is predominantly a political analysis. Near Vevey she notices a group of merrymakers singing the 'Marseillaise' 'with good humour and gaiety', and takes them for French visitors from across the lake. Later she discovers that they are natives and have subsequently been imprisoned. In the upper Valais, beside political abuses, she notices the diversion of a part of a waterfall to serve a mill, and exclaims against this 'sacrilegious attempt on the majesty of the cataract, never to be forgotten' (1798: 2: 184). Predominantly her sensibility is engaged in indignation at the bloody suppression of discontent in the various territories by their masters, usually aided by the power of Berne. This indignation is commonly levelled at the 'complaisant' sentimentalizing of former commentators. Of the Haute Valais she comments:

> I have often admired the charming picture which Rousseau traces of the inhabitants of those regions; but I confess that the knowledge of the hanging scene in the lower Vallais has very sensibly diminished my respect for the sovereigns of the mountain.
>
> (1798: 2: 187–8)

Another passage starkly contrasts sentimental associations with present realities:

> The soft image of the impassioned Julia no longer hovers around the castle of Chillon; which is now converted into a Swiss Bastile, and guarded by a stern soldiery. The tear of sensibility which has so often been shed over this spot for the woes of fiction, may now fall for sorrows that have the dull reality of existence. It is not the imaginary maternal shriek that pierces the air, it is the groan of the patriot rising from the floor of his damp dungeon that rends the heart.
>
> (1798: 2: 180)

There are few references to Greece and Rome, but many to images of feudal subordination. In an attempted contradiction of

Goldsmith, she indignantly exclaims against the constitution of Basle:

> What is remarkable enough in this celebrated land of freedom, where the poet tells us, that
>
> > 'Even the peasant boasts his rights to scan,
> > And learns to venerate himself as man',
>
> All the peasantry in the canton of Basil . . . are literally serfs and annexed to the soil.
>
> (Williams 1798: 1: 98-9)

The attack is rather blunted by the fact that Goldsmith applied the lines to England, but the concern for the peasantry is a genuine focus of her humanitarian politics, as it was for Wordsworth. When reckoning up the gains of the French Revolution, her primary example was the condition of landworkers. While she too responds to the 'patriarchal' life of the shepherds, she enjoys their hospitality as, for her, a delightful 'transition from the crimes of ferocious tyranny' (1798: 1: 345) rather than a healthy permanent state. She insists on their hardships and especially their lack of society, 'bereaved even of the most common enjoyments of social life'. The progress of intellectual and social life was important to Williams. Her salons in London and Paris had attempted to provide a focus for such improvement and she criticizes both the stultified peasant's life and the society of such places as Basle, where she discerns 'neither the love of arts, of literature, of liberty, or of any earthly good, but money' (1798: 1: 59).

In one manifestation of sensibility, however, Williams is very close to Wordsworth. Whatever the anti-sentimental attacks of the political part of the work, her response to the scenery is as fervid as ever, and contrasts with the more factual notations of Coxe. In Switzerland she experiences an ecstasy in which the very sensation of existence seems suspended, an experience very similar to Wordsworth's sublime mood when we seem laid asleep in body. At the Schaffhausen Falls, where Coxe had speculated about their formation and disputed their dimensions, Williams experiences moments 'when with a sort of annihilation of self, with every past impression erased from my memory, I felt as if my heart were bursting with emotions too strong to be sustained'

(Williams 1798: 1: 60). A more tranquil sensation is evoked by the glaciers:

> Meditation assumes, in those regions, something of a character great, and sublime, proportional to the objects which strike us; something of tranquil rapture, remote from all that is selfish, or sensual . . . the soul contracts something of their unchangable purity . . . we forget ourselves, and have scarce a consciousness of existence.
>
> (1798: 2: 7–8)

This sense of a spirit immanent within Nature is again reminiscent of Wordsworth, and the fact that it is adapted from Rousseau emphasizes the continuities of sensibility.

In her translation of Ramond de Carbonnière's *Observations on the Glacières and Glaciers,* which she appended to her *Tour,* one can sense that elevation of the imagination which implicitly rejects the limitations of reality and asserts the transcendent powers within man. In contemplating the immense size and age of the glaciers, reason fails and 'the soul, taking that flight which makes it contemporary with every age, and co-existent with all beings, hovers over the abyss of time'. Williams uses the 'what if . . .' construction with which Shelley typically affirmed that spirit within man at enmity with material death and decay, as the passage moves from the Rousseauistic description of the wanderings of the imagination in a land of chimeras, to its apotheosis as the source of all our religious and moral conceptions:

> Imagination seizes the reins which Reason drops, and in that long succession of periods, catches a glimpse of the image of eternity, which she hails with religious terror. How has every thing vanished, which occupies, enchants, and astonishes us here below, when we compare it with the objects of glory that are set before us! Thus our most extended ideas, and our most elevated and noble sentiments have their origin in the wanderings of the imagination; but let us forgive its chimeras, for what would there be great in our conceptions, or glorious in our actions, if finite was not, through its illusions, continually changed into infinite, space into immensity, time into eternity, and fading laurels into immortal crowns.
>
> (Williams 1798: 2: 351)

HELEN MARIA WILLIAMS

Helen Maria Williams is a good example of radical sensibility under stress, since she preserved her allegiance to the principles of the Revolution and perpetually looked for their implementation in society. At every check given by the shifting policies of the French she sought to explain or optimistically justify the course of events. Yet in her writings of the 1790s the techniques of radical sensibility, the appeal to images that include both an emotional and a radical content, seem progressively less effective as their basis in an optimistic conception of man's potentialities is eroded. She follows a trajectory common to many radical writers, from a relatively unthinking trust in the progressive reformation of society to a recognition that such hopes cannot rely merely on collective humanitarian feelings. In her writings, radical sensibility becomes a combative, critical force, using the methods of reason as well as the emotions to attack the traditional images revered by conservative sensibility. Though both radical and conservative sensibility stem from a line of thought which regards the 'social' feelings as paramount, the critical spirit of radical sensibility progressively found fewer and fewer examples of social reality which could legitimately represent these feelings. The most common feelings expressed by writers of this kind are indignation and pity – a pity which conservatives continually criticized as misplaced. Helen Maria Williams maintained a certain optimism in the course of history, but of greater value was her faith in the imagination as a source of ideals and a solace for the disappointments of reality. To some extent she follows the movements of Wordsworth and Coleridge from an idea of freedom realized in society to an idea of the individual freedom of the imagination in its relationship with nature, but, like Shelley, she put her faith in the 'subtle spark' and communicated lightning of the mind as a revolutionary agency. Wordsworth asserted that in his moods of sublime self-forgetfulness he could 'see into the life of things', just as he seemed to see into the living truth of idiots, inarticulate peasants, and beggars. The more sceptical Williams, like Shelley, can only assert the inner ideals of the imagination, not a perceived higher reality.

6
CHARLOTTE SMITH AS RADICAL NOVELIST

Charlotte Smith has usually been assigned to a peripheral position in the radical groupings of the 1790s. She has been seen as a sentimental novelist, a contributor to the Gothic mode, and a forerunner of Jane Austen.[1] As a professional novelist whose large family depended on her success, she was well aware of the restrictions imposed by her audience and – largely the same thing – the conventions of her medium. Throughout her novels she refers to such difficulties as drawing a heroine who might be at once interesting and beyond moral criticism, or how to describe affectionate scenes in ways which might avoid the usual reproaches. Charlotte Smith developed amidst a more liberal interpretation of sensibility, one nourished by Prévost (whose *Manon Lescaut* she translated), Rousseau, and Goethe. She became part of the London literary world at the time of the French Revolution, meeting most of the leading radicals at the salon of her friend Helen Maria Williams and, like many liberal and radical literati, she visited France before the publication of *Desmond* (1792). Her work, like that of Mary Wollstonecraft and Helen Williams, argues for greater equality in society, for the right of private judgment, and affirms the capacity of the individual to act from motives of an extensive benevolence, rejecting the narrow and customary objects of concern in pursuit of what Godwin defined as 'political justice'.

Smith uses her characters of sensibility to criticize the vices of the aristocracy, the mercenary values of middle-class trade, the iniquities of the legal system, and the inhumanity and irresponsibility of the military profession. She is not one of those writers whose championing of sensibility is part of the middle-class moral assault on aristocratic licence, since the middle class and their notions of respectability are one of her prime targets. She has a heterodox attitude towards female purity comparable to Bage, and is generally more lenient towards excessive sensibility than writers of the Burney mould. The democratic premise of radical sensibility is sustained throughout her work by reference to America as the land of equality, and she takes issue with writers who would restrict the privileges of sensibility to those who have money and leisure to cultivate its effete caricature. If one looks for a political programme in her writing, one finds only the most rudimentary radicalism, much of it based on liberal attitudes common to other writers of the period. It is her use of sensibility that aligns her with a more radical discourse, especially after radical sensibility had linked its own positive values with the ideals of the French Revolution. Smith focuses on issues which are crucial to the debate between the conservative and radical proponents of sensibility. In *Desmond, The Old Manor House, The Banished Man*, and *The Young Philosopher* she extends the techniques which had previously allowed her to emphasize the potentially subversive aspects of sensibility, while apparently adhering to a conventional pattern. The events of the 1790s also lead her, like most radicals, to re-examine the values of benevolence, individualism, and egalitarianism as they are called into question by historical events. Most prominently, she is forced to re-examine her egalitarian commitment and to distinguish the prejudices of the lower classes, as well as those of the higher, from the 'natural' enlightened view. Education can be seen as assuming greater importance throughout her work as these prejudices present a more formidable obstacle to enlightenment, and education comes to include the development of the reason and the study of history, as well as the romances and lessons of experience which usually constitute the sentimental education. From the intuitive virtuous responses of Emmeline she progresses to the rather tentative commitment to reason of D'Alonville and Marchmont until her last novel, written when she was cultivating Godwin, espouses the virtues of philosophy in both its intellectual and its popular senses.

From the outset, her attitude to the sentimental tradition was critical and her use of its conventions tricksy. Her most effective devices are those which might elude the critical awareness of her day. Irony is allowed to flicker around her major protagonists, and parallel situations within the novels reinforce radical themes or develop ideological tensions. Allusions to the political situations of America, France, and England, more usual in the polemical prose works of the time, suggest a radical message sometimes overtly enforced in footnotes. Aware of conventional expectations, she delights to contradict them, whether those expectations are of literary or social origin. While her characters frequently show a sensibility more akin to the passions of Werther, Julie, and Saint-Preux, so reprobated by conservative critics, these passions are shown to have a natural and noble restraint in situations which are viewed as shocking by other characters – and readers – dominated by a Burneyesque concern for propriety. The conflict between the 'partial passions' towards kindred and close connections and an active universal benevolence is implicit in her early work, but becomes more consciously stressed after Godwin had polemically highlighted the dispute, and the French War and British reaction had inhibited the direct expression of political views. Significantly, it is her supposed recantation of radical views, *The Banished Man* (1794), that most fully explores this conflict, and it remains a prominent issue in her work. Her last novel, *The Young Philosopher* (1798), presents a hero who has to be gradually weaned from an unjustified restricted fraternal loyalty to find a more satisfying exercise of universal benevolence in America.

The sophistication of her literary technique and her use of the coded language of sensibility cloaked her radical commitment and posed problems for conservative critics. Robert Bissett, one of the most violent of the anti-Jacobin writers, introduces her as a character in his *Modern Literature* (1804) under the name of Mrs Somerive (paying a tribute to the hero of *The Old Manor House*), and presents an appreciative discussion of *Emmeline*. The work contains scabrous caricatures of Godwin and Mary Wollstonecraft, and among their acolytes is numbered a 'Mrs Sonnet' whose novels 'have proposed to decry existing institutions, exalt the philosophers of France, and to debase what is called female virtue, by an attempt to show that it depends on accident and not principle' (Bissett 1804: 3: 213). This too seems to refer to Smith, and testifies to the mixed response of even a hardened conservative. In Charlotte Smith's novels the didactic technique of sensibility, seeking to educate by an identification with the feelings of the central characters, is often displaced by irony and parody, modes usually associated with an élitist art. She calculated on a popular audience but, like Godwin, also hoped that she might find a substantial readership among those still attached to radical attitudes in an age of officially enforced conservative standards.

In the heroine of *Desmond*, Geraldine Verney, Smith created one of the most extreme examples of the oppressed wife, who nevertheless seems to glory in her martyrdom, fulfilling the traditional Griselda role. Her husband neglects her, beggars her, and tries to prostitute her to his creditors. Even though he gives her *carte blanche* to do whatever she likes with herself and the children as long as she does not bother him for money, she still obeys his order to embark for France amidst the turmoil ensuing on the king's flight to Varennes. There she has the prospect of being 'sold' to the debauched ultra-royalist Duc De Romagnecourt. Her dedication to female propriety is so strong that, even when she is rescued by Desmond from the French civil conflict in which her husband dies, she has qualms about being escorted to safety by him alone. Such an example of devotion to conventional pieties might be thought a gift to the conservative camp, yet Geraldine is a Trojan horse. The dutiful woman, suffering the injustices of society, yet upheld by a conscious devotion to duty, was one of the most hackneyed, if revered, figures of the eighteenth-century novel, but at this stage in history, with the emergence of a more radical and feminist consciousness among readers, an author's use of this archetype was bound to be problematical. Smith could not offend the susceptibilities of her readers by making her heroine act as she herself had done in real life by separating from her husband, but she emphasizes the untenable rigour of the convention by presenting Geraldine's behaviour in exaggerated, even parodic, terms. Smith was well aware of a divided readership and perpetually played on ambiguities of response.

From the elevation of her position of martyr, Geraldine is used by Smith to give the most powerful critique of the enslavement under which she bows. When leaving for France, she comments 'after what I know and what I *suspect* of Mr Verney, I had rather meet death than be in his power'. But death has no terrors for her, nor is such danger to be feared from the French, 'those people, whose ferocity arises not from their present liberty, but their recent bondage'. ' Is it possible', she asks, 'to suppose that they will injure me, who am myself a miserable slave, returning with trembling and reluctant steps, to put on the most dreadful of all fetters? – Fetters that would even destroy the freedom of my mind' (Smith 1792: 3: 71). The parallel between her situation and that of the French people under the *ancien régime* has been noted by Diana Bowstead as one of Smith's typical thematic devices to enforce ideological tensions.[2] Smith also uses Geraldine to make an extreme radical affirmation when she asserts that the deaths of those who opposed the revolution were sanctioned by 'the tremendous decree of justice' (1792: 3: 130). The independence of Geraldine's mind is in direct contrast to the subservience of her actions, and she can give the clearest condemnation of the repressive nature of her education and bemoan with the young Fanny Waverley the intense supervision of a conventional girl's education. '*We* were always brought up as if we were designed for wives to the Vicar of Bray', she comments to Fanny (1792: 3: 133). She endorses Fanny's impatience with the restraint of her reading, asserting that it is salutary to read those works 'which represent human life nearly as it is', with all its vice and weakness (1792: 2: 166). Despite her copybook propriety, Geraldine, like Emmeline, co-operates in the lying-in of a 'fallen woman', in this case one who owes her condition to the man Geraldine later marries. Unlike the heroine of *Sydney Biddulph*, to which she refers in another context, she is not mistakenly and tragically alienated from her lover by his impulsive physical liaison. The revelation of Geraldine's complicity in this affair is carefully relegated to the last section of the novel.

As a character of sensibility, Desmond has clear links with Rousseau's Saint-Preux, especially in his 'innocent' devotion to a married woman; he even pens despairing letters from the Pays de Vaud. But his sensibility is also the source of his radicalism. This is based on sympathy for the poor and enslaved under the feudal system of France, and it has a basis in personal experience, as well as in a reading of pre-Revolutionary authors. Charlotte Smith herself in her Preface vouches for the fact that the political discussions of the novel are taken from experience: 'conversations to which I have been a witness in England, and in France, during the last twelve months'. The link between the American and French revolutions is made not only by ideological continuities but in the experience of Desmond's friend Montfleuri, who, like Montignac in Smith's *Celestina* (1791) and real figures like

Lafayette, had a hand in both revolutions: '[T]he men who were sent out to assist in the preservation of American freedom, would soon learn that they were degraded by being themselves slaves; and would return to their native country to feel and to assert their right to be themselves free' (Smith 1792: 1: 152-3). Desmond's concern is with happiness, not merely with reason and right. Just as Wordsworth sympathizes with the abject peasant girl in *The Prelude*, so Desmond's sympathies are with the oppressed, and his and the author's comments link the plight of the French peasants with that of the British lower classes. Desmond responds to a Breton peasant's first-hand account of feudal oppression, and Smith inserts a long note on the similar distresses of the London poor, commenting: 'Yet we are always affecting to talk of the misery and beggary of the French – And now impute that misery, though we well know it existed before, to the revolution. – To the very cause that will in a very few years remove it' (1792: 1: 177). When discussing the British Constitution, Desmond 'cannot pronounce it to be without imperfections, where I observe such dreadful contrasts in the condition of the people under it' (1792: 2: 124). Quoting *King Lear* on superfluity, he glances at the ideal of the benevolent landowner, revered alike by conservative and liberal writers: 'Were there, indeed, a sure appeal to the mercies of the rich, the calamities of the poor might be less intolerable' (1792: 2: 127). But, as Smith often pointed out, echoing Fielding's Booth, the artificial conditions of the rich contract their sensibility: 'How few do we meet with who can feel for miseries they cannot imagine, and are sure they can never experience?' (1792: 2: 127-8). In *Desmond* Montfleuri is exceptional in resisting the corruption of 'a system from the influence of which it was hardly possible for young men of property and title to escape' (1792: 1: 107). In conversation Desmond itemizes abuses in Britain that need reform: the inequality of representation, the penal laws, the laws defending property, the procedures of the courts of Equity and Chancery, and he would perhaps have added more if he had not been silenced by the acclamation which greeted the rejoinder that 'truth is not expedient' (1792: 2: 136). Charlotte Smith later referred back to this passage as expressing her view of the superiority of the British Constitution, but Desmond's is a decidedly qualified admiration.

Another criticism of Britain involves the status of the aristocracy. Desmond rejoices in the abolition of hereditary titles and the abolition of the 'gothic' feudal system in France, but, while affirming that the English aristocracy is not as oppressive as the French, he goes on to point out that the French never possessed a 'right of hereditary legislation, a strong, and to many, an obnoxious feature' (Smith 1792: 1: 69). The democratic egalitarianism of radical sensibility was mostly directed against the established inequalities of property and power which privileged the aristocracy, and most radicals did not see a substantial difference between the French and English aristocracies. The *nouveaux riches* of the commercial classes, including those enriched by East and West Indian trade and those administering the expanding financial and legal system which managed such wealth, were often allied to the aristocracy, especially in novels. As wealth endowed them with the same power over the happiness of the poor, they were subjected to the same criticism as the old aristocracy by those writers like Smith whose radicalism had its roots in sensibility. Other radicals like Paine championed the growing manufacturing and trading enterprises, largely the product of Dissenting industry, and argued for their fair representation in the prevailing power-structure. They directed their criticism almost exclusively at monarchical and aristocratic privilege. Smith has been criticized for directing her animosity against the league of financial and legal oppressors who figured so prominently in her personal misfortunes, but this criticism is similar to that of Godwin and Holcroft, and later that of Cobbett and Shelley, in being directed at the real interests that manipulate political power.

Desmond is the most outspoken of her novels in political terms, though still wary of a conservative audience. The epistolary form allows a representation of competing views, and the novel carries such a weight of reported conversation that it has similarities with Bage's novels of debate. The author's point of view, however, is not in doubt. The cautious Bethel, whom the reader identifies as the voice of moderation, is initially incredulous about both Geraldine's worthiness as Desmond's ideal and about the soundness of French principles. He is won over to Geraldine by a personal meeting which leaves him only marginally less fervid than Desmond, while his comments on the French become more appreciative of their virtue and justice, though he dreads the effect that foreign military pressure might have on their inexperienced and divided leadership. The epistolary form also enables Smith to juxtapose letters on different but subtly related subjects. Thus we pass from Desmond's strictures on the British Constitution to Fanny Waverley's complaints against the government of her reading and education, and from Desmond's affirmation of the right to dissolve a former contract of government to Geraldine's resolution to adhere to her contract of marriage. In Smith's later novels the heroes are less radical, more easily assimilable to the conventional type, and the multiple viewpoints and parallel situations are more artfully fashioned to produce ironic effects.

The Old Manor House (1793) was apparently produced in circumstances of greater serenity than many of her other works at a time when she enjoyed the friendship of William Hayley. In its early sections it shows Smith fully in control of her technique of indirect radical comment on seemingly conventional situations. The manor house functions as a picture of unreformed Britain. It is dominated by the figure of Mrs Rayland, in sympathy a Jacobite of the sort who were given fresh heart by Burke's defence of the monarchy and assertion of a minimal commitment to change in the settlement of 1689.[3] While it is set in the era of the American War, its parallels extend backwards to the English Revolution, as Mrs Rayland and the ecclesiastic Doctor Hollybourn, united in revering 'that cause for which Laud and his sacred master died' (Smith 1969: 169), view the Americans as descendants of the regicides, and forward to the French Revolution, as Smith sets the atrocities of the British campaign to subdue the Americans against the violence of the French in defence of their liberty. Another strong political parallel is the comparison between the Rayland household and the government of Britain. Mrs Lennard, Mrs Rayland's companion, runs the domestic establishment like a prime minister, managing the various cabals among the principal officers of the household. She keeps secret files on their nefarious activities and takes a cut of the profits of a smuggling enterprise run by the butler. This Fieldingesque parallel is extended by reference to the growing dominance of legal and financial interests. The Woodfords, a bourgeois commercial branch of the Rayland family, rise from humble beginnings in the wine trade to intimacy with the noble and powerful of the land. Mr Woodford eventually sells a parliamentary seat to become involved in the more lucrative cabals managing government contracts and finance. The passing of the old order is signalled by the passing of estates to the *nouveaux riches*, and lawyers and financial agents also infiltrate the management of the Rayland establishment. The imprisonment of Monimia under the auspices of the old regime of the Manor House is followed by the imprisonment of Mrs Lennard at the hands of her husband Roker, the rising young attorney.

Orlando Somerive is a hero whose conventional perfections are shaded by several equivocations and improprieties. The younger son of the despised branch of the Rayland family, he gains a hold on Mrs Rayland's affections in the same way that Waverley enters Waverley-Honour, but his sympathy with Mrs Rayland's prejudices is equivocal. He is perhaps too sophisticated in dutifully conforming to her ideas in public, while talking the language of reason and equality to the heroine, Monimia. He engages in clandestine night meetings with his beloved – for the purpose of educating her. His feelings for his father do not deter him from preventing his sister's favoured match with General Tracy by conniving at her elopement with Tracy's nephew, Warwick. Monimia herself persists in their nightly encounters, though she has that intuitive sensibility that recognizes their impropriety. An episode of bedroom farce points to the latent danger of such meetings in a typical parallel situation, when Orlando's brother and a flirtatious maid are rivals for the occupation of Orlando's chamber – and for no educational purpose.

The theme of education carries the most overt radical force in the book. Like many radicals, Smith insists on the connection of the American and French revolutions, in contrast with Burke, whose attack on the French resolutely ignores the fact that a commonwealth had been set up, as he asserted it could not be, on the grounds of reason, not the accumulated experience of generations. Orlando's education of Monimia is an assault on the prejudices that sustain the Rayland empire and monarchical government, full of condemnation of that usurped authority which cannot meet the eye of reason and has to defend itself by imposition, illusion, and coercion. His efforts to free Monimia from her dutiful submission to her aunt, the tyrannical Lennard, is conducted on lines similar to Paine's exhortations to the Americans to cut the leading strings which bound them to Britain and to learn an independent self-respect. Far from encouraging the Gothic mode, Smith links its superstitions with those of ancient despotism and refutes its terrors in one of

Orlando's pointedly political sallies: Monimia questions whether ghosts do not rise to avenge their murder and Orlando comments: 'Yes, Monimia, to the conscience of the guilty; but even that is not always ready to raise hideous shadows to persecute the sanguinary monsters who are stained with crimes; for if it were, Monimia, I am afraid not one of our kings or heroes could have slept in their beds' (Smith 1969: 49). The radical rhetoric is usually Painite, appropriate to the period, and directed at kingly power, though the reality of power in the Rayland household and in the state lies with politicians and commercial interests. In fact Mrs Rayland is progressively viewed more sympathetically as a victim of those around her, clinging to the more generous chivalric sentiments of public service as she finances Orlando's departure for the war, and later perhaps regretting her encouragement when he is feared dead. Smith comments, 'It seemed as if towards the close of her life, Mrs Rayland had acquired, instead of losing, her sensibility' (1969: 250).

Up to a point Smith manages fairly well in presenting her hero's equivocal appearance of loyalty to both the prejudices of Mrs Rayland and the ideals of sensibility. In one episode Orlando is reluctantly prepared to fight a duel, ostensibly in defence of Mrs Rayland's game, but really in response to an amorous assault on Monimia. His rejection of a position in the wine trade suits both his idealistic objections to commercialism and Mrs Rayland's aristocratic disdain of such low occupations. Orlando's entry into the ranks of the enemies of America and freedom, however, is a contradiction of the libertarian arguments which he has been rehearsing with Monimia. But arguments and ideas are no match for personal experience, and Smith presents him as one who had not thought deeply about such matters and is willing to accept the opinions of society and follow his father's profession. The military career had commanded respect in Smith's previous novels, and Orlando, while not sharing the chivalric enthusiasm of Mrs Rayland, has a general conviction of its honour. His education in the horrors of the war and its injustice quickly disabuses him. If Scott owed the title of *Waverley* to *Desmond*, surely much of the situation is derived from this novel, despite its Jacobinical tendencies. The descriptions of war perhaps reflect radical anti-war propaganda, but Smith is equally assiduous to link it with other themes of radical sensibility, as when she compares the conditions on the troop ships with those of slave transports. In General Tracy she glances at the military reputation for gambling which had featured in *Ethelinde* (1789). Although Monimia's eventual rescuer, Flemming, is a sailor, Smith emphasizes that he 'had not . . . been so long at sea as to acquire that steadiness of mind which enables men of that profession to look on all personal danger with indifference, and moral evil as a matter of course' (Smith 1969: 487). A disabled veteran plays a crucial role in Orlando's final unmasking of Roker, and he is introduced with a reference to Goldsmith's Old Soldier from 'The Deserted Village', but with the rider that his mutilation was suffered 'in the service of what is called his country, that is, in fighting the battles of its politicians' (1969: 461). From this publication onwards, the military career that so distinguished Godolphin and Lord Westhaven in *Emmeline* is no longer a satisfactory profession for Smith's heroes of sensibility.

The Banished Man (1794) marks an advance in ironic technique and a toning down of the radical criticism which had characterized the authorial voice. As in *Desmond*, political issues are debated by a variety of characters and although her secondary hero, Ellesmere, seems to present her own views, he is not allowed to dominate or conclude a debate. Her main hero, D'Alonville, unlike Orlando Somerive, is thoroughly impregnated with the aristocratic pride of his father. Though he has the capacity of the hero of sensibility to learn more enlightened lessons from experience, for the major part of the novel he is bound by these prejudices, while Smith endeavours to place his reactions to events in a critical radical perspective. It is probably the most complex of her novels in attempt, though not completely successful in execution. This complexity is due to her efforts to come to terms with the French betrayal of the ideals of the Revolution in the tyranny of Robespierre, and also to her efforts to circumvent the inquisitorial forces of reaction in Britain. In making her hero a French aristocratic émigré and following his attempt to join a royalist uprising in Brittany, she chose a centre of consciousness inimical to radical views. D'Alonville is even impatient of that close study of the progress of the Revolution which a less committed personality would be likely to make. For this reason the novel has been seen as her recantation of radicalism. In fact the novel could be seen as more radical than *The Old Manor House* in that it uses the contemporary French situation to reflect criticism of British conditions. The obviously autobiographical nature of the distress of Mrs Denzil (the Bodleian copy calls her Charlotte as well as Harriet) has for most readers, it seems, obscured the major structural parallel between her family, reduced to an insecure wandering life by Lord Aberdare's legal frustration of her just claims, and the situation of émigrés like D'Alonville, banished from their rightful place by those who have subverted the liberty promised by the Revolution. 'Alas! Sir,' expostulates Mrs Denzil, 'my children and I have also been wanderers and exiles. I know not whether we may not still be called so; for the victims of injustice, oppression, and fraud, we are now banished from the rank of life where fortune originally placed us' (Smith 1794: 2: 206). Another lachrymose passage claims that 'in every species of humiliation and mortification, none of the unhappy exiled French have suffered, perhaps, more than I have done' (1794: 3: 181).

In this novel, Smith exploits the conflict between private and universal benevolence in a way which shows her consciousness of its radical significance. Her hero is devoted to the memory of his father and loyal to the king. He condemns his brother, who resisted parental authority to join the Revolutionaries. Yet we continually meet examples of the pernicious effects of restricted affection among the enemies of French ideas. After escorting Mme D'Alberg from her threatened French castle to her husband in Coblentz, D'Alonville is astonished at the coldness of the latter. Mme D'Alberg explains that the Baron, his life spent between court and camp, has 'very little sensibility' (Smith 1794: 1: 191). To be sure, he is 'passionately attached to his daughter and her children' but he has no compassion for other sufferers, even those before his eyes. It is, she admits, 'an apparent hardness of heart; this tendency towards selfishness, and self-consequence, blemishes for which hardly any virtues can make amends' (1794: 2: 192). In England the Ellesmere establishment is a counterpart to that in *The Old Manor House* in its stagnation in an outmoded family pride that upholds the 'infallibility of powers and princes' (1794: 2: 98). This prejudice, as in the case of Orlando, raises difficulties for the marriage-choices of the children and also gives Ellesmere's elder brother the enhanced status of one born to primogeniture. Another aristocratic family, the exiled Touranges, show a similar restriction of sympathy. The height of their ambition is the prospect of 'seeing the house of De Touranges restored to its original splendor, and trampling in the dust the party to whom it owed its being eclipsed' (1794: 2: 195). The devaluing of family affection was held to be a fault of the radicals, but in these inward-looking aristocratic families we can see what the radicals were reacting against. If radicals did attack such 'partial affections', it was in the cause of a wider benevolence, whereas Ellesmere's brother shows us a contempt of such affections born of mere selfishness. A political manoeuvrer in the government of the day, he warns Edward against the 'boyish ebullitions' of friendship and advises him that for superior men 'all these attachments, nay, even what are called the ties of blood, are dissolved immediately on any political exigency' (1794: 3: 16), and that as a soldier he will learn to 'rejoice at the death of [his] brother officers' (1794: 2: 18).

The episode which best shows the irony with which Smith treats D'Alonville is that in which he sets out to join the émigré resistance group. As he reacts to democratic 'excesses', so the reader is reminded of former aristocratic oppression. On his journey through the countryside, D'Alonville is principally appalled by the depredation of the game which had been formerly appropriated to the pleasures of the great. Smith makes the comparison with Britain's forest laws, 'which, though not enforced, remain as records of our subjection; and from whence have sprung the subsequent game laws, the continual source of oppression and dispute' (Smith 1794: 3: 109). At the rendezvous he has to rescue a retainer from an oubliette into which the peasants had thrown him 'for a day or two' so that he might experience the 'places, where [his] ci-devant lord had it in his power to condemn to death any one who offended him' (1794: 3: 134). D'Alonville's family pride is grotesquely displayed in his reactions to those who hold power under the new government: 'the blood of a long line of illustrious ancestors, whom he had been taught to number till they were lost in the remote royalty of Merovingian kings, rose indignantly, and tempted him to spurn, rather than conciliate citizen Coreau the white-smith' (1794: 2: 95-6). When arrested, his brother happens to be one of the commissioners in charge of his case, and D'Alonville denounces in fulsomely anti-Jacobinical terms the 'cant of party, that Roman disregard of the ties of nature . . . the infamous maxims that tend to break the ties of blood and friendship' (1794: 2: 164-

5). In fact his brother treats him with quite fraternal benevolence, spiriting him away from execution and setting him down in Paris with a certificate of civism as a law student. In the early part of the novel the brother is referred to as Du Fosse, which would bring to many minds the story of the Du Fossé family related by Helen Maria Williams. In her account the elder son is a sympathetic victim of parental oppression under the old regime and participated in the liberal reforms of the first stages of the Revolution. Smith's Du Fosse, or Du Bosse as he is later called, tries to interest D'Alonville in the course which the Revolution is taking, but D'Alonville confounds all Revolutionary parties in an undiscriminating condemnation, refusing 'to have any connection with the men under whatever appellation, whether Girondists or Mountaineers, Modérés or Enragés, who called themselves legislators of France' (1794: 2: 221). It transpires that his brother is far from being a 'sans-culotte' and sufficiently foresees the disastrous course of events to employ D'Alonville to secure his property abroad. He is denounced and executed soon after D'Alonville has escaped.

This episode clearly invites a reading which conflicts with D'Alonville's impatient prejudices, and it is during this episode that Smith intervenes most prominently and clumsily to offer different perspectives on the course of the Revolution. D'Alonville's meditation is that of the embittered aristocrat:

> these are the boasted blessings of that liberty for which they have been four years contending – infatuated, misled people! The taille, the gabelle, the corvés, even the feudal services, however heavily imposed, what were they when compared to the oppressions under which you now labour! If ye had burthens under the government of an arbitrary monarch, ye danced gaily under them.
>
> (Smith 1794: 2: 92)

Smith contrasts this with the view of 'an Englishman', and it is the view which is persistently upheld by the co-hero Ellesmere:

> an Englishman might have thought the experiment right; and that the attempt to shake off such burthens . . . was a glorious attempt, and failed only because [of] the headlong vehemence of the French national character, and the impossibility of finding (in a very corrupt nation, and

among people never educated in notions of real patriotism) a sufficient weight of abilities and integrity to guide the vessel in the revolutionary tempest.

(1794: 2: 93)

Smith also offers us the probable opinion of 'a coarser Briton, a plain John Bull, [who] would say "Those French fellows have not sense enough to be as free as we are." ' Both Britons would unite in opposing any effort to reform Britain if the same violence were to be the consequence.

All radicals, and especially those who clung to benevolist ideas, had to come to terms with the apparent unleashing of human evil during the reign of Robespierre and to explain why an enlightened democracy might be possible in America, yet not in France. Smith, like Williams, Godwin, and Wordsworth, links the excesses of the new order with the corruption of the old regime. Her analogue of Robespierre, Heurthofen, is given a psychology of immense, frustrated ambition, perverted into power-lust and revenge by the constrictions of the old regime. She even makes him an abbé to link him more firmly with the corruptions of old Catholic France. To the brutalization of the lower ranks she would oppose the force of education, but an education which expanded rather than constricted their sympathies. Her footnote to the words 'real patriotism' in the passage quoted above shows that she did not follow Burke in ideas of unquestioning allegiance but, like Price, associated patriotism with ideas of universal progress and liberty: 'They had never been taught what was really liberty'.

Attacks on a restricted sensibility are prominent in *The Banished Man,* not only on the restricted sympathy of family feeling but also on the customary narrow loyalties to rank, country, and politics. In Britain D'Alonville meets the hostility of national and political prejudice, and Smith analyses it in terms of class and education. While the middle and higher classes contribute to the support of the emigrants, the uneducated lower classes combine their national prejudice with what they have been told of French atrocities and involve 'every one of that nation in universal condemnation' (Smith 1794: 2: 88). D'Alonville himself lacks sympathy for 'a person who has lately emigrated; for such he had learned to consider as persons who had been too much connected with the men and measures of the first revolution' (1794: 2: 185). The outspoken Mrs Denzil is ostracized as fair-weather friends drop off and even well-wishers demonstrate 'that estrangement which policy imposes on the sage and the prudent' (1794: 2: 233). Smith is here commenting on the mood of Britain in 1794 which affected herself and many others, including D'Arblay. In her poem *The Emigrants* (1793) Smith attempted to enlist sympathy for the bigoted French nobility and priesthood even while using them to remind 'hireling' British statesmen of the fate of oppressors.

The internationalism of Smith's sympathies is seen in the introduction of the figure of Carlowitz, the Polish freedom fighter, whose daughter marries Ellesmere. Carlowitz is a thinly disguised portrait of Kosciusko, one of Helen Maria Williams's heroes, who visited France in the vain hope of engaging Robespierre in the cause of Polish liberty. The disgust of Carlowicz with the French leadership and the marriage of his daughter to an Englishman who has consistently supported the initial stages of the Revolution possibly carries the hope that, while France no longer carries the torch of freedom, Britain might provide an asylum for those whose extensive views of liberty are not bounded by national prejudice. Smith's picture of Britain does not, however, encourage sanguine expectations. D'Alonville himself is in the jeopardy of British justice at one point. Installed as tutor in the household of Lord Aberdare, he wounds a guest in self-defence after the latter has insulted his wife. Secure in his naive trust in British law, he dreads no evil consequence: 'Am I not in England? . . . Is not my life guarded by its laws, if I only acted, as it will be found I have, in my own defence?' (Smith 1794: 4: 298). Mrs Denzil can only lament both his danger and his resort to violence, which she associates with his aristocratic prejudices. Her own situation has shown that there is no security in a legal system which can be manipulated by the rich and powerful.

The education of D'Alonville is far less radical than that of Orlando Somerive. At the end of the novel he is left regretting his prejudices and feeling the need of a mentor like Ellesmere to sustain his philosophy, since it is not based on 'reason and reflection':

> I fear that from disposition and education, I am as volatile, as inconsiderate, as impetuous, as the generality of young

men of my rank and country, who, born in the lap of
prosperity, were educated only to appear in those scenes of
life, where solidity of character would have impeded rather
than assisted their progress towards those objects to which
the ambition of the French nobility was directed.
(Smith 1794: 4: 339)

Only 'adversity', that schooler of sensibility, has taught him to
'conquer prejudice, and to feel for the sufferings of others' (1794:
4: 340). He has been sympathetic and benevolent throughout the
book, yet blinkered by aristocratic prejudices. Mrs Denzil pays
him the back-handed compliment that he 'has proper pride
enough to counteract every degree of false pride' (1794: 4: 311) – a
similar remark is made of D'Arcy in *Pride and Prejudice*. Smith
has provided the material which might have educated him, and a
multiplicity of viewpoints which suggest his deficiencies, but
this complex patterning seems to be for the benefit not of the
character himself, but of the discerning reader, and perhaps
designed to hoodwink the undiscerning reader. The faults of the
book are largely those of indirection and a justifiable caution in
not making the radical patterns clearer. D'Alonville, not fully
reacting to his educative experiences, becomes a static character,
and the irony of his presentation is only occasionally obvious.
Mrs Denzil's plight is not immediately or clearly enough linked
to British injustice. But the muffling of these more overtly radical
aspects of the work throws into relief the radical treatment of
sensibility in her commitment to the universal benevolence or
extended sympathies of the radicals and her opposition to the
narrow, habitual loyalties which were supposed by conservatives
to cement the fabric of society.

Smith's next novel, *Marchmont* (1796), also deals with the
French Terror, but is rather incoherent and perfunctory in its
patterning, a fault which may be ascribed to the fact that she was
in poor health and grieving for the death of her favourite
daughter. Smith had obviously been reading accounts of experiences under Robespierre, including those of her friend Helen
Maria Williams, and such experiences are shown as educative to
the main character. Marchmont has prejudices associated with
his cavalier ancestry, though it is one of the faults of the book
that we never see them motivating any reprehensible action
except his challenge to his oppressor Mohun, which lands him in

jail. In France he, like D'Alonville, is taught by adversity, but in Marchmont it promotes a 'habit of reflection' which leads him to a radical criticism of contemporary society and to misanthropy. Such reflection is

> a habit which, when once acquired, helps the possessor to divest himself of the prejudices (often destructive to happiness, and never, that I can discover, contributing to it) which are with so much pain inculcated by rote at the beginning of our lives – as if the only use of memory were to assist mankind in getting rid of their reason, and to substitute in its place systems which the cunning have invented for the subjection of the weak.
> (Smith 1796: 4: 36)

This clarity of vision seems to enable him only to see the world as a place of exploitation, and when he is imprisoned he gives way to misanthropic distraction. He does reach what he calls a 'sort of fluctuating philosophy' (1796: 4: 344) in putting his faith in reason as a practical remedy for abuses. He recognizes, however, that such reform can only be gradual and admits his own limitations of fortitude for such a task. The influence of Williams may be seen when he asserts that women have more of such fortitude than men, adducing her most prominent heroine of liberty, Mme Roland (1796: 4: 342).

Smith's final novel, *The Young Philosopher* (1798), is a more committed radical work, and amply justifies its inclusion in Gillray's 'New Morality'. She had been reading *Political Justice*, and the philosophy of the title is at once the stoic calmness of popular parlance and the attitude of Godwin's gradualist reformer, not over-elated or depressed by single events, but confident in the general trend of human progress. She is anxious to defend the 'new philosophy' from charges of licentiousness, which had been particularly urged against Godwin, with his ideas on marriage. She stresses the purity of George Delmont's love for Medora, and gives Armytage, the Godwinian philosopher of the novel, a pointed rebuttal of such charges. She draws attention to the fact that it is aristocratic rakes and soldiers who speak the 'rationalistic' language of licentiousness, not philosophers. The major parallel structure of the book also owes something to Godwin, this time a perceptive response to one of Godwin's main points of discussion: the medium between 'individuality and concert', the extent to which one can or should divest oneself of the natural and habitual ties that, perhaps irrationally, bind one to society as it is and inhibit efforts towards self-education and the reform of society.

By the beginning of the novel, Delmont's radical education has already been completed by the exertions of his mother and by his own reading and experience. He is content to remain a farmer 'whose talk is of bullocks' - but 'of other things as well', he adds (Smith 1798: 1: 5), in a reference to Burke's dismissal of 'dishonourable' occupations.[4] Rodney Baine has drawn attention to the apparent collusion between Holcroft's *Hugh Trevor*, Godwin's *Enquirer* essay 'On Trades and Professions', and Smith's *The Old Manor House* in their attacks on the venal employments possible in a corrupt society (Baine 1965: 81), but *The Young Philosopher* is even more scathing in its criticism: 'I shall not feel a single emotion of envy', asserts George,

> when I see one on the bench of Themis condemning wretches legally to die on the gallows, or on the bench of bishops, lending their weight to laws that send forth myriads to slaughter in the field; nor shall I once regret, that I do not with a truncheon in my hand preside myself at those human sacrifices, either by land or sea, where men are collected together by hundreds and by thousands; are ordered to destroy each other, they know not, they dare not enquire, why?
>
> (Smith 1798: 1: 93-4)

George leaves the trade of blood to his father and brother, and despises all the professions which profit from man's injustice and inhumanity. Disabused of the false values of society, he stands alone and independent. Secure in his own content and liberty of thought, he accepts his uncle's marriage, which cuts off the prospects of his branch of the family, with an equanimity which is regarded by his relations as scarcely human. Nevertheless, he has strong family feelings which 'had formed part of the system grown up in his mind' and which he carries 'perhaps to excess' (Smith 1798: 3: 63). In particular, he is always having to rescue his elder brother Adolphus from the merited consequences of his dissolute life and engage himself for the debts incurred ' "in the course of a man's living" (that is playing and betting every night)' (1798: 3: 20). His feelings for Medora and her mother Mrs Glenmorris further engage him in a struggle with social injustice. Glenmorris himself, after unavailingly combating the corruptions of Europe, has made his home in America, but sends his wife and child to England to recover family money which is rightfully theirs. A conversation between Delmont and Mrs Glenmorris focuses the problem: George, in the spirit of the quotations from Rousseau scattered throughout the book, despises the world ('monde') and the 'imaginary atmosphere' of 'prescriptive prejudice', asserting his 'contempt of all such prejudices as enslave the mind, and restrain man's best prerogatives, that of thinking, saying what he thinks, and where he can, acting up to his thoughts' (1798: 1: 229). Mrs Glenmorris interposes the limitations of 'existing circumstances' and, with Glenmorris as an example, asserts that there is 'hardly any case wherein it is possible for a man, however determined he may be, to shake off the fetters which are for the most part wantonly imposed, so entirely to emancipate himself, as not to be dragged back in some instance to the forms of society' (1798: 1: 232). George concedes the truth of this but hopes that 'the period may not be far off, perhaps, when its truth may be disputed'.

The irony that is directed at George and at Mrs Glenmorris for giving way to their anxieties for the abducted Medora is a recognition of the dependence of the individual on others. Godwin himself admitted this dependence and the anxieties which it causes: 'He . . . who regards all things past, present, and to come as links of an indissoluble chain', he asserts, will 'find himself assisted to surmount the tumult of passion and be enabled to reflect upon the moral concerns of mankind with the same clearness of perception, the same firmness of judgement, and the same constancy of temper, as we are accustomed to do upon the truths of geometry.' But, he adds, this 'must be expected to be no more than a temporary exertion', and when a man experiences the loss of an object endeared to him by association and habit he will inevitably find 'his thoughts in some degree unhinged' (*PJ*98: 1: 396).

After encounters with inordinately oppressive family pride, rapacious lawyers, and libertine aristocrats, involving such adventures as abduction, incarceration in a mad-house, and imprisonment for debt, the corruption of society is amply proved. At the conclusion of the novel, Delmont, terminally disillusioned with his dissolute and uncaring brother, determines to go with Glenmorris to America. Glenmorris entices him by quoting Crèvecoeur on the democratic liberty of America, where 'farmer' is the most common and honourable title, and by painting it as the place most propitious to universal benevolence. 'True philanthropy', he says in Godwinian vein, 'does not consist of loving John, and Thomas, and George and James, because they are our brothers, our cousins, our neighbours, our countrymen, but in benevolence to the whole human race' (Smith 1798: 4: 393-4). He cannot live where he sees 'the miseries of the social compact greatly exceed the happiness derived from it' (1798: 4: 344), and he propounds the maxim that 'wherever a thinking man enjoys the most uninterrupted domestic felicity, and sees his species the most content, *that* is his country' (1798: 4: 395). 'I do not love to live', says Glenmorris, 'where I see a frightful contrast between luxury and wretchedness; where I must daily witness injustice I cannot repress, and misery I cannot relieve' (1798: 4: 391).

These passages might derive from Godwin's denunciation of narrow patriotism. A wise man's attachment, he asserts:

> will be to the cause, as the cause of man, and not to the country. Wherever there are individuals, who understand the value of political justice, and are prepared to assist it, that is his country. Wherever he can most contribute to the diffusion of these principles and the real happiness of mankind, that is his country.
>
> (*PJ*98: 2: 147)

But a helpless withdrawal from the task of reform is not what *Political Justice* teaches. It is the Rousseauistic Glenmorris who persuades the party to emigrate. He, like Hermsprong, who proposes a similar kind of American pantisocracy, is a cosmopolitan figure who values above all the freedom of America. The other more central characters here acquiesce, which is perhaps a reflection of the disillusioned mood of 1798, a notably low point in radical morale. Delmont, however, has a firm faith in reason and progress. His Rousseauistic sensibility is qualified by the inspiration of Godwin and Wollstonecraft.

Godwin had faith in man's ability to transform the real world, to 'act up to his thoughts', and regarded the imagination with suspicion when it was used not to envisage future amelioration but to inhibit it. Both Godwin and Wollstonecraft viewed the conceptions of the imagination as the inspiration of progress, although Wollstonecraft acknowledged that such conceptions might have to be their own reward in a society which thwarted active reform. Both impulses come together in *The Young Philosopher*, as they later came together in the ideas of Shelley. Armytage, the rather isolated representative of Godwinian progressive philosophy, gives a long defence of his political views at the conclusion of the novel. Like Hermsprong, he tends to be disappointingly conventional when he is explicit about the political leanings of his ideas, but he does strike the authentic Godwinian note in his rejection of violence: 'Far from thinking that such measures are likely to establish liberty and the general rights of mankind', he asserts, 'I hold them to be exactly the means that will delay the period when rational freedom, and all that its enjoyment can give to humanity, shall be established in the world' (Smith 1798: 4: 16). The hope for the future is not in political measures, as in *Desmond*, but in the human faculties of reason and sensibility. Delmont's faith in reason is not just a complacency in his own clarity of vision but a faith in a general awakening which is irreversible. In his dispute with the Burkean Dr Winslow, he remonstrates that if progress is impossible and undesirable then we should still be Papists, but since the French Revolution 'the gloomy and absurd structures raised on the basis of prejudice and superstition, have toppled down headlong; many are crushed in their fall . . . but the bastilles of falsehood, in which men's minds were imprisoned, are levelled with the earth, never, never to rise again' (1798: 1: 147).

The hope of sensibility is embodied in Medora. Her sensibility, Smith insists, 'was not the exotic production of those forced and unnatural descriptions of tenderness, that are exhibited by the imaginary heroine of impossible adventures'. It is hailed as 'that intuitive sense by which she knew how to put herself, in imagination, in the place of another, and to feel for all who were unhappy, [which] made her active in doing all the good that her age and situation admitted' (Smith 1798: 3: 38). Her mother recognizes the danger that such sensibility runs of 'suffering her imagination to outrun her reason', leading her to 'bewilder herself among ideal beings'. This is the fate foreseen by Mary Wollstonecraft for those whose imaginative conceptions transcend the possibilities of reality. Nevertheless, Mrs Glenmorris would prefer her daughter to be regarded as a 'strange, romantic girl', rather than for her to give up any claim to 'an opinion of her own . . . and go through the world with prudery', resigning, 'because she is a woman . . . all pretensions to being a reasonable being' (1798: 2: 14-15). In considering the education of such a sensibility, Smith picks up the issues debated by Geraldine and Fanny in *Desmond,* and reiterates her contempt for a cloistered virtue. Lessons of the callousness and perfidy of men are necessary to develop 'female fortitude', whereas 'ignorance of the ways of the world would occasion a feebleness of spirit' (1798: 3: 41).

When Medora is abducted by a libertine, she amply demonstrates that union of sensibility with heroic active virtue which Mary Wollstonecraft and Williams celebrate, far exceeding the conventional passivity of 'female fortitude'. Feats such as wrenching iron bars asunder and swinging to earth on a creeper are the least of her achievements. Delmont fears her exposure to the conversation of 'waggoners and hackney coach drivers' (Smith 1798: 4: 125), but Medora has none of the fastidious delicacy of a constricted sensibility. She even braves the infection of a sick family moved on by parish officers, and sympathy provokes her to indignation against the laws which authorize such inhumanity (1798: 4: 282). She is going through the same educative process that George had followed, from a sensibility that responded to suffering individuals, whether impostors or not, to criticism of the system of laws under which such misery existed (1798: 1: 54). Like Godwin and Marchmont, Delmont comes to view modern history as the 'annals of fraud and murder, of selfish ambition, or wicked policy, involving millions in misery for the gratification of a few' (1798: 1: 90). Like Godwin too, he has to look to ancient history to find magnanimous virtues, the impressions of which, 'made thus early on the mind, are never likely to be erased or enfeebled, if reason is suffered to stifle all those paltry passions by which men coming into life are induced to follow blindly where their interest leads them, and to become the mere creatures of convenience and convention' (1798: 1: 91-2).

The personal development of George and Medora is exceptional, however, and in *Political Justice* Godwin had emphasized the difficulties of education. The insinuation of the spirit of government into every aspect of life, counteracting the benevolent tenets of the educator, made the existence of virtue very precarious. Smith seems to be more aware of this point in

The Young Philosopher than in her previous novels, perhaps because the lesson was reiterated by Enfield in his 'Enquirer' section of *The Morning Chronicle* during 1798. Unexpectedly virtuous characters are found in her previous novels, such as the young solicitor who aids Orlando Somerive to gain his inheritance, but they do not play a crucial role in the winding up of the plot, nor is much stress placed upon their exceptional nature. In explaining the phenomenon of Medora, Smith offers, instead of 'sensibility', the phrase 'integrity of understanding' (Smith 1798: 3: 251), which she defines as 'that natural strength and rectitude of mind, seldom seen, because it must be strong indeed where it has resisted the early counteraction of what is called education; but which, where it does survive, forms characters which are capable of every thing that is good and great'. For *The Young Philosopher* to reach a happy conclusion they need to find in the heiress of the Glenmorris fortune, Miss Cardonnel, another such 'rare instance' of one who, despite her ogre of a mother, has resisted efforts to instil prejudice (1798: 4: 207).

The natural sensibility which had been an adequate guide to Smith's early heroines is now seen as a rare quality which needs the concurrence of other virtues, of energy, resistance, and a strong understanding, to survive in a world which makes one doubt the humanity of man, that 'little spark of friendship for human kind', as Smith writes, quoting Hume, 'that particle of the dove kneaded into our frame, along with the elements of the wolf and the serpent' (Smith 1798: 4: 365). The novel is ambiguous in its resolution. Despite its commitment to the progressive powers of reason and an educated sensibility, the main characters of the novel retreat to the Rousseauistic dream of Crêvecoeur's America. It marks the end of the decade of revolutionary optimism.

With the disintegration of a widely shared moral consciousness the novelist could no longer have confidence in the reactions of the reader. The didactic art of sensibility relied on the identification of the reader with a character whose emotional and moral responses might refine their own and strengthen the social passions which were hailed as the forces of progress. Charlotte Smith often employed her heroes and heroines in exemplary roles, but in her response to the changing attitudes of her readership she developed more sophisticated techniques. Her unity of theme enabled her to structure telling parallel situations, and she employed a play of irony and allusive satire which disturbed the expectations of the reader and the conventions of the genre. As a female author highly conscious of her reception, she could be seen as progressively cultivating the 'private' authorial persona, abjuring commitment on public issues in a knowing exploitation of literary technique and manipulation of emotional response. Her many autobiographical passages in the novels as well as the prefaces emphasize her female limitations and vulnerability. This indirection caused some confusion in her critics – Bissett in particular seems not to know where to have her. The taint of Jacobinism, however, had been early established with *Desmond* and, despite the later red herrings, her political views were not concealed. Jane Austen adopted similar indirect techniques more successfully, and her use of wit, irony, and satire drew on the legacy of liberal practitioners like Bage and Smith, as well as the more heavy-handed anti-Jacobins.

7

WORDSWORTH AND SENSIBILITY

To situate Wordsworth in the context of sensibility is a task both facilitated and complicated by his ambiguous use of the terms 'nature' and 'feeling', and by the fitfully precise yet generally undependable chronology of *The Prelude*. The massive argument of the poem, foreshadowed by 'Lines written above Tintern Abbey' and manuscript material dating from 1798, is that love of nature leads to love of man, that nature's education leads to a sympathy of the widest extent and a moral balance in which impulse and duty are reconciled. Nature provides a sure refuge in times of calamity in which it may, in imagination and memory, preserve a continuity of personal being and a sense of quasi-divine purpose in the universe. The growth of the poet's mind is charted, following both the events of Wordsworth's life, as far as he wishes to reveal them, and a more general pattern of maturation to which, in general, the incidents of the life adhere or are compelled to conform. Its culmination is the achievement of imaginative insight which allows the poet to participate in the creative power of nature and in the benevolence or love it inspires, which is the root of moral feelings.

The development of this conception is credited in the poem to the years 1793–8, a confused and ill-documented period of his life which provides the crisis of *The Prelude*, where it is the subject of three separate accounts. Scholars have pointed to some contradictions in his representation of this period, the most glaring being between *The Prelude* and 'Tintern Abbey' in their descriptions of his condition in 1793. According to the very precise dating of both poems it was a time of unreflecting animal instincts ('Tintern Abbey') and a time of the triumphant accession of love for man (*Prelude*).¹ Since we have the evidence of the unpublished 'Letter to the Bishop of Llandaff', his letters to Mathews, and 'Salisbury Plain' available to us, we might well accept the account of *The Prelude*, since these show a fervid concern with man, a radical humanitarianism which he presents as a legacy of his experiences in France. Yet these works of 1793-4 show a revolutionary indignation at social injustice. They are not part of the growth of that calm confidence in a beneficent universal scheme which the 1805 *Prelude* points towards but an interruption of it. His radical questioning of society is generally regarded as a kind of sickness, an impairment of his imagination, and the philosopher whose influence he felt most, Godwin, is seen as the arch-rationalist whose contagion had to be escaped. Yet in striking ways the ideas of Godwin and radical sensibility are incorporated into the descriptions of his early awakenings to benevolence and into the teachings of nature which became his ultimate authority.

Even in *The Prelude*'s account of the growth of the two principles, love of nature and love of man, there is room to doubt the priority which Wordsworth gives to love of nature, while the evidence of his early poems and manuscripts shows that the specifically Wordsworthian sense of nature's own life developed *after* 1793 and was based not only on the deistic sense of nature as shadowing forth the Creator but also on the expansive human sympathies of the tradition of sensibility deriving from Shaftesbury. In Shaftesbury's *The Moralists*, often taken as the inspiration for the eighteenth-century worship of nature, the progress of Palemon's 'aspiring soul' is a model of the expansion of the affections, first towards individual beauty and perfection, then to the 'beautiful society', considering 'by what Harmony of Particular Minds the general harmony is composed, and *Common-Weal* established'. It advances towards 'a nobler Object, and with enlarg'd Affection seeks the *Good of Mankind*'. This search involves the study of 'Laws, Constitutions, Civil and Religious Rites; whatever civilizes and polishes rude Mankind' and eventually seeks the source of universal order and perfection in Nature and the divine will (*Char*: 2: 211-12). Such a progressive expansion of human sympathies is assumed by many of the writers of sensibility. The attributes of Nature and the divinity are expressed in terms of human ideals by Shaftesbury, Hutcheson, and Rousseau, and it became a commonplace of sentimental writing to express the moral effect of nature in terms linking beauty and human virtue. Mary Wollstonecraft, who had a deeply religious response to nature, nevertheless asserts that it is from human affections that the true sublime sense of God in Nature derives, human love being, in Miltonic phrase, a 'scale to heavenly'. In her essay *On Poetry* she states: 'Love to man leads to devotion – grand and sublime images strike the imagination – God is seen in every floating cloud' (Wollstonecraft 1989: 7: 8). The derivation of love of man from love of nature seems to me to be a later notion which Wordsworth used to order the experience of *The Prelude*, just as later conceptions of patriotism confusingly intrude into the account of his ideas of the early 1790s. Struggling within the poem are the ideas of sensibility, that man 'naturally' feels his affinity with the wider systems of mankind and universal nature, and the idea, probably derived from Coleridge, that man's being is 'built up' for him by the process of association, guided by a benevolent nature through which God matures His purpose of bringing all things to perfection. In the latter Hartleyan theory the development of the moral sense is the last stage of human development. The privileging of Nature above humanity is also a product of Wordsworth's later exaltation of the poet's imagination, which creates a new world restored to the Paradisal state by the faculty divine working in harmony with nature's creative powers. A faith in such harmony could reconcile Wordsworth to the tragedies of humanity. Like his pedlar he could afford to suffer with those whom he saw suffer, reconciled to their fate by his acknowledgement of a benign system of natural loss and renewal in nature. The poetry of the 1790s is not suffused with this spirit, however, and the focus of *Lyrical Ballads* is predominantly a human one. *The Prelude* itself shows patterns associated with the growth of a humanistic, liberal sensibility, though its development into a revolutionary force is obfuscated and reinterpreted as a deviation from previous latent principles of development associated with 'Nature'.

The early books of *The Prelude* are anxious to establish the link between the child and nature. Mostly this is done by 'extrinsic' means: nature is associated with the joy of the social events for which it provided a setting. It is based on an association of sense impressions which is analogous to the formation of allegiances to home and country. His feelings for the moon, associated with youthful dreams of joy, are 'humble though intense, / To patriotic and domestic love / Analogous' (*Prelude*: ii.194-6), just that kind of attachment that Kames had censured as 'vulgar', based on sense rather than the generalizing faculty. But Wordsworth insists that his feelings for nature were also influenced by a more intrinsic principle: those affinities that 'fit / Our new existence to existing things' (i.582-3). The account of the 'infant babe' shows the influence of both theories. The feelings of the babe towards external things seem to be explained in an associationist way as the love for the mother irradiates all objects which move their mutual feelings, and binds all things in a reprocity and 'discipline' of love. Yet the figure of the mother is progressively etherialized from a 'presence' to a 'Presence', and the filial bond becomes a 'gravitational' one, binding the babe to the 'active universe'. In his own case, Wordsworth was left alone, the 'props' of his affections removed: 'And yet the building stood, as if sustained / By its own spirit!' (ii.295-6). This cryptic reference to his mother's death rather undermines her role in the process as she becomes a mere 'prop'. The associationist 'conjecture' might be an analogy of the development of love of nature rather than an account of its source. It is, confessedly, an attempt to fathom a feeling which he asserts 'in the words of reason deeply weighed, / Hath no beginning' (ii.236-7). Tom Wedgwood was fond of tracing the source of love to the desire of the baby for the breast, and in his associationist theory desire was caused by the removal of the breast: love/desire was fundamentally Locke's uneasy feeling caused by the absence of a desired object. Little of this anxious desire is shown by Wordsworth, to whom the world of nature gives ample recompense for this loss. The child's awakened affections impart strength and power to sentiments of joy and exultation as well as of grief and fear. However it is engendered, this sympathy with nature is a universal birthright of our being, an 'infant sensibility' which is 'the first / Poetic spirit of our human life' (ii.275-6). Like Blair, he attributes a discriminating power to this sensibility. It appreciates nature's finer influxes in the 'more exact / And intimate communion' of the heart, and can discern 'manifold distinctions, difference / Perceived in things, where to the common eye, / No difference is' (ii.318-20). Likewise it also observes 'affinities / In objects where no brotherhood exists / To common minds' (ii.403-5). This sensibility relishes a sublime which is connected with the growth of the faculties and a beauty which is described in Shaftesburyan terms as 'that universal power / And fitness in the latent qualities / And essences of things, by which the mind / Is moved by feelings of delight' (ii.343-6). When speculating on the growth of creative imagination and insight into the life of nature Wordsworth refers to the habit of perceiving affinities, and the 'great social principle of life, / Coercing all things into sympathy' (ii.408-9).

In one of Wordsworth's typical alternative explanations for the sense of the 'one life' he canvasses 'the power of truth / Coming in revelation' by which he conversed 'with things that really are' (ii.411-12). Eventually the 'social' aspect of his link with nature diminishes from the time of boyhood companionship and human love which initiated it until he uses the word 'social' in a way which might better be expressed as 'associative'. By the end of Book II, the conclusion of the 1799 *Prelude,* the 'social' origin of his feelings for nature is so occluded as to make it possible for him to claim a kinship with Coleridge, whose 'pious mind' rejected Wordsworth's naturalism. Though he appeals to 'human sentiments' and proclaims a 'more than Roman confidence' in our nature, his condemnation of those who had fallen away from the cause of virtue to selfishness 'disguised in gentle names / Of peace, and quiet, and domestic love' (ii.453-4) affirms not a renewed hope in humanity but the inspirational values of solitary communion with nature.

His conception of the interaction of man and nature is dated to his seventeenth year, 1787, in *The Prelude.* This preoccupation colours his presentation of Cambridge and London, which are seen as environments at odds with the development of vision. Their social life is competitive and divisive, and the picture we are given is of a youth exploring the worlds of the imagination and intellect, detached from immediate or wider social concerns. It comes as quite a surprise that Wordsworth was moved to interrupt his studies at a crucial stage for a walking tour of the Continent inspired both by the prospect of the sublimity of the Alps and by the wish to see Revolutionary Europe. In Book VIII, devoted to the growth of his love of man, and in the subsequent account of his experience in France, a very different picture of the young Wordsworth emerges, a picture more in tune with the development of radical sensibility in which Nature has social and humanitarian significance.

Wordsworth describes the growth of his love for humanity not as a development of domestic feelings in the way that Coleridge saw benevolence, a process of 'concretion', but as a pure gift of nature. It was 'Nature' that led him to love his fellow beings:

> Beyond the bosom of my Family,
> My friends and youthful Playmates. 'Twas thy power
> That raised the first complacency in me,
> And noticeable kindliness of heart,
> Love human to the Creature in himself
> As he appeared, a Stranger in my path,
> Before my eyes a Brother in this world.
>
> (viii.73-9).

The extended sympathies of sensibility typically yield a 'complacency' that has little to do with selfish pleasure. The picture of the shepherd with which he illustrates this sympathy suffers from Wordsworth's attempts to recommend him to the audience which proved so unsympathetic to his figures of low and rustic life in *Lyrical Ballads*. The remote, statuesque figure, buttressed by allusions to Theocritan and Shakespearean pastorals, later eclogues, and German shepherds, is hardly humanized by an anecdote of common shepherding heroism. The distance from which he views the shepherd, almost as an aesthetic object, is a purifying remove which is calculated to produce reactions suitable to the sublime, the classical, and the sentimental. When Wordsworth writes of his good fortune in seeing man 'through objects that were great and fair' (viii.451) rather than in the crowded life of cities, the 'objects' he has presented, the sublime scenes of nature, have in fact been supplemented by a weight of scholarly apparatus. But the point of the passage, however tailored to its audience, is that man's essential nature is worthy of 'admiration and respect' and that without this 'prepossession' no valuable insight into human life can be gained (viii.460-8). After this intensely worked section it comes as something of a disappointment to learn that at 'this' time both man and nature were only secondary in Wordsworth's mind to his own pursuits 'And animal activities' (viii.477). The next advance in his feelings for man is the development of what he calls an 'adulterate power' (viii.592) which peopled the scenes of nature with appropriate human characters. This operation of the fancy, in which the appearances of Nature suggest human passions, is very similar to the more exalted insight which saw the very stones feel or linked them to some feeling, and spread the sentiment of Being over all things. Yet Wordsworth criticizes his early creative exercises of this humanizing faculty for their sensationalism. These 'tragic super-tragic' creations who haunted melancholy situations are reminiscent of the widow in *An Evening Walk* and the consciously exaggerated spectre of despair in 'The Thorn'. Wordsworth is willing to grant that such shapes of wilful fancy were 'grafted' upon feelings of the imagination and so rose in 'worth', but they were vitiated by his slender knowledge of human passions. Moreover, they were unfaithful to what he 'knew' was the natural course of events. Wordsworth invokes his Cumberland 'reality', the 'real solid world / Of images' (viii.604-5), as a standard of natural passion as well as of external nature. Woodmen died for love in his fancy, but in reality from disease. The use of this construct of nature and reality to limit the claims of an over-ardent imagination is seen later in a political context. Here it is adduced as a healthy control in comparison with Coleridge's position in the unnatural city, where he is presented as 'in endless dreams / Of sickliness, disjoining, joining things / Without the light of knowledge' (viii.608-10).

The countryside was, of course, the favoured environment of sensibility, but those who were moved by the new evaluation of human feeling and inspired with the idea of progress looked to a universal evolution of social life, not the stagnation of rural communities. Wordsworth's own contact with the great world, in little in Cambridge, in large in London, is presented negatively in the books devoted to them, but in Book VIII this movement is dramatically reversed. Both environments are credited with major contributions to his love of man:

> As of all visible natures crown; and first
> In capability of feeling what
> Was to be felt; in being rapt away
> By the divine effect of power and love,
> As, more than anything we know, instinct
> With Godhead.
>
> (viii.634-9)

The images which Wordsworth uses to describe this period combine that of an expansion of life and 'Being', which is used to describe his feelings for nature, and the images of sun and light, which come to characterize the moral unity of man on which social progress is based:

> The pulse of Being everywhere was felt,
> When all the several frames of things, like stars
> Through every magnitude distinguishable,
> Were half confounded in each other's blaze,
> One galaxy of life and joy.
>
> (viii.627-31).

Cambridge brought him 'more near . . . to guilt and wretchedness' (viii.657-8) and awakened an active pity: 'seeing, I essayed / To give relief'. He is careful to note that his human sympathy was not self-centred, 'not for the mind's delight' (viii.668), and a thing 'Common to all' (viii.666). London presents itself now not as a bewildering chaos overmastering the individual sensibility but as a source of sublime conceptions. Wordsworth's mind, oppressed by the weight of experience, develops an inner power to apprehend the manifestations of the human spirit in the great metropolis and its history:

> A weight of Ages did at once descend
> Upon my heart; no thought embodied, no
> Distinct remembrances; but weight and power,
> Power growing with the weight.
>
> (viii.703-6)

Whereas Book VII concentrates on the outward pageantry and opulence that gilded vice and squalor, and seems to be designed to counter any Dick Whittington illusions, Book VIII sets his sublime awakening to the significance of the city on the roof of an 'itinerant vehicle' with 'vulgar men about me, vulgar forms / Of houses, pavement, streets, of men and things, / Mean shapes on every side' (viii.694-7). His vision of the human spirit is very similar to his conception of nature as a presence widely 'diffused':

> The human nature unto which I felt
> That I belonged, and which I loved and reverenced,
> Was not a punctual Presence, but a Spirit
> Living in time and space, and far diffused.
> In this my joy, in this my dignity
> Consisted; the external universe,
> By striking upon what is found within,
> Had given me this conception, with the help
> Of Books, and what they picture and record.
>
> (viii.761-9)

Here, rather than in the sections on books, schooldays, or Cambridge, he pays tribute to the histories of Greece and 'popular Rome' for presenting him with a worthy image of humanity. The result of this experience was 'elevating thoughts / Of human nature' and a 'trust / In what we may become' (viii.801-7) which could not be shaken by the guilt and misery which he saw around him.

At this point the phrase 'what we may become' has a more collective meaning than other similar phrases in the poem. Elsewhere human progress has been linked with the regeneration of the individual through the discipline of Nature and the power of imagination, a process not aided by city life. Here regeneration, prophesied with a reference to *Paradise Lost* (viii.822-3), has a more communal dimension, inspired by the spirit of congregated humanity. To his experience in the city Wordsworth ascribed his sense of the unity of man and the unity of the moral sense, not as a faculty generated by association but as a natural bond of social union:

> One spirit over ignorance and vice
> Predominant, in good and evil hearts
> One sense for moral judgements, as one eye
> For the sun's light. When strongly breathed upon
> By this sensation, whencesoe'er it comes
> Of union or communion, doth the soul
> Rejoice as in her highest joy: for there
> There chiefly, hath she feeling whence she is,
> And passing through all Nature rests with God.
> (viii.828-36)

This passage seems to suggest that the moral feelings associated with human unity give a more joyous and direct sense of the divine than the intimations of nature, or that such feelings ascend through an analogous sense of unity with nature to the divine. In either sense it makes a claim which sits uneasily with Wordsworth's statement that his fellow-men were still less important to him than nature. Not until his experiences in France had awakened his radical humanitarianism could he state quite simply that: 'my heart was all / Given to the People, and my love was theirs' (ix.24-5). This is an extraordinarily bold admission, given the public mood in 1805, and contradicts the attempts to distance his republican enthusiasm from the education of nature. What qualifies this boldness is that the radical documents which Wordsworth produced in 1793-5 were unpublished, as was *The Prelude.*

In Book IX all the influences of Wordsworth's early life, including those of Nature, mature into a definite political stance. The inspiration of poetry and history which exalted heroes, not kings or nobles; the equality of Cumberland life, mountain liberty; even the equality of conditions at Cambridge, which are here viewed more favourably than before: all made him a 'Patriot' in the radical sense of the term, devoted to 'the government of equal rights / And individual worth' (ix.248-9). As if aware of the competing senses of terms like 'patriot', the passage goes on to contrast the senses of the term 'honour' as the royalist officers of Orleans fail to 'make my understanding bend / In honour to their honour' (ix.258-9).

Michel Beaupuy is presented as Wordsworth's first political instructor, though Nicholas Roe's investigations might suggest some scepticism as to Wordsworth's claim that he was 'scarce dipped' into controversy (ix.339). Beaupuy, as a French soldier of noble birth, adds authority to the ideas attributed to his conversation, especially when pointing the contrast between 'self-respect and virtue in the Few / For patrimonial honour set apart, / And ignorance in the labouring Multitude' (ix.334-6) and in expatiating on the corruption of courts, cut off from all the 'natural inlets of just sentiment, / From lowly sympathy, and chastening truth ' (ix.358-9). In Beaupuy Wordsworth creates a figure which, in the manner of Williams and Godwin, links old chivalric virtues with modern universal benevolence. His love for the 'mean and the obscure' seemed 'a courtesy which had no air / Of condescension, but did rather seem / A passion and a gallantry, like that / Which he, a Soldier, in his idler day / Had paid to Woman' (ix.316-20). It is in response to the famous words which are put into Beaupuy's mouth about the Revolution being for such as the hunger-bitten peasant girl that Wordsworth reveals that the 'earth' has some kind of political programme. If Wordsworth believed that the Revolution was 'nothing out of nature's certain course' (ix.253), the spirit that animated the Revolution for him was Nature's wish:

> that poverty
> At least like this, would in a little time

> Be found no more, that we would see the earth
> Unthwarted in her wish to recompense
> The industrious, and the lowly Child of Toil,
> All institutes for ever blotted out
> That legalised exclusion, empty pomp
> Abolished, sensual state and cruel power
> Whether by edict of the one or few,
> And finally, as sum and crown of all,
> Should see the People having a strong hand
> In making their own Laws, whence better days
> To all mankind.
>
> (ix.522-34)

The expansive sympathy for humanity and the identification of a moral and beneficent force in nature come together in a political context here, just as the poems written immediately after his French experiences show new developments in his consciousness of nature's own life and a deeper sympathy with humanity.

The early version of *An Evening Walk* (1793) contains many accurate and evocative pictures of nature, but the poetic pose is highly derivative. The melancholy poet, revisiting the scenes of past joys, parades the tear on his cheek and luxuriates in scenes of peace in which rustic characters play walk-on roles. Celebrating the calm domestic contentment of the vales, passages are typically introduced by phrases such as 'I love' or 'Sweet are', yet the poet is distanced from the scenes and characters he describes; he does not sympathetically inhabit their consciousness nor does he explore the impact of the scenery on his own sensibility. He often uses the contrast, prominent in Gray and Smith, between the delight of the scene and the melancholy of the poet. The principal episode is a harrowing tale of the death of a widow and her two children in a snowstorm. This has considerable overtones of social protest. She mourns her husband, dead on 'Bunker's charnel hill', and is 'deny'd to lay her head, / On cold blue nights, in hut or straw-built shed' (*EW*: 62, ll. 254-7). Wordsworth concludes the story with the mother vainly attempting to shelter her children: 'Thy breast their death-bed, coffin'd in thine arms' (*EW*: 66, l. 300), and then abruptly invites us to contemplate the tranquillity of the lake. The alternation of excitation and calm, like that of sublimity and beauty, later becomes a Wordsworthian pattern, and his later work usually attempts to impose some continuity, provided by the concept of a humanized nature or the transcendent power of human passion. This early poem remains disturbingly unaccommodating to the feelings raised by the woman's fate. It seems to be influenced by eighteenth-century theories such as the value of exercising humanitarian responses and to exploit the emotional pleasure of contrasting scenes, each wrought up to their height, as recommended by Kames. The poet of the 1793 *Evening Walk* is an onlooker, 'pensive' in the passive eighteenth-century sense, invoking only stereotyped responses, not the strong personal emotional reactions which move the poet to active thought. The revisions which Wordsworth made to this poem during 1793-4 establish the pattern for his more mature verse in which events are reflected on and emotional response yields knowledge. In the manuscript version of the poem published by Averill and in the contemporaneous *Salisbury Plain* we can see not only the effect of his new political commitment but the influence of writers in the line of sensibility.

On his return from France Wordsworth was fired with a sense of political mission, and the 'Letter to the Bishop of Llandaff' well represents the political opinions he had absorbed. Rousseau, perhaps discussed with Beaupuy, Paine, one of the 'master pamphlets' he must have read, the declarations of the Assemblée Nationale, and the more immediate influence of Bishop Grégoire at Blois, all colour his defence of the Revolution and the execution of the king. Dominating the work is a strong republican antagonism to monarchy, aristocracy, and large accumulations of wealth and property. His defence of violence is understandable for one who had been moved to tears by the domestic severings of families whose menfolk were bound to the defence of their newly won freedom. Nevertheless, his regrets at the prodigious waste of talents consequent on the subordination of moral to political virtues shows a susceptibility to the more peaceable faith of Godwin that revolutions need not always be the work of violence. While the 'Letter' testifies to a strength of mind that could stand by the Revolution even during its most bloody and despotic periods, it is clear that Wordsworth soon reverted to a less violent faith and apparently became an ardent disciple of Godwin in 1793 or early 1794.

While the proposals for the 'Philanthropist' of mid-1794 demonstrate the influence of Godwin as a political thinker, the poetry produced over this period reflects the assimilation of Godwin's ideas into the wider framework of thought provided by the tradition of sensibility. Godwin's conception of justice is linked with the expansive sympathies which urge benevolence towards wider systems of being; Godwin's reverence for individual human potential and condemnation of restrictive institutions and traditions merges with the wish to assert a more personal critical relationship to poetic tradition. Godwin's appeal to Truth as an irresistible force leading to virtue and benevolence merges with the common sentimental appeal to nature as a benign system and with the progressive, revolutionary spirit which Wordsworth had glimpsed in France. Wordsworth's poetry enters into a relationship with philosophic discourse and no longer aspires to the poetic imitations of his youth.

The first poetic expression which Wordsworth gives to his sense of Nature as a living force, an active universe, is in the revisions to *An Evening Walk*. Here the expansion of the affections is presented in a thoroughly Shaftesburyan way:

> A Mind, that in a calm angelic mood
> Of happy wisdom, meditating good,
> Beholds, of all from her high powers required,
> Much done, and much designed, and more desired;
> Harmonious thoughts, a soul by Truth refined,
> Entire affection for all human kind;
> A heart that vibrates evermore, awake
> To feeling for all forms that Life can take,
> That wider still its sympathy extends,
> And sees not any line where being ends;
> Sees sense, through Nature's rudest forms betrayed,
> Tremble obscure in fountain, rock, and shade;
> And while a secret power those forms endears
> Their social accents never vainly hears.
>
> (*EW*: 135, ll. 119-32)

As in Shaftesbury's description of the extension of Palemon's sensibility, the 'harmonious' mind rises to the contemplation of the harmony of society and then to the harmony evident even in the rudest appearances formed by that empowered creatress, nature. The phrase 'entire affection' is Shaftesbury's, used to describe the universal as opposed to the partial affections: 'That PARTIAL AFFECTION, or social love *in part*, without regard to Society or *a Whole* is in it-self an Inconsistency, and implies an absolute contradiction ... INTIRE AFFECTION (from whence *Integrity* hath its name) as it is answerable to itself, proportionable, and rational; so it is irrefragable, solid, and durable' (*Char*: 2: 110-11). Shaftesbury is perhaps only an ultimate source, since Wordsworth's passage incorporates the terms of later developments of Shaftesbury's ideas in theories of expansive sympathy and the 'vibrations' of sympathetic emotional response, here innocent of Hartleyan physiology.

A further significance of the passage is that it is introduced in a critical allusion to a literary source, Horace's 'Ode to the Bandusian Spring', which describes a sacrifice to the spirit of the spring. While Wordsworth invokes the classical sense of a spirit in nature which inspires reverence and sacrifice, his sacrifice is to be the exertions of his mind, not a kid 'Stabbed when desire first wantons in his blood' (*EW*: 135, l. 115). This humanitarian criticism of classical customs is one of the first occasions when Wordsworth refers to a literary source in any other but a reverential way. Wordsworth's own translation of the ode, given in his note, describes the kid: its brow 'where the first budding horns appear, / Battles and love portends – portends in vain'. Beneath the reverence for nature might lie more potent sources of rebellion against tradition and custom awakened by his French experiences, and suggest an additional motive for his allegiance to the philosopher who attacked the present mode of sexual relations and the interference of social distinctions.

In many passages of the revised poem there is an easy assimilation of Godwin's stress on reason and universal benevolence to the values of feeling and domestic love. Favoured souls, taught 'By active Fancy or by patient Thought', whose 'sense no trivial object knows', mount 'through the fields of thought on wings of fire' but nevertheless behold 'with tenfold pleasure ... The powers of nature in each various mould'. Thought and sense are reconciled in passionate speculation, just as domestic love may coexist with universal benevolence:

If, like the sun, their [ ] love surrounds
The [ ] world to life's remotest bounds,

Yet not extinguishes the warmer fire
Round which the close domestic train retire;
If but to them these farms an emblem yield,
Home, their gay garden, and the world, their field;
While that, more near, demands minuter cares,
Yet this its proper tendance duly shares.
                              (*EW*: 138, ll.204-20)

Wordsworth's later manner is also foreshadowed in a greater intensity of sympathy with the lowly, which threatens the inherited poetic persona:

– Who now, resigning for the night the feast
Of Fancy, Leisure, Liberty, and Taste,
Can pass without a pause the silent door,
Where sweet Oblivion clasps the cottage poor?
Here, while I bend o'er this half useless gate,
And muse on human being's various state;
This path, that door, those peaceful precincts own
A charm at any other hour unknown;
Now subtle thought a moral interest sheds
On the cool simples of these garden beds.
                              (*EW*: 156, ll. 771-80)

The complacent gentleman-poet of sensibility is made uncomfortably aware that the things which make life a feast to him are denied to the poor, whose lives are so miserable that night and sleep are their best friends and oblivion their happiest state. If Cowper was the model for *An Evening Walk*, as Goldsmith was for *Descriptive Sketches*, the valetudinarian self-absorption of his poetic persona is being displaced by one which in fellow-feeling can see deeper into the misery of others. If Wordsworth does echo the sentimental commonplace 'From love of Nature love of Virtue flows', the love of nature is linked as firmly as it is in Shaftesbury with a virtue which implies universal benevolence, expanded beyond Shaftesbury's limited formulations into the egalitarian sympathy of radical sensibility.

Godwin, while the most systematic exponent of universal benevolence and a benevolent Truth, was not the only influence on Wordsworth in this period. *Salisbury Plain* shows the influence of other writers in the tradition of sensibility. The startling introductory stanzas comparing savage life with civilization have been thought to show the influence of Rousseau, and certainly the general point is the one Rousseau makes in the *Discourse of Inequality* that the development of society entails inequality, misery, and social injustices of which savage life is innocent. It is, however, Rousseau seen through Adam Smith, since it is the *sympathy* of equality that is valued. For Rousseau pity and sympathy decline with refinement; for Smith, as for Wordsworth, it is refinement that 'calls / The soft affections from their wintry sleep' (*SP*: 21, ll. 28-9). For Rousseau the animals of the wild have few terrors for the savage whose strength and agility make him a match for most; Wordsworth's savage hears their cries with fear. Rousseau's stress is on the hardy physique of the savage, Wordsworth's is on the firmness of his mind. Smith's view of savage life (which had been used by Mackenzie in *The Man of the World*) emphasizes the role which the compassion of others and that of the 'impartial spectator' plays in governing the passions. Wordsworth's savage is 'strong to suffer' because all others share his hard lot. It is not a subject of commiseration but a shared condition of life. Sensibility to suffering, whether one's own or that of others, is more acute in the varying fortunes of a complex commercial state, and personal suffering gains its sting from comparison, especially

> from reflection on the state
> Of those who on the couch of Affluence rest
> By laughing Fortune's sparkling cup elate,
> While we of comfort reft, by pain depressed,
> No other pillow know than Penury's iron breast.
> (*SP*: 21, ll. 23-7)

In stanza 49 Wordsworth links himself with those like Wollstonecraft and Williams, as well as Godwin, in criticizing the practice of charity and in lamenting the stunting of human worth by inhuman toil:

> How many at Oppression's portal placed
> Receive the scanty dole she cannot waste,
> And bless, as she has taught, her hand benign?
> How many by inhuman toil debased,
> Abject, obscure, and brute to earth incline
> Unrespited, forlorn of every spark divine?
> (*SP*: 35-6, ll. 436-41)

In a survey of colonialist oppression he singles out India, one of the favourite targets of humanitarian sentiment, and also Peru, a seemingly remote subject, but one which had been treated by Helen Maria Williams in a poem of 1784. Peru also figures in *An Evening Walk*, where the sun, viewing 'Thrones, towers, and fanes in blended ruin lie', is urged to roll to Peruvian vales to see temples to the sun itself mouldering in decay, and resign itself to the replacement of superstitious worship by 'triumphant Truth' (*EW*: 142, ll. 334-9). Such is the vagueness of Wordsworth's abstractions that Gill has speculated that his target in this passage is religion and Godhead itself (Gill 1990: 82). In *Salisbury Plain* it is acknowledged that those who destroyed the temples of the sun were not heroes of Truth but slaves of a different superstition. In both poems any religious connotations are borne by the landscape itself, that of *An Evening Walk* evoking 'religious awe' (*EW*: 150, l. 595), while in *Salisbury Plain* nature is given the peace and beauty of 'The Spirit of God' diffusing quiet through balmy air. Nature, however, is unable to minister to the female vagrant and her companion. Such diffused quiet, she says, echoing one of Charlotte Smith's most famous lines, 'might have healed, if ought could heal, Despair' (*SP*: 33, l. 360), but her despair is beyond such remedy. Save for one 'faint red smile' and a 'meek dawn' of gladness in her eyes, the smiling dawn has little restorative power. Her moments of relief come from human sympathy. In the conclusion of the story the sun puts on 'a show / More gorgeous still!' but the traveller is impervious to its beauty: 'Human sufferings and that tale of woe / Had dimmed the traveller's eye with Pity's tear' (*SP*: 34, ll. 397-9): their comfort is in the hospitality of the 'lowly cot'. Wordsworth seems to be making a point of the fact that the power of nature here is weaker than that of humanity. Nature has not yet developed that restorative power that he claims for it in 1798.

His position at this point might be compared with that of Charlotte Smith in *The Emigrants* (1793). She too has an enthusiastic response to a nature dominated by 'omniscient goodness'. Her faith is the common sentimental one that did not need 'declamatory essays' of divinity but read God through nature. But man's self-created horrors, specifically the turmoils of the Revolution, have, she laments, 'taught me so much sorrow, that my soul / Feels not the joy reviving Nature brings; / But, in dark retrospect, dejected dwells / On human follies, and on human woes' (Smith 1793: 4-5). Her powers of natural description are impressive, but after each evocation of the beauty of nature and the beneficence of God she interposes the barrier of human suffering:

> every leaf
> That Spring unfolds, and every simple bud,
> More forcibly impresses on my heart
> His power and wisdom - Ah! while I adore
> That goodness, which design'd to all that lives
> Some taste of happiness, my soul is pain'd
> By the variety of woes that Man
> For Man creates.
>
> (Smith 1793: 64-5)

Wordsworth was later to lament what man has made of man in similar vein, while spring buds burgeoned about him.

In *Salisbury Plain* this contrast between the calm of nature and the pain of human suffering is presented in a strongly radical, if not revolutionary, context, just as Charlotte Smith's poem consciously assumes a radical stance. But in the revisions of *An Evening Walk*, confronting a similar contrast in the death of the widow and her children, Wordsworth seems to employ methods which look back to eighteenth-century theories and forward to *The Ruined Cottage* and *Lyrical Ballads*. In the 1794 version the widow is turned into a spectacle, viewed by a wandering rustic the next morning frozen in the posture in which she had attempted to shelter her children. Her 'stedfast form' is a monument to the 'love whose providence in death survives' (*EW*: 148, ll. 533-6) and the transcendent power of that love mingles the response of horror with one of reverence. Wordsworth's passage in the Preface to *Lyrical Ballads* about the complex delight which flows from sympathy with pain has similarities with formulations like that of Blair, which derive this pleasure from the social affections. Sympathy itself has pleasure as a social passion, and when it is evoked by the sufferings of one who illustrates the same worthy feelings to a heightened degree the pleasure is intensified. Nature plays little role in reconciling us to the fate of the 'Mad Mother', the 'Forsaken Indian Woman', or even, arguably, Margaret in *The Ruined Cottage*. Any comfort must come from a recognition that they portray feelings which do honour to humanity.

The ministry of nature is still paired with human values in the later version of the Salisbury Plain material, *Adventures on Salisbury Plain*. Nature here manages to cheer the female vagrant more successfully, but the focus of the poem has changed. Nature now brings no comfort to her companion; in fact it heightens his unease. He is now characterized as a sailor whose oppression by press-gang and navy has so corrupted him that he commits robbery and murder. As most commentators note, it is a Godwinian theme, though the commonly quoted maxim 'the assassin cannot help the murder any more than the knife' is only half the story. Godwinian necessity does not proclaim the gloomy inevitability of corrupt states producing corrupt individuals: men can seldom be so corrupt as never to feel the return of more 'natural' benevolent feelings, nor (in the 1793 edition of *Political Justice*) can society become so corrupt as not to perpetually suggest motives of benevolence. The guilt felt by Tyrell, Falkland, and by Caleb Williams himself is a testimony to this essential human benevolence. Similarly, nature's evidence of a universe of love recalls the sailor to the humanitarian ideals betrayed in his crime. It hardly needs the melodramatic appearance of his wife, expiring as a further indirect victim of his crime, to impel him to expiation. *Adventures* shares with *Caleb Williams* the critical attitude towards the law which provides a conclusion that is 'just' only in the legal, not the human, sense.

The response of Mortimer in *The Borderers* is another example of guilt testifying to an essential humanity, but the perversion of Rivers is a product of Wordsworth's meditations on the examples of terrorists such as Robespierre, Saint-Just, and Marat, who had perverted reason, benevolence, and nature into a code of slaughter. In Wordsworth's reaction against the utopian rationalism of reformers, Godwin, with his non-violent gradualism and attempts to avoid extremism, might well have been an important influence, though he has been condemned for a precipitant optimism which was more the property of his disciples. The strategy which Wordsworth adopts is largely to abandon the claims of reason to better the human condition, but to infuse his concepts of feeling, nature, and imagination with the attributes of benevolence, reason, and gradual progress. Vital aspects of reason as a critical force are lost, but in his nostalgic and pastoral construction of 'nature' certain principles linked with reform survive. The independence of his characters, morally and economically, marks their distinction from any Burkean construction of dependent loyalty, and the habits and traditions which he presents as native to rustic life, such as the communal care of orphans and beggars, are evidence of extended benevolence which does not pauperize or demean. The major object of the *Lyrical Ballads* is to extend the sensibility of its readers beyond the limits of sympathy posited by Adam Smith. The important exchange of letters between Wordsworth and John Wilson in 1802 highlights this purpose. Wilson had objected to some of the characters in *Lyrical Ballads*, especially the Idiot Boy, as unfit to raise the sympathy of the 'impartial spectator'. He felt that his inability to sympathize was based on the general feelings of human nature established by Smith. Wordsworth's reply asserts the poet's duty to 'rectify men's feelings, to give them new compositions of feeling'. He refers to feelings which might have prevailed 'hundreds of years', yet which the 'philosopher' can look upon as 'accidents' not inherent in human nature. Among the feelings which Wordsworth mentions as in need of rectification are the 'excessive admiration' of 'personal prowess and military success', feelings connected with 'birth and innumerable other modes of sentiment, civil and religious' (*OA*: 622-3). Humanity is the focus of the collection, not external nature; it is human feelings that give life to the heap of stones with which 'Michael' begins and to the eponymous thorn tree. 'Tintern Abbey' first yields that sublimity of vision in which the harmony of universal life incorporates but subdues the still, sad music of humanity, and initiates the celebration of a continuum in which tragic figures like Margaret can be seen as 'passing shows of Being'.

The idea of love of nature leading to love of man is persuasively presented in *The Prelude*, but as an account of Wordsworth's personal progress it is a hoax. Of course it is difficult to disprove experiences which are described as remembered feelings, senses, and latent visions, but in his poetry the sense of nature as a living, active universe develops at exactly the same time as his revolutionary humanitarianism, if indeed the radical enthusiasm which expanded sympathy to the lowest forms of human life did not itself awaken analogous feelings for the lesser celandine. It may be a pardonable elision to confuse the date of his accession to a radical humanitarian sensibility with that of similar feelings towards nature. It is, however, a patent falsification to suggest that the love of nature which was the source of his humanitarianism was the same as that which provided a sure relief for the defeat of humanitarian goals in an inner ecstasy that lifted the burden of an unintelligible world and stimulated the literary celebration of the power to create literature.

Wordsworth's accounts of his revolutionary years in *The Prelude* are a typical mixture of fidelity to experience and the projection of later ideas on to earlier development. The first account in Book X describes a relatively coherent development towards radicalism to which both nature and human sympathy impel him. The second account, beginning with line 657, gives a much more self-reproachful analysis of the war within him. Universal benevolence is seen as the foe of native feelings of allegiance, and reason as a delusive enchantress which, in promising to regenerate humanity, erodes traditional moral principles. In Book XI a third account of his development over the period attacks critical reason and the domination of the eye as immature stages of a mental progress which may be taken as universal rather than individual.

His first account is continuous with his French experiences and affirms a faith in progress towards a more just and egalitarian society based on man's social affections. He credits the Revolution with this aim, and still feels in 1803 that the influence of 'one paramount mind' might have guided the Revolution to that end, quelling internal faction and resisting external aggression. On the declaration of war with France he writes of the 'most unnatural strife / In my own heart' as his sympathies are wrenched from his own countrymen. He talks in terms of 'apostasy' of the supplanting of narrow insular 'patriotism' by the new cosmopolitan ideal. Nevertheless, he blames not himself but politicians for the 'change and subversion' which he and 'all ingenuous youth' experienced during the war. His disaffection took the form of prophetic denunciations of England, and even a 'kind of sympathy with power'. Like a Hebrew prophet celebrating the just wrath of God, he viewed the devastation within France as 'in the order of sublimest laws' as retribution for the oppressions of the old regime, while the reverses of the allied armies seemed fit punishment for attempting to strangle the infant republic. The death of Robespierre heralded a new optimism about the course of the Revolution and, though disappointed with the Directory, Wordsworth concludes his account of French affairs by affirming his faith in the French people and their irresistible, universal triumph. The focus then shifts to Wordsworth's mistaken faith that the triumph of egalitarian, benevolist ideas would be as irresistible in England. Here he seems to be confessing some 'juvenile errors', but again the predominant criticism is of British politicians. The only 'errors' he mentions are the radical party's loss of heart and his own over-confidence. Here the account stops and Wordsworth introduces another version of his progress.

The second narrative presents an account of values which he asserts were established in his youth, which faltered under pressure, and were confirmed only by thought and experience. He formulates this faith as a confidence in:

> What there is best in individual Man,
> Of wise in passion, and sublime in power,
> What there is strong and pure in household love,
> Benevolent in small societies,
> And great in large ones also, when called forth
> By great occasions.
>
> (x.666-71)

It is a cautious statement. Valuing the individual is qualified by valuing what is 'best' in him; the social affections are stressed in their household and local attachments, while the exertions of universal benevolence are only evident on great occasions. The wisdom of the passions may be the wisdom of Burke or that of radical sensibility, the sublime of power may be the sublimity of Burke or the 'moral' sublime.

In this version of events the outbreak of war is far more subversive. Before the conflict Wordsworth presents himself as erring only in indulgence, tolerating both the excesses of reformers and the prejudice of error (hardly a true reflection of his opinions in the 'Letter to the Bishop of Llandaff'). He is still expanding his sympathies, still 'a child of Nature as at first, / Diffusing those affections wider / That from the cradle had grown up with me, / And losing, in no other way than light / Is lost in light, the weak in the more strong' (x.752-6). But now the war divides his affections. His feelings for the ideals of the

Revolution are no longer a commitment to the greater cause of humanity which strengthens him in his fight against entrenched prejudice. Instead they are presented as vitiating his feelings for his native land. The patriotism which Wordsworth developed in 1802-3 included criticism as well as piety, and was very different from the unreflecting prejudice he was attacking in the early 1790s. In this section of *The Prelude*, however, Wordsworth is projecting the values of 1803 back into 1793 and contradicting his first account of his progress. The eclipse of patriotism in his support for the universal cause is now described as a crippling perversion of his affections: 'not, as hitherto, / a swallowing up of lesser things in great, / But change of them into their opposites' which 'Soured and corrupted upwards to the source / My sentiments' (x.761-4). The mechanisms of sensibility are still invoked, but the assertion that his affections now 'Ran in new channels, leaving old ones dry' (x.770) suggests the priority of the 'old', the individual and local attachments.

Wordsworth's turn to Godwin for evidence of his optimistic faith 'Safer, of universal application, such / As could not be impeached' (x.789-90) is the major cause adduced for his falling off from the inspiration of nature. Much has been written on the use of Rivers' lines about the independent intellect in *The Prelude* and the responsibility of Godwinian reason for driving Wordsworth to despair and geometry. But there is scant external evidence for the crisis Wordsworth depicts. One might speculate that, in evoking despair comparable with Smith's Marchmont, Wordsworth is searching for the representative status that he claims for his own experience. Most scholars have seen the process as a long period of progressive disillusionment. What have been less noticed are the continuities between the independent reason and the new emphasis on natural feelings which would continue the work of reason in the context of daily life. In 1805 Wordsworth asserts that he still feels the expansive hope of his his Godwinian days, that: 'Man should start / Out of the worm-like state in which he is, / And spread abroad the wings of Liberty, / Lord of himself, in undisturbed delight' (x.835-9). The means by which he earlier attempted to further this aspiration, his plans for the 'Philanthropist', his immersion in the controversies of the day, his poetry of protest, are rejected as 'microscopic', not 'comprehensive' enough, and lying outside the limits of 'experience'. The limits of the world of experience are used to discipline his fancy in Book II; here they impose limitations on aspirations towards progress. Yet, lest this appeal to experience seem too Burkean, he leaves the reader in no doubt that for him the decent drapery of a conservative sensibility no longer veiled the oppressions of society or their connection with 'moral sentiments' that were in need of rectification:

> Enough, no doubt, the advocates themselves
> Of ancient institutions had performed
> To bring disgrace upon their very names;
> Disgrace of which custom and written law,
> And sundry moral sentiments, as props
> And emanations of these institutes
> Too justly bore a part. A veil
> Had been uplifted; why deceive ourselves?
>
> (x.849–56)

The restless inquisition which he conducted into 'all passions, notions, shapes of faith' (x.889) is, as Roe suggests, strongly reminiscent of the Revolutionary Tribunals of the Terror, and he is also demanding 'proof' in the same manner as Mortimer in *The Borderers*, proof which, of inner truths like passion and faith, cannot be provided by reason, though reason can shake them.

Wordsworth returns to his efforts to guillotine aristocratic notions in Book XI, where he describes himself criticizing the heroes of the past and of poetic tradition in the light of reason, becoming a 'Bigot to a new idolatry' (xi.75) and cutting off his heart from 'all the sources of her former strength' (xi.78). The language here is far more Burkean as he laments his mistrust of 'the elevation which had made me one / With the great Family that here and there / Is scattered through the abyss of ages past, / Sage, Patriot, Lover, Hero' (xi.61-4). Here too later ideas are being projected on to the earlier period. In the sonnets of 1802-3 Wordsworth was resuscitating ancient heroes and gilding them with the colours of the moral imagination, a process later extended to modern heroes, the Church, and the aristocracy. His poetry of the 1790s introduced far different heroes to his audience and affronted their prejudices with idiot boys, village wives, pedlars, and shepherds.

In Book XII of *The Prelude* Wordsworth still rests his egalitarian doctrine on a far more extended idea of sensibility than any other author. He claims not only the rights of equal humanity for the village characters of his tales but an elevation above his 'gentle readers'. Other writers had held that sensibility and strong feelings were not dependent on 'Retirement, leisure, language purified / By manners thoughtful and elaborate' (xii.189-90) or a life abounding in the 'light and air / Of elegances that are made by man' (xii.192-3). Others, too, had argued that taste, if not genius, was the birthright even of 'souls of humblest frame ' (xii.15). Wordsworth takes these claims to an extreme. Convinced of the defects of modern education and the 'talking world', he finds his highest examples of human nature and natural inspiration in inarticulate characters whose language is 'of the heavens, the power, / The thought, the image, and the silent joy; / Words are but under-agents in their souls' (xii.270-2). He is insistent that these characters are 'real', not abstractions, and subject to the hardest lot of mankind, condemned to daily labour 'under all the weight / Of that unjustice which upon ourselves / By composition of society / Ourselves entail' (xii.102-5). He recognizes that his model is in fact a favoured example of such labourers, and that their virtuous feelings depend on economic circumstances. They are not subjected to unintermitted toil which, he acknowledges, stifles sensibility. They have an economic independence in land-ownership which, he thought, gave greater strength to family feelings. His overtly political pleas, like the letter to C. J. Fox of 1802, are in defence of this achieved paradise of equality and fraternity; only rarely and tentatively does he speculate on generalizing these conditions to society at large.

Grasmere is a happy valley where healthy feelings can be nurtured, and it is by these feelings and by experiencing the creative power of man in union with nature that the 'ordinary' world can be regenerated. The egalitarian vision which Wordsworth now promulgates is a revolution of sensibility which extends the previously envisaged range of social sympathy and human potentiality, yet seems restricted to this model of reality. Politically, an idealized Grasmere offers no particular advance in considering the leading problems of the age, though it can provide a 'real' embodiment of abstract doctrines. Wordsworth's return to nature is not to unsocialized Rousseauistic man but to a society much like that praised by Scottish philosophers as the stage of social progress most suited to the natural social feelings. Here 'they who want, are not too great a weight / For those who can relieve; here may the heart / Breathe in the air of fellow-suffering / Dreadless' (*OA*: 184, ll. 447–50). Relief can be a matter of individual sharing, not the organized alms-giving of the opulent or the state. Individual independence can be maintained for the beggar whose last wish is to avoid the workhouse. Yet these conditions have an economic basis in property and a political basis in the principle of heredity. Though Wordsworth seems to wish to disturb the aristocratic prejudices of his readers by giving them a 'tale of honour' clothed in rustic garb (xii.183), the use of the discourse of aristocracy is a two-edged weapon. Michael talks of his forefathers as 'not loth / To give their bodies to the family mold' (*OA*: 234, l. 380) as if to a family crypt when passing on the land to him. Heredity is seen more as a transmission of love and trust than a property transaction. In later years, as he condemned the materialism of the age and settled his own accounts with aristocracy, Wordsworth turned to them as guardians of inherited rural traditions, and credited them with the enlarged sympathies which in the 1790s he had used to attack them.

Wordsworth developed the habit of abjuring criticism of others, preferring to appeal to common traditions which could be idealized. He was capable of more critical attitudes in Book X of *The Prelude*, where a parallel is suggested between England and the degenerate condition of Sicily, a land 'Strewed with the wreck of loftiest years' (x.960). In such a land 'indignation works where hope is not' (x.966). The idealization of rural life is balanced by indignant criticism of present realities and a residual commitment to reason and progress. Even when affirming the 'mysteries of passion' which make 'One brotherhood of all the human race' he also looks forward to what reason 'shall perform to exalt and to refine' (xi.84–8). In asserting his faith in a surviving natural sensibility he also attacks what Godwin called the 'crimping-house of oppression' which thwarts the growth of sensibility and genius:

> True it is, where oppression worse than death
> Salutes the being at his birth, where grace
> Of culture hath been utterly unknown,
> And labour in excess and poverty
> From day to day pre-occupy the ground

Of the affections, and to Nature's self
Oppose a deeper nature, there indeed,
Love cannot be.

(xii.194-201)

Coleridge too had been impressed with Godwin's demonstration of the brutalization of the oppressed and the vengeful retaliation that it provoked. As a necessitarian, he considered this an inevitable result of the prevailing state of society and sought a means of containing this violence and encouraging an educative process initiated from above, guided by religious ideals. Wordsworth followed Godwin rather than Coleridge in trusting to the humanity of the lower classes, but went beyond both in his faith in a natural sensibility which had no need of formal education. In his protest against the 'outside marks by which / Society has parted man from man, / Neglectful of the universal heart' (xii.217-19) we might again find an echo of Shaftesbury's condemnation of the 'marks set upon men' which divide our common nature, but extended beyond Shaftesbury's limits in the development of egalitarian sensibility.

Wordsworth seems to have followed the tradition of sensibility in his theory of natural morality, though his ideas have a similarity with Coleridge's derivation of benevolence from Hartleyan association. Passages which Wordsworth composed in 1798 and later incorporated into *The Excursion* show particular continuities with the ideas of sensibility. He maintains that man works in the spirit of Nature, not presuming to anticipate progress which is unrealistic, but he insists on man's capacity to act according to laws of his own nature. In one passage he seems to be echoing Godwin's criticism of Rousseau's negative idea of virtue as abstention from evil: 'we were never made to be content / With simple abstinence from ill' (*OA*: 677, ll. 25-6). Our active powers, when unconstrained by 'chains / Shackles and bonds', actually become 'Subversive of our noxious qualities, / And by the substitution of delight / And by new influxes of strength suppress / All evil' (*OA*: 677, ll. 33-6). The passage evokes Godwin's confidence that man does not require the coercion of chains and gallows to dragoon him into virtue but that his own developing moral sense will lead him to see the insufficiency of sensual and selfish enjoyments to produce the greater happiness of benevolence. If we are bound by a law, it is one 'Allied to our own nature' (*OA*: 677, l. 29), one of beneficence:

> There is one only liberty, 'tis his,
> Who by beneficence is circumscribed;
> 'Tis his to whom the power of doing good
> Is law and statute, penalty, and bond,
> His prison and his warder; his who finds
> His freedom in the joy of virtuous thoughts.
> (*OA*: 677, ll. 39-44)

In following the inner law of benevolence there is no contradiction between adhering to general laws and acting in the light of circumstances: 'we shall read / Our duties in all forms, and general laws / And local accidents shall tend alike / To quicken and to rouze, and give the will / And power which by a [ ] chain of good / Shall link us to our kind' (*OA*: 679, ll. 36-41).

These passages are particularly useful in disentangling the thought of Wordsworth and Coleridge. Patton and Mann in their edition of Coleridge's lectures of 1795 show numerous instances of Coleridge using language and concepts which could be attributed to Godwin (or the tradition of sensibility) and interpreting them in terms of Hartleyan association. Wordsworth in the lines above emphasizes man's active powers and sees them as 'natural'. Coleridge sees the transformation of selfish desires into purer motives as a 'magical' process performed by association and directed in the last instance by the divine Providence that educes good out of evil:

> It is with virtue precisely as it is with money. Originally money is not valued but for its use in the procuring of something else, but in old age, many love and pursue that as an end which at first was only a means. So virtue is first practiced for the pleasures that accompany or the rewards that follow it – and Vice avoided as hateful from the punishment attach[ed]. But in length of Time by the magic power of association we transfer our attachment from the Reward to the action rewarded and our fears and hatred from the Punishment to the Vice Punished. Hence it is that gross self-interest rises gradually into pure Benevolence, and Appetence of Pleasure into Love of Virtue.
> (*Lect*: 113-14)

Godwin had used Hartley's example of the miser, just as Wordsworth appealed to the habit of charity in *The Cumberland Beggar*, but for both there was an additional pleasure in a benevolent habit that was associated with rational approval. Coleridge's optimistic faith in mechanism and habit as a means of spiritual progress was only a temporary phase, but it dominated his response to Godwin's ideas in the 1790s. To him they ignored essential facts of human nature, its selfishness, sensuality, and exclusiveness of sympathy, which could only be transformed by a divine force.

Wordsworth seems happy to accept Coleridge's associationism, yet it coexists with a faith in the human mind's natural moral and creative powers. There is no conflict if one accepts that man and nature share the same life and power. Stones do feel, and man does link them with some feeling. But by the time of *The Prelude* Wordsworth was beginning to accept the authority of Nature as a limiting control on the powers of the mind. The famous 'spots of time' passage begins with a claim that they demonstrate the mastery of the human mind, but they bear a message of limitation and even of chastisement. The moments of transcendence, which in 'Tintern Abbey' had been seen as a gift of nature and the world of 'sense', become moments when the mind rebels against the limits of reality. The imagery of the Simplon Pass passage links the rebellious human imagination with the sublime hopes of the French Revolution. Nature, having already disappointed the imagination by imprinting a real Mont Blanc on a mind possessed by its sublime image, disappoints Wordsworth even more in the anticlimax of crossing the Alps. The apocalyptic vision retrospectively imposed on the incident and embodied in images of the descent through the pass is ascribed to the 'unfathered vapour' of the imagination, owing nothing to memory or association. Wordsworth memorably asserts the mind's independence in language which exalts its transcendence of nature and of society, yet still contains the 'social' images of 'home' and the more indirect references to revolutionary activity:

> Our destiny, our nature, and our home,
> Is with infinitude – and only there;
> With hope it is, hope that can never die,
> Effort and expectation, and desire,

> And something evermore about to be.
> The mind beneath such banners militant
> Thinks not of spoils or trophies, nor of aught
> That may attest its prowess, blest in thoughts
> That are their own perfection and reward –
> Strong in itself, and in the access of joy
> Which hides it like the overflowing Nile.
>
> (vi.538–48)

Roe (1988: 61) links the passage with Wordsworth's French experience through the image of the 'banners militant' of the patriot army of 1792. He asserts that Wordsworth is 'acknowledging its formative revolutionary influence but discarding the mundane paraphernalia of politics'. It is also linked by the 'overflowing Nile' as an image of apocalyptic renewal, an image developed from a brief allusion in the 1793 *Descriptive Sketches* into a more explicit revolutionary image in the later version. In this Wordsworth calls on God to preside

> Over the mighty stream now spreading wide:
> So shall its waters, from the heavens supplied
> In copious showers, from earth by wholesome springs,
> Brood o'er the long-parched lands with Nile-like wings!
> And grant that every sceptred child of clay
> Who cries presumptuous, 'Here the flood shall stay,'
> May in its progress see thy guiding hand,
> And cease the acknowledged purpose to withstand;
> Or, swept in anger from the insulted shore,
> Sink with his servile bands, to rise no more!
>
> (*DS*: 117–19, l.l.655–64)

The image which in the mid-decade had represented a 'natural' social and political tranformation had by the end become a vision of the mind's capacity to transcend nature, a sublime which found little in nature and reality to support its social aspirations. The apocalyptic vision of the early decade might well have been influenced by the millennial hopes current among many Dissenting radicals which have been explored by H. W. Piper. The development of Hartley's ideas by Darwin and Priestley saw nature actively participating in the universal march towards perfection, earthquakes and inundations anticipating the eventual transformation of all things natural and social.

What characterizes Wordsworth's thought as apocalyptic is not so much the doctrines of progress gleaned from Paine and Grégoire but his acceptance of the violence necessary to produce this 'natural' transformation. The final description of the ascent of Snowdon has justifiably been seen as a 'set-piece', a too appropriate image of the mind in harmony with the creative power of nature, but it is noteworthy that it is an elegiac attempt to recapture an experience of the early decade when nature and human aspirations were in harmony.

Wordsworth's idea of nature does change from a faith in the world of 'sense' as an avenue to visions of possible sublimity associated with human and social aspirations, to a more remote conception of all-encompassing continuity, bearing human tragedy and loss within a stream of tendency whose ultimate goodness is disclosed to the eye of imaginative faith. It comes to sanction habits and traditions which Wordsworth had sought to combat and transform during the 1790s, and exercises an increasingly severe discipline on the imagination. But his 'more than Roman confidence' in human nature did not suddenly collapse, nor were his aspirations confined to the apocalypse of the inner vision. Roe suggests that Wordsworth's Godwinian gradualism, his political involvement, and even the theory of the 'One Life' 'would be seen to have usurped the promptings of personal vision as a means of access to redeemed experience' (Roe 1988: 62). He further suggests that his turn to the apocalypse of the mind was produced by the 'consciousness of human weakness and fallibility' and that 'it was failure [presumably both personal and social] that made Wordsworth a poet' (Roe 1988: 274-5). I would agree that his faith in human progress was intimately connected with his sense of the 'One Life' of nature in its genesis, but I would not see it as extinguished by the failure of revolutionary hopes in 1798 nor even in 1802, the date by which Wordsworth felt that the war against Napoleon had been nationally recognized as 'just and necessary'.

When British armies, instead of liberating Spain, gave free passage for French troops back to France, Wordsworth responded to the national mood of revulsion. *The Convention of Cintra* (1809) provided an occasion when Wordsworth could feel again that he was voicing the thoughts of men in opposition to constituted authority. In 1793 he had thought that 'one paramount mind' might have saved the Revolution from Terror by appealing to truths which are evident to the humblest eyes, transcending 'all local patrimony / One Nature as there is one Sun in heaven' (*Prelude*: x.139-40). Such a spirit, remaining 'thoroughly faithful to itself', could become 'as an instinct among men, a stream / That gathered up each petty straggling rill / And vein of water' (x.147-51). In 1809 he tried to represent such a spirit in voicing the widespread indignation with the Convention and felt again the inspiration of the French Revolution's early years in championing the patriot army of the Peninsula, betrayed by politicians and career generals.

He asserts that a natural fellow-feeling supported the efforts of the Spaniards for freedom. Though this freedom is national, Wordsworth tries to link the love of country with universal goals. Though their former institutions were oppressive and superstitious, Wordsworth affirms that the struggle for liberty, like that of the French, inspires aspirations to more egalitarian government and a purified religion. The experience of the sublime is again evoked in a context of social aspiration: 'the vigour of the human soul is from without and from futurity, - in breaking down limit, and losing and forgetting herself in the sensation and image of Country and of the human race' (*Prose*: 292). He reproaches British statesmen, schooled in managing the selfish passions, for neglecting virtues such as the 'instincts of natural and social man; the deeper emotions; the simpler feelings; the spacious range of the disinterested imagination' (*Prose*: 305). Referring to the American War and the 'war against the French People in the early stages of their Revolution', he condemns 'the same presumptuous irreverence of the principles of justice, and blank insensibility to the affections of human nature, which determined the conduct of our government in those two wars *against* liberty, [which] have continued to accompany its exertions in the present struggle *for* liberty' (*Prose*: 308-9).

In appealing to the values of sensibility against expediency, Wordsworth is primarily appealing to that sensibility which, 'formerly a generous nurseling of rude Nature, has been chased from its ancient range in the wide domain of patriotism and religion' (*Prose*: 325). But the urge to link patriotic sensibility with a wider benevolence which can claim universal justice and reason involves him in some awkward constructions. An image of a spider's web, whose 'outermost and all-embracing circle of benevolence' is linked to inner concentric circles round the centre of self 'which sustains the whole', presents us with a most incompetent spider. While the 'higher mode of being does not exclude, but necessarily includes, the lower', the 'sublime and disinterested feelings' nevertheless do not 'trust long to their own unassisted power' but 'condescend', 'adopt', and 'know the time of their repose' (*Prose*: 340). Wordsworth looks forward to the unification and freedom of Germany and Italy, but he can also appreciate the benefits of a more highly civilized nation assimilating a less civilized one, and sees justice and progress in the unification of Britain.

Wordsworth struggled to maintain the faith which had inspired him in France, a faith in social progress supported by a trust in human sensibility. When he eventually met Helen Maria Williams in France in 1820, he delighted her by repeating from memory her poem 'To Hope'. Hope in social progress in the later period was less easy to affirm. Called upon in 1809 to formulate such a hope in answer to the letter of 'Mathetes' in *The Friend*, Wordsworth could claim only limited support from history. His account of the meandering path of human progress (so like his own) required the aid of Godwin to affirm an unquenched faith in human potential. We may be reconciled to the apparent tardiness of human progress by historical examples of transcendent human powers demonstrated by individuals:

> In fact it is not, as a Writer of the present day has admirably observed, in the power of fiction, to portray in words, or of the imagination to conceive in spirit, Actions or Characters of more exalted virtue, than those which thousands of years ago have existed upon earth, as we know from the records of authentic history. Such is the inherent dignity of human nature, that there belong to it sublimities of virtue which all men may attain, and which no man can transcend: And, though this be not true in an equal degree, of intellectual power, yet in the persons of Plato, Demosthenes, and Homer, – and in those of Shakespeare, Milton, and Lord Bacon, – were enshrined as much of the divinity of intellect as the inhabitants of this planet can hope will ever take up its abode among them.
>
> (Coleridge 1969: 2: 232)

In the context of Godwin's *Thoughts Occasioned* the achievements of genius are an illustration of man's capacity to act up to his imagination whatever the circumstances of society. Considering the same question as Wordsworth – whether 'any extraordinary improvement can ever be expected to take place in society' – Godwin puts his faith in imagination: 'The human imagination is capable of representing to itself a virtuous community, a little heaven on earth. The human understanding is capable of developing the bright idea, and constructing a model of it' (Godwin 1968: 372–3). In one of the many passages which look forward to Shelley, Godwin proclaims:

> what the heart of man is able to conceive, the hand of man is strong enough to perform. There is no beauty of literary and poetical composition which we can so much as guess at, that excels what we find executed in the divinest passages of Milton and Shakespear. There is no virtuous action which we can figure to ourselves, that surpasses that virtue and elevation of mind which we find over and over again recorded in the faithful page of history. Fiction here labours in vain; it never equals what men have acted and felt, in the great vision and awe-creating presence of reality.
> (1968: 373)

Both Godwin and Wordsworth emphasize the historical reality of these monuments to the human spirit, though both had reservations about the historicity of recorded heroism. In *The Prelude* Wordsworth says that he viewed history in the same light as poetry, only valuable as far as it inspires the imagination. Godwin doubted whether even a contemporary figure could be correctly estimated, let alone an object of historical controversy like Cato. Both, however, had felt the pressures of historical reality in their time, and responded with a creative visionary power which marked them for life.

NOTES

INTRODUCTION

1 Scholars such as R. S. Crane, Louis Bredvold, and Arthur Sherbo produced some of the first examinations of the area. More modern studies referred to in the text are Brissenden (1974), Sheriff (1982), Todd (1986), and Mullan (1988).
2 *ELH* (June 1956), 144–52.
3 *The Lounger* 20 (18 June 1785).

1 VARIETIES OF SENSIBILITY

1 Sheriff asserts that after Hume 'the distance between the rationalists and the sentimentalists, which was never great, was diminished' (Sheriff 1982: 77).
2 Stewart observes that Godwin's theory is 'the system of Hutcheson, disguised under a different and much more exceptionable phraseology', in which 'the duty of justice is supposed to coincide exactly as a rule of conduct with the affection of benevolence' (Stewart 1854: 599).
3 See Abrams (1953: 95–6); Jacobus (1976: 186–93).

2 TOWARDS REVOLUTION

1 Mackenzie (1791: 20). Another letter, of 22 November 1790, reviews the *Reflections* and criticizes the support Burke gives to a constitution of absolute rule and his neglect of the distresses of the masses. He does, however, praise Burke's fear of 'the inconsiderate desire for reform; a jealousy of needless innovation, which it seems to me extremely useful to keep awake at the present time' (1791: 60). Subsequent letters are loud in defence of the Constitution, the culture and civilization of centuries, and vituperative against the opposition, the last calling for war with France (Mackenzie 1793: 150).

3 SENSIBILITY IN REVOLUTION: GODWIN AND WOLLSTONECRAFT

1 See especially Paulson (1983) and O. Smith (1984).
2 Abinger MSS Dep. b. 227/2. This copy is marked by many corrections, repositionings, and scorings out. Two further copies exist, one a fair copy incorporating the corrections, and the other replacing passages marked in both other copies by pencil brackets with ellipses. This last copy is included with copies of the other 'Letters of Mucius' as if for publication, but the ellipses produce nonsense and an attempt to annotate references to opposition speeches from the *Parliamentary Register* is abandoned (probably because some of the speeches referred to in the letter do not appear in that publication).

4 SENSIBILITY IN REACTION

1 Abrams (1953: 191) quotes a description of the process by Gerard which accounts for 'inspiration' without 'violating the assumptions of the associationist theory of mind'.
2 Quotations from Thomas Wedgwood's letter to Godwin are from Abinger MSS Dep. c. 507/11.
3 Wedgwood MSS 28475-40. This material exists in a number of versions, one of which was submitted to Godwin for stylistic correction in 1796.
4 Wedgwood MSS 28515/118-40.
5 'As the herd of mankind are stripped of everything, in body and mind, so are they thankful for what is left; as is the desolation of their hearts and the wreck of their little all, so is the pomp and pride which is built upon their ruin, and their fawning admiration of it' (Howe: 7: 148).

5 HELEN MARIA WILLIAMS: RADICAL CHRONICLER

1 Woodward (1930) gives the fullest account of her milieu.
2 See Harper (1916: 1: 149-50).
3 Abinger MSS Dep. b. 214/3.
4 H. M. Williams, *Letters Containing a Sketch of the Politics of France from the 31st May 1793 till the 28th July 1794 and of the Scenes which have passed in the Prisons of Paris* (London, G. G. and J. Robinson, 1795), vol. 2, p. 117. All further references to this work appear in the text as Williams (1795).
5 H. M. Williams, *Letters from France . . .*, vol. 2 (London, G. G. and J. Robinson, 1792), p. 70. The publication history of the four volumes of this series of letters is complicated. The first volume appeared in 1790, published by T. Cadell, who continued to issue subsequent editions. The second volume of letters was published by G. G. and J. Robinson in 1792. The Robinsons also published the letters of 1793 in two

volumes, numbered 3 and 4, in 1793, an edition which is rarely cited. Woodward suspected the existence of letters published in 1793 from references in the letters of Mrs Piozzi and Anna Seward but was unable to locate them (Woodward 1930: 88-9). The Scholars' Facsimile and Reprint edition (New York, 1975) reproduces the second edition of the 1793 letters, published in 1796. There is a copy of the first edition of the 1793 letters in the British Library which is identical to the later edition. I have also seen an edition of these two volumes published by J. Chalmers in Dublin in 1794. Scholars have laid more stress on the letters of 1790-1, yet the 1793 letters are obviously important for their influence on radicals reacting to the progress of the Revolution. I have used the 1792 edition of the letters of 1790-1 (Williams 1792) and the 1793 edition of the letters of that year (Williams 1793).
6 *Gentleman's Magazine* 65, 2 (Aug. and Dec. 1798), 672; 1030.
7 *Monthly Magazine* 5 (1798), 492. It had presented the cause of friction in February as the violation of the 'social compact' between the Pays de Vaud and 'the aristocratical Cantons of Berne and Fribourg', and interpreted French military moves as a reply to the 'hostile measures' of the cantons (145).

6 CHARLOTTE SMITH AS RADICAL NOVELIST

1 The only full-length study of Charlotte Smith is Hilbish (1941). This efficiently establishes Smith's place among the literary genres of the period, though its appreciation of the social and political context is weak. Gregory (1915) pays particular attention to Desmond as 'the first and fullest expression of Charlotte Smith's Revolutionary politics' (214), and to *The Young Philosopher* as an expression of 'philosophic' Revolutionism (222). Like many critics, Gregory bases her estimate of Smith's radicalism on the specific political doctrines found in her work rather than on the political implications of her themes and techniques. Ernest Baker links Smith with Radcliffe and the Gothic school in *The History of the English Novel* (Edinburgh, H. F. and G. Witherby, 1924-38), 5: 187-92; Lionel Stevenson in *The English Novel* (London, Constable, 1960) assimilates Smith to the novel of sensibility, acknowledging that the 'incidental social satire' (161) of her early works became more prominent when she 'succumbed to the ferment of the new ideas' (168). Anne Ehrenpreis, in the introduction to her edition of *The Old Manor House* (Smith 1969: xi), has asserted that 'literary historians who try to "place" Charlotte Smith as a Gothic novelist do so only by ignoring three-quarters of her work'. Many works on Jane Austen deal with Smith's novels, especially *Emmeline*, though most fail to acknowledge that, in choosing Emmeline as a 'model' heroine of sensibility, Austen was satirizing a creation which already had an almost parodic relationship to established models.
2 Bowstead suggests that 'the radicalisation of her heroine' is the 'central action' of the novel (Bowstead 1986: 261), and that her

marriage to Desmond is an indication of her enlarged political awareness. I fail to see any such growth in Geraldine, who seems to me to be always radical in her perceptions, though her actions never cease to be governed by social convention – with the marked exception of her treatment of Josephine.

3 Gunn (1983) explores the survival of Jacobitism during the eighteenth century as the 'Spectre at the Feast'. See Gunn (1983: 177–80) for an estimate of the Jacobite tendencies of *The British Critic*, the *Anti-Jacobin*, and figures such as John Reeves. He points out that Burke was erroneously taken as a supporter of these High Tory views.

4 She is echoing Burke's *Reflections* (1803: 105). The text mentions hairdressers and tallow-chandlers, and asserts that 'the state suffers oppression, if such as they, either individually or collectively, are permitted to rule', but Burke also quotes Ecclesiasticus 35: 25 in his footnote: ' "How can he get wisdom that handleth a plough, and that glorieth in the goad; that driveth oxen; and is occupied in their labours; and whose talk is of bullocks?" '

7 WORDSWORTH AND SENSIBILITY

1 See Gill (1990: 10) and Chandler (1984: 9–12).

BIBLIOGRAPHY

For eighteenth- and nineteenth-century works, place of publication is London unless otherwise stated.

Abrams, M. H. (1953), *The Mirror and the Lamp*, London, OUP.
Abrams, M. H. (1973), *Natural Supernaturalism*, New York, Norton.
Aikin, J. and Barbauld, A. L. (1792), *Miscellaneous Pieces in Prose*, 3rd ed.
Bage, R. (1788), *James Wallace*, 3 vols.
Bage, R. (1824), *Mount Henneth*, Ballantyne's Novelists' Library.
Bage, R. (1979), *Man as He Is*, 1792, repr. New York, Garland.
Bage, R. (1985), *Hermsprong*, ed. P. Faulkner, London, OUP.
Baine, R. M. (1965), *Thomas Holcroft and the Revolutionary Novel*, Athens, University of Georgia Press.
Belsham, T. (1801), *Elements of the Philosophy of the Human Mind*.
Bissett, R. (1804), *Modern Literature: A Novel*, 3 vols.
Blair, H. (1813), *Lectures on Rhetoric and Belles Lettres*, 3 vols, Edinburgh.
Blum, L. A. (1980), *Friendship, Altruism and Morality*, London, Routledge & Kegan Paul.
Bowstead, D. (1986), 'Charlotte Smith's *Desmond*: the epistolary novel as ideological argument', in *Fetter'd or Free?*, ed. M. A. Schofield and C. Macheski, Athens, Ohio University Press, 237-63.
Brissenden, R. F. (1974), *Virtue in Distress*, London, Macmillan.
Brooke, F. (1769), *The History of Lady Julia Mandeville*, 2 vols.
Burke, E. (1803), *Reflections on the Revolution in France*, vol. 5 of *Works*, ed. W. King and F. Laurence, 16 vols, 1803-27.
Burke, E. (1990), *A Philosophical Enquiry into the Origin of our Ideas of the Sublime and the Beautiful*, ed. A. Phillips, Oxford, OUP.
Burney, F. (1968), *Evelina*, ed. E. A. Bloom, London, OUP.
Butler, M. (1975), *Jane Austen and the War of Ideas*, London, OUP.
Chandler, J. K. (1984), *Wordsworth's Second Nature*, Chicago, University of Chicago Press.
Coleridge, S. T. (1956-71), *Collected Letters of Samuel Taylor Coleridge*, ed. E. L. Griggs, 6 vols, Oxford, Clarendon.
Coleridge, S. T. (1969), *The Friend*, ed. B. E. Rooke, 2 vols, London, Routledge & Kegan Paul.

Coleridge, S. T. (1971), *Lectures 1795 on Politics and Religion*, ed. L. Patton and P. Mann, London, Routledge & Kegan Paul.
Coleridge, S. T. (1972), *On the Constitution of Church and State*, ed. J. Barrell, London, Dent.
Coleridge, S. T. (1974), *Poems*, ed. J. Beer, London, Dent.
Coleridge, S. T. (1983), *Biographia Literaria*, ed. J. Engell and W. J. Bate, 2 vols, London, Routledge & Kegan Paul.
Coxe, W. (1780), *Sketches of the Natural, Civil, and Political State of Swisserland*, 2nd ed.
Dobrée, B. and Manwaring, G. E. (1937), *The Floating Republic*, London, Penguin.
Edgeworth, M. (1795), *Letters for Literary Ladies*.
Edgeworth, M. (1805), *The Modern Griselda*.
Edgeworth, M. and R. L. (1801), *Practical Education*, 2nd ed., 3 vols.
Elledge, S. (1961) (ed.), *Eighteenth Century Critical Essays*, 2 vols, Ithaca, Cornell University Press.
Erametsa, E. (1951), 'A study of the word "sentimental" and of other linguistic characteristics of eighteenth-century sentimentalism in England', *Annales Academiae Scientiarum Fennicae*, ser. B, no. 74, Helsinki.
Ferguson, A. (1792), *Principles of Moral and Political Science*, 2 vols, Edinburgh.
Ferguson, A. (1966), *An Essay on the History of Civil Society*, ed. D. Forbes, Edinburgh, Edinburgh University Press.
Fielding, H. (1972), *Miscellanies*, ed. H. K. Miller, 2 vols, Oxford, Clarendon.
Fielding, H. (1983), *Amelia*, ed. M. C. Battestin, Oxford, Clarendon.
Gill, S. (1990), *William Wordsworth*, Oxford, OUP.
Godwin, W. (1793), *Political Justice*, 2 vols.
Godwin, W. (1797), *The Enquirer*.
Godwin, W. (1799), *St Leon*, 4 vols.
Godwin, W. (1946), *Political Justice*, 3rd ed., 1798, ed. F. E. L. Priestley, 3 vols, Toronto, University of Toronto Press.
Godwin, W. (1966), *Four Early Pamphlets*, Gainesville, Florida, Scholars' Facsimiles and Reprints.
Godwin, W. (1968), *Uncollected Writings*, Gainesville, Florida, Scholars' Facsimiles and Reprints.
Godwin, W. (1970), *Caleb Williams*, ed. D. McCracken, London, OUP.
Gregory, A. (1915), *The French Revolution and the English Novel*, New York, Knickerbocker Press.
Gunn, J. A. W. (1983), *Beyond Liberty and Property*, Kingston and Montreal, McGill-Queens University Press.
Harper, G. M. (1916), *William Wordsworth*, 2 vols, London, John Murray.
Hays, M. (1974), *Letters and Essays Moral and Miscellaneous*, New York, Garland.
Hazlitt, W. (1930-4), *The Complete Works*, ed. P. P. Howe, 21 vols, London, Dent.

BIBLIOGRAPHY

Hilbish, F. M. (1941), 'Charlotte Smith, poet and novelist', PhD thesis, University of Pennsylvania.
Hume, D. (1888), *Hume's Enquiries*, ed. L. A. Selby-Bigge, Oxford, Clarendon.
Hume, D. (1888), *A Treatise of Human Nature*, ed. L. A. Selby-Bigge, Oxford, Clarendon.
Hutcheson, F. (1753), *A Short Introduction to Moral Philosophy*, 2nd ed., Glasgow.
Hutcheson, F. (1969), *An Essay on the Nature and Conduct of the Passions*, 3rd ed., 1742, Gainesville, Florida, Scholars' Facsimiles and Reprints.
Hutcheson, F. (1971), *Illustrations on the Moral Sense*, ed. B. Peach, Massachusetts, Harvard University Press.
Jacobus, M. (1976), *Tradition and Experiment in Wordsworth's Lyrical Ballads*, Oxford, Clarendon.
Jones, V. (1990) (ed.), *Women in the Eighteenth Century*, London, Routledge.
Kames, H. Home, Lord (1782), *Loose Hints upon Education*, 2nd ed., Edinburgh.
Kames, H. Home, Lord (1805), *Elements of Criticism*, 8th ed., 2 vols.
Kames, H. Home, Lord (1813), *Sketches of the History of Man*, 3 vols, Edinburgh.
Kelly, G. (1976), *The English Jacobin Novel*, Oxford, OUP.
Kelly, G. (1989), *English Fiction of the Romantic Period*, London, Longman.
Knox, V. (1779), *Essays Moral and Literary*, 2nd ed., 2 vols.
Legouis, E. (1939), 'Some remarks on the composition of the Lyrical Ballads of 1798', in *Wordsworth and Coleridge*, ed. E. A. Griggs, Princeton, Princeton University Press.
Lloyd, C. (1798), *Edmund Oliver*, 2 vols, Bristol.
Locke, D. (1980), *A Fantasy of Reason*, London, Routledge & Kegan Paul.
Logan, J. (1781), *Elements of the Philosophy of History*, Edinburgh.
Macdonell, D (1986), *Theories of Discourse*, Oxford, Blackwell.
Mackenzie, H. (1791), *The Letters of Brutus*, 1st series, Edinburgh.
Mackenzie, H. (1793), *The Letters of Brutus*, 2nd series, Edinburgh.
Mackintosh, J. (1791), *Vindiciae Gallicae*, 3rd ed.
Mackintosh, J. (1799), *A Discourse on the Study of the Law of Nature and Nations*.
Marshall, P. H. (1984), *William Godwin*, New Haven and London, Yale University Press.
Millar, J. (1803), *An Historical View of the English Government*, 4 vols.
Millar, J. (1806), *The Origin of the Distinction of Ranks*, 4th ed., Edinburgh.
More, H. (1801), *Strictures on the Modern System of Female Education*, in *Works*, 8 vols.
More, H. (1809), *Coelebs in Search of a Wife*, 2nd ed., 2 vols.
Mullan, J. (1988), *Sentiment and Sociability*, Oxford, Clarendon.

Paine, T. (1969), *Rights of Man*, ed. H. Collins, Harmondsworth, Penguin.
Parr, S. (1801), *A Spital Sermon preached at Christ Church April 15 1800*.
Paulson, R. (1983), *Representations of Revolution*, New Haven, Yale University Press.
Philp, M. (1986), *Godwin's Political Justice*, London, Duckham.
Piper, H. W. (1962), *The Active Universe*, London, Athlone Press.
Poovey, M. (1984), *The Polite Lady and the Woman Writer*, Chicago, University of Chicago Press.
Pratt, S. J. (1779), *Shenstone-Green; or the New Paradise Lost*, 3 vols.
Pratt, S. J. (1788), *Humanity or, The Rights of Nature*.
Pratt, S. J. (1807), *Sympathy and Other Poems*.
Price, R. (1789), *A Discourse on the Love of Our Country*.
Rescher, N. (1975), *Unselfishness: The Role of Vicarious Affects in Moral Philosophy and Social Theory*, Pittsburgh, University of Pittsburgh Press.
Roe, N. (1988), *Wordsworth and Coleridge: The Radical Years*, Oxford, Clarendon.
St Clair, W. (1989), *The Godwins and the Shelleys*, London, Faber.
Seward, A. (1811), *Letters of Anna Seward: written between the years 1784 and 1807*, 6 vols, Edinburgh.
Shaftesbury (1711), *Characteristicks of Men, Manners, Opinions, Times*, 3 vols.
Shelley, P. B. (1977), *Shelley's Poetry and Prose*, ed. D. H. Reiman and S. B. Powers, New York, Norton.
Sheriff, J. K. (1982), *The Good-Natured Man*, Alabama, University of Alabama Press.
Smith, A. (1976), *The Theory of Moral Sentiments*, ed. D. D. Raphael and A. L. MacFie, Oxford, Clarendon.
Smith, C. (1789), *Ethelinde, or the Recluse of the Lake*, 5 vols.
Smith, C. (1790), *Elegiac Sonnets*, 6th ed., Dublin.
Smith, C. (1791), *Celestina, A Novel*, 4 vols.
Smith, C. (1792), *Desmond*, 3 vols.
Smith, C. (1793), *The Emigrants, A Poem in Two Books*.
Smith, C. (1794), *The Banished Man*, 4 vols.
Smith, C. (1795), *Montalbert, A Novel*, 3 vols.
Smith, C. (1796), *Marchmont*, 4 vols.
Smith, C. (1798), *The Young Philosopher*, 4 vols.
Smith, C. (1969), *The Old Manor House*, ed. A. Ehrenpreis, London, OUP.
Smith, C. (1971), *Emmeline, The Orphan of the Castle*, ed. A. H. Ehrenpreis, London, OUP.
Smith, O. (1984), *The Politics of Language 1791-1819*, Oxford, Clarendon.
Stanton, J. P. (1989), 'Introduction' to C. Smith, *The Old Manor House*, ed. A. H. Ehrenpreis, Oxford, OUP.
Stewart, D. (1854), *Elements of the Philosophy of the Human Mind*, ed. G. N. Wright.

Stone, L. (1979), *The Family, Sex and Marriage in England 1500-1800*, London, Penguin.
Todd, F. M. (1957), *Politics and the Poet*, London, Methuen.
Todd, J. (1986), *Sensibility: An Introduction*, London, Methuen.
Todd, J. (1989), *The Sign of Angellica*, London, Virago.
Voitle, R. (1984), *The Third Earl of Shaftesbury*, Baton Rouge and London, Louisiana State University Press.
Wilberforce, W. (1805), *A Practical View of the Prevailing Religious System of Professed Christians*, 8th ed.
Williams, H. M. (1790), *Julia, A Novel*, 2 vols.
Williams, H. M. (1792), *Letters from France*, series 1, vols 1 and 2.
Williams, H. M. (1793), *Letters from France*, series 1, vols 3 and 4.
Williams, H. M. (1795), *Letters from France*, series 2, 4 vols.
Williams, H. M. (1798), *A Tour in Switzerland*.
Williams, H. M. (1801), *Sketches of the State of Manners and Opinions in the French Republic towards the Close of the Eighteenth Century*.
Williams, H. M. (1815), *A Narrative of the Events which have taken place in France from the Landing of Napoleon Bonaparte to the Restoration of Louis XVIII*.
Williams, H. M. (1823), *Poems on Various Subjects*.
Williams, I. (1968) (ed.), *Sir Walter Scott on Novelists and Fiction*, New York, Barnes & Noble.
Wollstonecraft, M. (1790), *A Vindication of the Rights of Men*.
Wollstonecraft, M. (1794), *An Historical and Moral View of the Origin and Progress of the French Revolution*.
Wollstonecraft, M. (1975), *A Vindication of the Rights of Woman*, ed. M. Kramnick, Harmondsworth, Penguin.
Wollstonecraft, M. (1976), *Mary* and *The Wrongs of Woman*, ed. G. Kelly, Oxford, OUP.
Wollstonecraft, M. (1989), *The Works of Mary Wollstonecraft*, ed. M. Butler and J. Todd, 7 vols, London, Pickering.
Woodward, L.-D. (1930), *Hélène-Maria Williams et ses amis*, Paris, Honoré Champion.
Wordsworth, W. (1967), *The Letters of William and Dorothy Wordsworth. The Early Years 1787-1805*, ed. De Selincourt, rev. C. L. Shaver, 2nd ed., Oxford, Clarendon.
Wordsworth, W. (1974), *The Prose Works of William Wordsworth*, ed. W. J. B. Owen and J. W. Smyser, 3 vols, Oxford, Clarendon.
Wordsworth, W. (1975), *The Salisbury Plain Poems*, ed. S. Gill, Ithaca, Cornell University Press.
Wordsworth, W. (1978), *The Letters of William and Dorothy Wordsworth. The Later Years*, ed. De Selincourt, rev. A. G. Hill, Oxford, Clarendon.
Wordsworth, W. (1979), *The Prelude 1799, 1805, 1850*, ed. J. Wordsworth, M. H. Abrams, and S. Gill, New York, Norton.
Wordsworth, W. (1984), *Descriptive Sketches*, ed. E. Birdsall, Ithaca, Cornell University Press.
Wordsworth, W. (1984), *An Evening Walk*, ed. J. Averill, Ithaca, Cornell University Press.

Wordsworth, W. (1984), *The Oxford Authors: William Wordsworth*, ed. S. Gill, Oxford, OUP.

INDEX

Abrams, M.H. 1, 113
Addison, J. 5
Aikin, J. 65-6
American Revolution 60-1, 64, 80, 140, 164-5, 167-8, 216
anti-Jacobin 4, 16-17, 162, 172, 184
association of ideas 26, 28-9, 52, 116-17, 123-7, 187-91, 212-13
Austen, J. 16-17, 68, 75, 120, 160, 184

Bage, R. 64-5, 68-9, 80-4
Baine, R.M. 178
Belsham, T. 90
benevolence: limited 12, 14, 21-3, 27, 42, 45-7, 60-1, 96, 110-11, 114-15, 117, 171-2, 207; universal 6, 9, 13, 21-2, 26, 50, 60, 62-3, 73-4, 79, 81, 83, 91-4, 100, 102, 110, 132, 139, 162, 190, 198-9, 205-7, 216-17
Bissett, R. 112, 162
Blair, H. 3, 54-8
Bowstead, D. 164
Brissenden, R.F. 4-6
Brooke, F. 77-8
Burke, E. 4, 9, 12, 16, 23, 29, 31, 48-9, 63, 72, 85-6, 102-5, 112, 134-5, 139, 208
Burney, F. 69-70, 78, 131
Burns, R. 67, 112
Butler, J. 24, 62

charity 13, 31, 46, 52, 79, 92, 115, 133, 200, 210
Coleridge, S.T. 5, 9, 12, 40, 52, 103, 108-9, 112-13, 124, 128-9, 140, 143-4, 211-13
Cowper, W. 67, 199
Coxe, W. 154-5
Crèvecoeur, M.-G. de 61, 180

Danton, G. 146
David, J.-L. 150-1
delicacy, delicate 3, 55, 69
Dissenters 7, 9, 73, 90, 108, 166

Edgeworth, M. 16, 25, 68, 116-20, 132, 135
education 13, 16, 25, 44, 56, 98-9, 102, 112, 116-32, 135, 150, 161, 164, 168-9, 175-6, 178, 182-3, 185, 211
egalitarianism 6, 8-9, 24, 35, 92, 105, 111, 132, 149-50, 161, 166, 180, 194, 199, 205-6, 208-9, 211, 216
Evangelicals 4, 12, 102, 110, 113-15

Ferguson, A. 7, 34-9
Fielding, H. 62-3
Forbes, D. 35
Fox, C.J. 9, 40, 88, 209
French Revolution 3, 9, 11, 14, 23, 40, 64, 86-9, 101, 111-12, 136, 138-51, 165, 173-4, 201, 205-7

gender constructions: female 5, 26, 41-2, 47, 64, 69-70, 72, 74, 76, 80, 82, 85, 106, 145, 147,

INDEX

182; male 18, 32–3, 44, 68–70, 74
genius 49, 53, 56, 102, 112, 117, 123, 150-1, 209, 217–18
Gill, S. 125, 142, 201
Godwin, W. 108-9, 137, 186, 197, 203, 207; *Letters of Mucius* 87-9, 104; *PJ* 9-10, 12, 16, 23-4, 26-7, 29-30, 40, 62, 89-101, 149, 177-82; *Caleb Williams* 44, 95; *Enquirer* 64, 101,120-35; *St Leon* 69, 98, 134-5; *Thoughts Occasioned* 98, 110-11, 217-18
Goethe, J.W. van 74, 160
Goldsmith, O. 63, 154, 157, 170

Hartley, D. 24, 60, 90-1, 94, 126, 131, 187, 198, 211-13
Hays, M. 17
Hazlitt, W. 14-15, 49, 62, 65-6, 133, 135
Holcroft, T. 64, 77
honour 44-5, 71, 78, 114, 119, 135, 194
Hume, D. 5-6, 15, 22, 26-34, 59, 62, 94, 99-101
Hutcheson, F. 5, 8-9, 12, 15-16, 21, 24-6, 32, 61-2, 67-8, 89-94, 96, 111

imagination 23, 28-9, 49-50, 56, 65-6, 90, 93-4, 102-4, 113-18, 123, 125, 128-9, 158-9, 180-1, 191, 203, 213-16, 218
India 63, 80-1, 201

Johnson, S. 50, 60, 148
Jones, V. 16
justice 6, 25, 29-30, 32, 35, 39, 42, 49, 91, 100, 160, 197, 203, 216

Kames, H. Home, Lord 8, 43-54, 82, 131, 188
Kelly, G. 15
Knox, V. 15-16

Legouis, E. 133
Lloyd, C. 108
Locke, J. 20-2
Logan, J. 122

Mackenzie, H. 2-3, 33, 57, 63, 78
Mackintosh, J. 109
marriage 7, 17, 73, 101, 171, 177
Millar, J. 9, 38-43, 86-7
Montesquieu C., Baron de 36
moral sense 20-1, 24-5, 44-8, 50, 105, 132, 211
More, H. 4, 10, 26, 114-15, 119-20
Mullan, J. 6, 15
mutiny 17-18

Newman, J.H. 102-3

Paine, T. 8, 76, 83, 105, 113, 166
Parr, S. 15, 110-11
patriotism 14, 31, 36, 43, 45-6, 85, 108, 110, 174, 194, 207, 216
Philp, M. 89
Piper, H.W. 214
Poland 16, 147-8, 175
Poovey, M. 5
Pratt, S.J. 78-80
Prévost, A.F., l'Abbé 160
Price, R. 62, 90, 108, 113
Priestley, J. 24, 60
primitivism 1, 9, 34-5, 59-61
progress 1-2, 8-9, 26, 30, 36-45, 60-1, 128, 139, 157, 181, 191, 193-5, 203, 210, 214, 217

Radcliffe, Mrs A. 148
Reid, T. 3-4
Richardson, S. 15
Robespierre, M. 9, 140-5, 170, 174, 176, 203, 206
Roe, N. 108, 113, 142, 194, 208, 214-15
Roland, M. 118, 144, 147, 177
Rousseau, J.-J. 3, 8, 16, 61, 67, 72, 74-5, 103-4, 118, 128, 132, 154-6, 179, 186, 200

Scott, S. 80
Scott, Sir W. 3, 68, 82, 168-9
Seward, A. 136, 141
Shaftesbury, A.A Cooper, 3rd Earl of 5, 8-9, 15-16, 20-4, 59-62, 119, 186, 197-8

INDEX

Shelley, P.B. 26, 55, 101, 122-3, 129
Sheridan, R.B. 87-9
Sheriff, J.K. 5-6, 33
slavery 2, 40, 43, 66, 78, 136, 138, 170
Smith, A. 5, 12, 21-2, 29-34, 59, 73, 90, 94, 111, 116, 200
Smith, C. 10, 65, 136-7, 160-84, 201-2; technique 161-3, 166-7, 170, 176, 183-4; *Banished Man* 170-6; *Desmond* 64, 163-7; *Emigrants* 175, 201; *Emmeline* 69-71; *Ethelinde* 66-7, 75-6; *Marchmont* 176-7; *Old Manor House* 76-8, 167-70; *Young Philosopher* 177-83
Stanton, J.P. 76-7
Sterne, L. 33, 57, 63, 90
Stewart, D. 30, 89
Stone, L. 7
sublime 1, 12, 48-9, 56-7, 73, 85, 118, 158-9, 187-90, 192, 196, 204-6, 213-17
sympathy 13, 22, 26-33, 37, 40, 47-8, 53-4, 57-8, 62, 65-6, 90, 130, 174-5, 182, 190, 199, 202, 204

taste 16-17, 48-50, 53, 55-6, 115, 126, 188, 209
Thelwall, J. 108
Todd, F.M. 141-2
Todd, J. 5-6, 78

utility, utilitarian 6, 38, 100-1, 119

Voitle, R. 8

Wedgwood, T. 27, 125-8, 134, 188
Wharton, J. 54, 59
Wilberforce, W. 4, 113-14
Williams, H.M. 10, 136-59, 173, 201; *Julia* 66, 74; *Letters from France* 65, 139-51; *Tour in Switzerland* 152-8
Wollstonecraft, M. 4, 9-10, 12, 15-16, 67, 71-4, 187; *Historical and Moral View* 79; *Maria* 64, 106-7; *Mary* 72-4, 78; *Vindication . . . Men* 40, 65, 78-9, 103; *Vindication . . . Woman* 103, 106
Wordsworth, W. 13-14, 23, 55, 58, 68, 94-5, 112-13, 125-7, 131-4, 136, 141-3, 145-6, 150, 153-4, 185-218; *An Evening Walk* 191, 195-9, 202; *Convention of Cintra* 14, 153, 215-7; *Descriptive Sketches* 86, 154, 214; *Lyrical Ballads* 27, 65, 94, 202-3; *Prelude* 18, 141-2, 150, 185-95, 204-11, 213-14, 216; *Salisbury Plain* 186, 199-203

Young, E. 53, 123